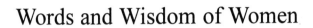

Words and Wisdom of Women

Words and Wisdom of Women

Selected Quotations

Compiled by
Charlotte K. LeBaron

Woodbine Books
P.O. Box 923
Deming, New Mexico 88030
www.cameolady.com

ISBN Number 1-57087-575-8

Library of Congress Control Number 01-132668

First edition
Printed on acid-free, recycled paper

Woodbine Books
P. O. Box 923
Deming, New Mexico 88030
www.cameolady.com

Manufactured in the United States of America
01 02 03 04 05   10 9 8 7 6 5 4 3 2 1

Dedicated to:

My mother, Rhea Allred Kunz, who gave me life,
taught me of its beauties, and set me upon a quest for learning

my paternal Grandmother, Maren Sophia Nielsen Kunz

and

my maternal Grandmother, Charlotte Susannah Pead Allred

And he [Elijah] shall turn the heart of the
fathers to the children, and the heart
of the children to their fathers, lest
I come and smite the earth with a curse.
—Malachi 4:6

Introduction

At what instant or point in life does one consciously resolve to make a book? In my case it was a sudden and clear decision. I had secured a particularly impressive book of quotations about life and its many facets and had spent hours reading, rereading and contemplating its wisdom, when suddenly I knew that I must make a book. Not for one second did I wonder about its contents. It would be on *my* topic—women—and must help define their role, be a source of comfort, insight and inspiration.

From the time I learned that little girls grew up to become mothers, I was fascinated and intrigued by a woman's place in life, even to the point of troubling Mother, wondering if I would become a mother.

In my growing up years I had begun to keep a mental log of biographies of great women, their words, and incidents in their lives that had inspired and motivated me. Actively collecting, seeking, and recording was a natural transition. Following the admonition of Paul, I have sought that which is pure, lovely, and of good report.

I have gathered and gleaned information on this subject from the King James version of the Holy Bible, from libraries, magazines, doctors' offices, wall plaques, journals and biographies; in airplanes, buses, and homes.

Packed with wisdom, practicality, humor, courage, and a measure of spunk, these selections have been chosen with care. From philosophers and sages; the Founding Fathers, their wives, daughters and granddaughters; from literature, both classic and modern; from the intellectual to the commonplace wisdom of simple souls, have come gems that virtually cry out to be shared.

I present my work—an effort which covers a period of twenty-nine years. It is my desire that it will bring a sense of equilibrium and direction in an age that seems to have lost its bearing. May it enlighten, inspire, refine, and ennoble the feminine sex through whom virtuous qualities are so beautifully displayed.

—Charlotte K. LeBaron

Acknowledgments

My gratitude goes to:

—Elizabeth Ann Carson, who believed in my book from the first and typed its beginnings on a manual typewriter. She encouraged me to improve my typing skills, convinced me that I needed an electric typewriter and later a computer.

—Linda Craig, who saw me through two computers and came to the rescue. She typed large portions of the manuscript, did the initial sorting of labeled quotations into chapters, and much more.

—Helen Leany, who helped me proofread most of the manuscript from its sources.

—Donna K. Mackert, my sister, who proofread several copies of the manuscript and whose literary skills refined and polished it.

—My nine children, who helped and encouraged in numerous ways. My six daughters maintained an unfailing confidence in the final outcome of the project.

—All those, past and present, whose words are included in this work.

There are others who deserve thanks for their assistance, encouragement, and support. Though not mentioned, they played a part and are appreciated.

Contents

Love

Caring and Compassion

Chapter One
Love
Caring and Compassion

Man's love is of man's life a thing apart;
'Tis woman's whole existence.

—Lord Byron

Love is a great thing, a good above all others, which alone maketh every burden light... Love is watchful, and whilst sleeping, still keeps watch; though fatigued, it is not weary; though pressed, it is not forced... Love is...sincere...gentle, strong, patient, faithful, prudent, long-suffering, manly... Love is circumspect, humble, and upright; not weak, not fickle, nor intent on vain things; sober, chaste, steadfast, quiet, and guarded in all the senses.

—Thomas á Kempis

It [love] is the rule for fulfilling all rules, the new commandment for keeping all the old commandments, Christ's one secret of the Christian life.

—Norman Vincent Peale

The sky is like a woman's love,
    The ocean like a man's;
Oh, neither knows, below, above,
    The measure that it spans!

—Maurice Thompson

ॐ

Love is the only way to grasp another human being in the innermost core of his personality. No one can become fully aware of the very essence of another human being unless he loves him. By the spiritual act of love he is enabled to see the essential traits and features in the beloved person; and even more, he sees that which is potential in him, that which is not yet actualized but yet ought to be actualized. Furthermore, by his love, the loving person enables the beloved person to actualize these potentialities.

—Viktor E. Frankl

*L*ove is an act of endless forgiveness, a tender look which becomes a habit.

—Peter Ustinov

*L*ove asks faith and faith firmness.

—George Herbert

*L*ove sought is good, but given unsought is better.

—William Shakespeare

*B*etter is a dinner of herbs where love is, than a stalled ox and hatred therewith.

—Proverbs 15:17

❧

*L*ove is, above all, the gift of oneself.

—Jean Anouilh

*L*ove for our neighbor consists of three things: to desire the greater good of everyone; to do what good we can when we can; to bear, excuse, and hide other's faults.

—John Vianney

*T*hey say if one understands himself, he understands all people; but I say to you, when one loves people, he learns something about himself.

—Kahlil Gibran

❧

*V*irtue is nothing but well-directed love.

—St. Augustine

*T*he love we give away is the only love we keep.

—Elbert Hubbard

*I*t is not the most lovable individuals who stand more in need of love, but the most unlovable.

—Ashley Montague

What we love we grow to resemble.

—*St. Bernard*

Love is a little blind; when we love someone dearly we unconsciously overlook many faults.

—*Beatrice Saunders*

The best proof of love is trust.

—*Dr. Joyce Brothers*

God so loved the world, that he gave his only begotten Son, that whosoever believeth in him should not perish, but have everlasting life.

—*John 3:16*

The giving of love is an education in itself.

—*Eleanor Roosevelt*

☙

Love calls us to the things of this world.

—*Richard Wilbur*

To love is to receive a glimpse of heaven.

—*Karen Sunde*

You give but little when you give of your possessions. It is when you give your heart that you truly give.

—*Kahlil Gibran*

Love must be learned, and learned again and again; there is no end to it.

—*Katherine Ann Porter*

When you love someone all your saved-up wishes start coming out.

—*Elizabeth Bowen*

To love deeply in one direction makes us more loving in all others.

—*Madame Swetchine*

Giving is the essence of loving.

—*Peter R. Stone*

The first condition of human goodness is something to love; the second, something to reverence.

—*George Eliot*

Love is but the discovery of ourselves in others, and the delight in the recognition.

—*Alexander Smith*

❦

The heart has its reasons which reason knows nothing of.

—*Blaise Pascal*

If there be any other commandment, it is briefly comprehended in this saying, namely, Thou shalt love thy neighbor as thyself. Love worketh no ill to his neighbor: therefore love is the fulfilling of the law.

—*Romans 13:9,10*

Love, even genuine love, is a fragile thing. It must be maintained and protected if it is to survive.

—*James Dobson*

Music is love in search of a word.

—*Sidney Lanier*

Love never reasons, but profusely gives; gives, like a thoughtless prodigal, its all, and trembles lest it has done too little.

—*Hannah More*

Love is like a violin. The music may stop now and then, but the strings remain forever.

—*June Masters Bacher*

To love and be loved is to feel the sun from both sides.

—*David Viscott*

8

They are the true disciples of Christ, not who know most, but who love most.

—*Fredrick Spanheim*

The Eskimo has fifty-two names for snow because it is important to him; there ought to be as many for love.

—*Margaret Atwood*

Age does not protect you from love. But love, to some extent, protects you from age.

—*Jeanne Moreau*

If you cannot work with love but only with distaste, it is better that you should leave your work and sit at the gate of the temple and take alms of those who work with joy.

—*Kahlil Gibran*

I have found that if you love life, life will love you back.

—*Arthur Rubinstein*

Absence makes the heart grow fonder.

—*Sextus Aurelius Propertius*

Love is a gentle courtesy.

—*Anonymous*

There is no fear in love; but perfect love casteth out fear...
We love Him because he first loved us.

—*1 John 4:18,19*

He drew a circle that shut me out—
Heretic, rebel, a thing to flout.
But love and I had the wit to win;
We drew a circle that took him in!

—*Edwin Markham*

Love I say, is energy of Life.

—*Robert Browning*

9

If music be the food of love, play on.

—*William Shakespeare*

To love abundantly is to live abundantly, and to love forever is to live forever.

—*Norman Vincent Peale*

It is possible to give without loving, but it is impossible to love without giving.

—*Richard Braunstein*

True love in this differs from gold and clay,
That to divide is not to take away.

—*Percy Bysshe Shelley*

Before love blooms
    it gets its start—
    deep within
A mother's heart.

—*Patricia J. Hacker-Harber*

ॐ

Love isn't love till you give it away.

—*Oscar Hammerstein*

Love is the only flower that grows and blossoms without the aid of seasons.

—*Kahlil Gibran*

Love cannot be begged, bought, borrowed or stolen.
It can only be given away.

—*Walter Rinder*

By some working of the universal law, as you give of love, you are given more love and happiness to go on with!

—*Albert Schweitzer*

Charity suffereth long, and is kind; charity envieth not; charity vaunteth not itself, is not puffed up, doth not behave itself unseemly, seeketh not her own, is not easily provoked, thinketh no evil; rejoiceth not in iniquity, but rejoiceth in the truth; beareth all things, believeth all things, hopeth all things, endureth all things.

—*I Corinthians 13:4-7*

Love is the only ray of light on life's dark cloud. It is the morning and evening star. It shines upon the cradle of the babe, and sheds its radiance upon the quiet tomb. It is the Mother of Art, inspirer of poet, patriot and philosopher. It is the air and light of every heart, builder of every home, kindler of every fire on every hearth. It is the first dream of immortality. It fills the world with melody, for music is the voice of love. Love is the magician, the enchantor, that changes worthless things to joy, and makes right royal queens and kings of common clay. It is the perfume of the wondrous flower—the heart, and without it we are less than beasts, but with it, earth is heaven, and we are Gods.

—*Robert Ingersoll*

ॐ

The ways of nature and of life are strange and deep. They are not to be understood. In the midst of angers and wars love's secret work goes on, and binds us all by blood and this whether love is denied or love is bestowed.

—*Pearl S. Buck*

Love is loveliest when embalmed in tears.

—*Sir Walter Scott*

Divine love is a sacred flower, which in its early bud is happiness, and in its full bloom is heaven.

—*Hervey*

Love is one of the chief characteristics of Deity, and ought to be manifested by those who aspire to be the sons of God. A man filled with love of God is not content with blessing his family alone, but ranges through the whole world anxious to bless the whole human race.

—*Joseph Smith*

When love and skill work together expect a masterpiece.

—John Ruskin

They do not love that do not show their love.

—William Shakespeare

The supreme thing...[love] is not a thing at all, but the giving of a further finish to the multitudinous words and acts which make up the sum of every common day.

—Norman Vincent Peale

If we truly care for others we need not be anxious about their feelings for us. Like draws to like.

—Andrew Carnegie

Genuine love demands toughness in moments of crisis.

—James Dobson

Whom the Lord loveth, he chasteneth.

—Hebrews 12:6

Love is the salt of life; a higher taste
It gives to pleasure, and then makes it last.

—Buckingham

Nuptial love maketh mankind, friendly love perfecteth it; but wanton love corrupteth and embaseth it.

—Francis Bacon

Love did his reason blind,
And love's the noblest frailty of the mind.

—John Dryden

To love and to be wise is scarcely granted to the highest.

—Laberius

That you may be loved be amiable.

—Ovid

The chemist who can extract from his heart's elements compassion, respect, longing, patience, regret, surprise and forgiveness and compound them into one can create that atom which is called Love.

—*Kahlil Gibran*

Where love is there is no labor; and if there be labor, that labor is loved.

—*Jane Austen*

One of the great qualities about genuine love is that it grows and deepens over time. Time is life's nursery for love.

—*W.B. Freeman Concepts*

Alas! they had been friends in youth;
But whispering tongues can poison truth;
And constancy lives in realms above;
    And life is thorny, and youth is vain,
And to be wroth with one we love,
    Doth work like madness in the brain.

—*Samuel Taylor Coleridge*

Beloved, let us love one another, for love is of God, and every one that loveth is born of God and knoweth God.

—*I John 4:7*

Was it something said,
    Something done,
Vexed him? was it touch of hand,
    Turn of head?
Strange! that very way
    Love began.
I as little understand
    Love's decay.

—*Robert Browning*

Could we forbear dispute and practice love,
We should agree as angels do above.

—*Waller*

Even love unreturned has its rainbow.

—*Sir James M. Barrie*

Love seeketh not itself to please.
Nor for itself hath any care,
But for another gives its ease,
And builds a heaven in hell's despair.

—*William Blake*

Many waters cannot quench love, neither can the floods drown it; if a man would give all the substance of his house for love, it would utterly be contemned.

—*The Song of Solomon 8:7*

No cord nor cable can so forcibly draw, or hold so fast, as love can do with a twined thread.

—*Robert Burton*

Love is an Art, and the greatest of the Arts.

—*Edward Carpenter*

I think true love is never blind,
    But rather brings an added light,
An inner vision quick to find
    The beauties hid from common sight.

—*Phoebe Cary*

Who walks a road with love will never walk
That road alone again.
Old lonely things will garb them in the guise
Of beauty glowing with remembered eyes.

—*Charles Thomas Davis*

Alas! that men must see
    Love, before Death!
Else they content might be
    With their short breath.

—*Margaret Wade Deland*

To the man who has the religion of peace, the supreme value is love.
—*Goldsworthy Lowes Dickinson*

All mankind love a lover.
—*Ralph Waldo Emerson*

Love goes toward love, as schoolboys from their books;
But love from love, toward school with heavy looks.
—*William Shakespeare*

Love that is hoarded molds at last
   Until we know some day
The only thing we ever have
   Is what we give away.
—*Louis Ginsberg*

After you have been kind, after Love has stolen forth into the world
and done its beautiful work, go back into the shade again and say nothing
about it. Love hides even from itself. Love waives even self-satisfaction.
—*Norman Vincent Peale*

Love is a proud and gentle thing, a better thing to own
Than all of the wide impossible stars over the heavens blown.
—*Orick Johns*

Love is the part, and love is the whole;
   Love is the robe, and love is the pall;
Ruler of heart and brain and soul.
   Love is the lord and the slave of all!
—*George Macdonald*

A new commandment I give unto you, That ye love one another.
—*John 13:34*

Let those love now who never loved before;
Let those who always loved, now love the more.
—*Thomas Parnell*

*N*ever change when love has found its home.

—*Sextus Aurelius Propertius*

*W*e pardon in the degree that we love.

—*Francois de la Lochefoucauld*

*T*he heart's affections are divided like the branches of the cedar tree; if the tree loses one strong branch, it will suffer but it does not die. It will pour all its vitality into the next branch so that it will grow and fill the empty place.

—*Kahlil Gibran*

*T*hey sin who tell us love can die;
With life all other passions fly,
    All others are but vanity...
        Love is indestructible.

—*Robert Southey*

*T*o love is the great Amulet that makes this world a garden.

—*Robert Louis Stevenson*

*L*ove does not have to be tethered, either in time or eternity.

—*Anna R. Brown Lindsay*

*L*ove supreme defies all sophistry.

—*George Eliot*

*R*iches take wings, comforts vanish, hope withers away, but love stays with us. Love is God.

—*Lew Wallace*

*E*ye hath not seen, nor ear heard, neither have entered into the heart of man, the things which God hath prepared for them that love him.

—*I Corinthians 2:9*

*L*ove is the beginning, the middle, and the end of everything.

—*Lacordaire*

O love, resistless in thy might, thou triumphest even over gold!
—*Sophocles*

*I*f there is anything better than to be loved it is loving.
—*Anonymous*

*T*he way to love anything is to realize that it might be lost.
—*Gilbert K. Chesterton*

*L*ove is always lonely in crowds.
—*Albert Schweitzer*

*T*o love is to place our happiness in the happiness of another.
—*Gottfried Wilhelm Leibnitz*

*L*ove gives itself; it is not bought.
—*Henry Wadsworth Longfellow*

❦

*T*he days grow shorter, the nights grow
    longer, the headstones thicken along
    the way; but love grows stronger
For those who walk with us day by day.
—*Ella Wheeler Wilcox*

*L*ove is friendship set to music.
—*Channing Pollock*

*A*nd when Love speaks, the voice of all the gods
Makes heaven drowsy with the harmony.
—*William Shakespeare*

*L*ove may be beset by anxieties and doubts, but of itself it stimulates all the noblest and greatest qualities of which human nature is characterized at its best. It is the greatest power in the world, and without it the races of mankind would finish in but a few generations.
—*Grantly Dick-Read*

If you wish to be loved, be lovable.

—*Benjamin Franklin*

'Tis better to have loved and lost,
Than never to have loved at all.

—*Alfred, Lord Tennyson*

This is my commandment, That ye love one another, as I have loved you. Greater love hath no man than this, that a man lay down his life for his friends.

—*John 15:12,13*

ಀ

Hatred never yet was overcome by hatred, but hatred is always overcome by love.

—*Buddha*

Love is to the moral nature what the sun is to the earth.

—*Honore de Balzac*

ಀ

We are all born for love; it is the principle of existence and its only end.

—*Benjamin Disraeli*

Faults are thick where love is thin.

—*English Proverb*

To make oneself beloved is after all the best way to be useful.

—*French Proverb*

Love is never lost. If not reciprocated it will flow back and soften and purify the heart.

—*Washington Irving*

So long as we love, we serve. So long as we are loved by others I would almost say we are indispensable; and no man is useless while he has a friend.

—*Robert Louis Stevenson*

The best way to know God is to love many things.

—*Vincent van Gogh*

The best portions of a good man's life are his little, nameless, unremembered acts of kindness and love.

—*William Wordsworth*

Love is the only freedom in the world because it so elevates the spirit that the laws of humanity and the phenomena of nature do not alter its course.

—*Kahlil Gibran*

This is the true measure of love: when we believe that we alone can love, that no one could ever have loved so before us, and that no one will ever love in the same way after us.

—*Johann Wolfgang von Goethe*

❧

He that plants trees loves others besides himself.

—*English Proverb*

His banner over me was love.

—*Song of Solomon 2:4*

Love comforteth like sunshine after rain.

—*William Shakespeare*

Listening is a primitive act of love in which a person gives himself to another's word, making himself accessible and vulnerable to that word.

—*William Stringfellow*

Love, and a cough, cannot be hid.

—*George Herbert*

*K*nowledge is gained by learning; trust by doubt; skill by practice; and love by love.

—*Thomas Szasz*

*N*ever close your lips to those to whom you have opened your heart.

—*Charles Dickens*

*T*he entire sum of existence is the magic of being needed by just one person.

—*Vii Putnam*

*L*ove is a fruit in season at all times, and within the reach of every hand.

—*Mother Teresa*

A friend hears the song in my heart and sings it to me when my memory fails.

—*Pioneer Girls Leaders' Handbook*

*R*eal love stories never have endings.

—*Richard Bach*

*M*ichael J. Arlen, a wonderful writer, said to me once that the greatest act of love is to pay attention. That's so true. I think the one lesson I have learned is that there is no substitute for paying attention.

—*Diane Sawyer*

*W*hen one loves somebody, everything is clear—where to go, what to do—it all takes care of itself and one doesn't have to ask anybody about anything.

—*Maxim Gorky*

*H*e that loveth his brother abideth in the light, and there is none occasion of stumbling in him.

—*I John 2:10*

*G*enuine love demands caring, commitment, and giving unselfishly to the other person.

—*James Dobson*

Where Love is, God is. He that dwelleth in Love dwelleth in God. God is love. Therefore *love*. Without distinction, without calculation, without procrastination, love. Lavish it upon the poor, where it is very easy; especially upon the rich, who often need it most; most of all upon our equals, where it is very difficult, and for whom perhaps we each do least of all... Any good thing therefore that I can do, or any kindness that I can show to any human being, let me do it now. Let me not defer it or neglect it, for I shall not pass this way again.

—Norman Vincent Peale

☙

All our loves are first loves.

—Susan Fromberg Schaeffer

Love is like quicksilver in the hand. Leave the fingers open, and it stays. Clutch it, and it darts away.

—Dorothy Parker

☙

Darkness may hide the trees and the flowers from the eyes but it cannot hide love from the soul.

—Kahlil Gibran

There isn't even enough time for love, so what does that leave for hate?

—Bill Copeland

☙

There is no surprise more magical than the surprise of being loved. It is God's finger on man's shoulder.

—Charles Morgan

When the satisfaction or security of another person becomes as significant to one as one's own satisfaction or security, then, the state of love exists.

—Harry Stack Sullivan

21

$\mathcal{L}$ove is not love
Which alters when it alteration finds.

—*William Shakespeare*

$\mathcal{G}$od is love; and he that dwelleth in love dwelleth in God.

—*I John 4:16*

$\mathcal{I}$ don't think love is "never having to say you're sorry." If we're human, we all hurt each other—even when we don't mean to. True love is understanding and being willing to say, "I'm sorry."

—*Marjorie Holmes*

$\mathcal{H}$e prayeth well who loveth well
Both man and bird and beast.
He prayeth best who loveth best
All things both great and small;
For the dear God who loveth us,
He made and loveth all.

—*Samuel Taylor Coleridge*

$\mathcal{L}$ove? Why...it is what everybody feels for everybody else.

—*Helen Keller*

$\mathcal{T}$he power to love is God's greatest gift to man, for it never will be taken from the blessed one who loves.

—*Kahlil Gibran*

$\mathcal{L}$ove reckons hours for months, and days for years; and every little absence is an age.

—*John Dryden*

$\mathcal{O}$, the toils of life!
How small they seem, when love's restless tide
Sweeps brightly o'er them! Like the scattered stones
Within a mountain streamlet, they but serve
To strike the hidden music from its flow,
And make its sparkle visible.

—*Anne Katharine Green*

*L*ove is the master key that opens the gates of happiness.

—*Oliver Wendell Holmes*

I like not only to be loved, but to be told that I am loved; the realm of silence is large enough beyond the grave.

—*George Eliot*

A loving heart is the truest wisdom.

—*Charles Dickens*

*L*ove is the reward of love.

—*Schiller*

*T*he course of true love never did run smooth.

—*William Shakespeare*

ॐ

*T*o feel the love of people whom we love is a fire that feeds our life. But to feel the affection that comes from those whom we do not know, from those unknown to us, who are watching over our sleep and solitude, over our dangers and our weaknesses—that is something still greater and more beautiful because it widens out the boundaries of our being, and unites all living things.

—*Pablo Neruda*

ॐ

*T*here is no power of love so hard to get and keep as a kind voice. Watch it day by day as a pearl of great price, for it is worth more than the finest pearl hid in the sea.

—*A.L. Alexander*

O, there be many things
    That seem right fair, below, above;
But sure not one among them all
    Is half so sweet as love.

—*Oliver Wendell Holmes*

Leave me a little love;
A voice to speak to me in the day-end,
A hand to touch me in the dark room,
Breaking the long loneliness...
Let me go to the window,
Watch there the day-shapes of dusk,
And wait and know the coming
Of a little love.

—*Carl Sandburg*

Love makes all hard hearts gentle.

—*George Herbert*

You will find as you look back upon your life that the moments that stand out...are the moments when you have done things in a spirit of love. As memory scans the past...there leap forward those supreme hours when you have been enabled to do unnoticed kindnesses to those around you...but which you feel have entered into your eternal life. I have seen almost all the beautiful things God has made; I have enjoyed almost every pleasure that he has planned for man; and yet as I look back I see standing out above all the life that has gone four or five short experiences when the love of God reflected itself in some poor imitation, some small act of love of mine, and these seem to be the things which alone of all one's life abide.

—*Norman Vincent Peale*

All work is empty save when there is love;
And what is it to work with love?
    It is to weave the cloth with threads drawn from your
heart, even as if your beloved were to wear that cloth.
    It is to build a house with affection, even as if your
beloved were to dwell in that house.
    It is to sow seed with tenderness and to reap the harvest
with joy, even as if your beloved were to eat the fruit.
    It is to charge all things you fashion with a breath of your
own spirit,
    Work is love made visible.

—*Kahlil Gibran*

24

*F*aces are but a gallery of pictures, and talk but a tinkling cymbal where there is no love.

—Sir John Lubbock

*L*ove and you shall be loved.

—Ralph Waldo Emerson

*L*ove is lost in immensities; it comes in simple, gentle ways.

—Joseph Fort Newton

*T*here is only one sort of love, but there are a thousand copies.

—Francois de la Rochefoucauld

❧

*L*ove is not getting, but giving, not a wild dream of pleasure, and madness of desire... It is goodness, and honor, and peace and pure living.

—Henry Van Dyke

❧

*B*lessed it is to know that neither distance nor death can truly separate those who love.

—John Muir

❧

*O*nce in the dear dead days beyond recall,
When on the world the mists began to fall,
Out of the dreams that rose in happy throng,
Low in our hearts, Love sang an old sweet song...

Just a song at twilight, when the lights are low,
And the flick'ring shadows softly come and go.
Tho' the heart be weary, sad the day and long,
Still to us at twilight comes Love's old song,
Comes Love's old sweet song.

—Clifton Bingham

Thou blind fool, love, what doest thou to mine eyes, that they behold and see not what they see.

—*William Shakespeare*

There is no significance to love that knows no alternative.

—*James Dobson*

A little word; a simple word;
And yet it means so much;
Love is the strongest force,
And underneath its magic touch—
A heart unfolds just like a flower
That opens to the sun...
This is the sweetest thing in life—
When all is said and done.

—*Patience Strong*

❧

Oh how deep is the wound of not being loved! From generation to generation the newborn heart is wounded afresh and cannot be healed until love is found, in someone, somewhere.

—*Pearl S. Buck*

❧

The supreme happiness of life is the conviction of being loved for yourself, or more correctly, being loved in spite of yourself.

—*Victor Hugo*

No worse fate can befall a man in this world than to live and grow old alone, unloving and unloved. To be lost is to live in an unregenerate condition, loveless and unloved, and to be saved is to love.

—*Norman Vincent Peale*

Love is a passion
Which kindles honor into noble acts.

—*John Dryden*

Talk not of wasted affection;
affection never was wasted.
If it enrich not the heart of another,
its waters, returning
Back to their springs, like the rain,
shall fill them full of refreshment;
That which the fountain sends forth
returns again to the fountain.

—Henry Wadsworth Longfellow

They that love beyond the world cannot be separated by it. Death cannot kill what never dies. Nor can spirits ever be divided that love and live in the same divine principle, the root and record, of their friendship.

—William Penn

There is no difficulty that enough Love will not conquer.
No disease that enough Love will not heal.
No door that enough Love will not open.
No gulf that enough Love will not bridge.
No wall that enough Love will not throw down.
No sin that enough Love will not redeem.

—Emmet Fox

I have heard birds calling their mates in the still forests,
    and insects chirping to their loves in the tangled grass
    of meadows;
I have seen mothers caressing their babes, and aged men
    supporting with devotion the slow steps of stooping women;
I have seen cheerful hearthstones surrounded by laughing
    children and strong men and happy women;
I have heard the tender words of lovers in the pure passion
    of youth;
And I have cried in my heart, "The world is love!"

—Max Ehrmann

$\mathscr{A}$re you willing to believe that love is the strongest thing in the world—stronger than hate, stronger than evil, stronger than death—and that the blessed life which began in Bethlehem nineteen hundred years ago is the image and brightness of the Eternal Love?

—Paul Harvey

č

Home and Family

Woman's Heritage

Chapter Two
Home and Family
Woman's Heritage

This is the true nature of home—it is the place of Peace; the shelter, not only from all injury, but from all terror, doubt, and division. As it is not this, it is not home...it is then only a part of that outer world which you have roofed over, and lighted fire in. But so far as it is a sacred place, a vestal temple, a temple of the hearth, watched over by Household Gods, before whose faces none can come but those whom they can receive with love—so far as it is this, and roof and fire are types only of a nobler shade and light—shade as of the rock in a weary land, and light as the Pharos in the stormy sea—so far it vindicates the name and fulfills the praise of home.

And wherever a true wife comes, this home is always round her. The stars only may be over her head; the glowworm in the night-cold grass may be the only fire at her foot; but home is yet wherever she is; and for a noble woman it stretches far round her, better than ceiled with cedar, or painted with vermilion, shedding its quiet light far, for those who else were homeless.

—John Ruskin

I have been led to believe that it is for homes and families our people will cry out... The greatest force behind the peace and prosperity of a nation emanates unseen and unheard from the mothers in their homes.

—Grantly Dick-Read

It is in the love of one's family only that heartfelt happiness is known.

—Thomas Jefferson

What work is greater for woman—or man—than the creating and maintaining of the center of human life, a home? Into this home children are born. It is their world, the only world they know for the most important years of their lives, and as long as they live it will continue the most important influence upon them.

—Pearl S. Buck

33

At the end only two things really matter to a man, regardless of who he is; and they are the affection and understanding of his family. Anything and everything else he creates are insubstantial; they are ships given over to the mercy of the winds and tides of prejudice. But the family is an everlasting anchorage, a quiet harbor where a man's ships can be left to swing in the moorings of pride and loyalty.

—*Richard E. Byrd*

Where does the family start? It starts with a young man falling in love with a girl. No superior alternative has yet been found.

—*Winston Churchill*

I was born to a woman I never knew and raised by another who took in orphans. I do not know my background, my lineage, my biological or cultural heritage. But when I meet someone new, I treat them with respect. For after all, they could be my people.

—*James Michener*

Choose ye this day whom ye will serve...but as for me and my house, we will serve the Lord.

—*Joshua 24:15*

I would say to all: use your gentlest voice at home.

—*Elihu Burritt*

Where there is room in the heart there is always room in the house.

—*Moore*

Rejoice with your family in the beautiful land of life.

—*Albert Einstein*

Better do a kindness near home than go to a far temple to burn incense.

—*Chinese Proverb*

There has emerged no institution that can replace the family in turning children into civilized human beings or in retrieving the wreckage of our current disorder.

—*George Gilder*

34

It's time to get back to some old-fashioned values, like commitment and sacrifice and responsibility and purity and love and the straight life. Not only will our children benefit from our self-discipline and perseverance, but we adults will live in a less neurotic world, too!

—*James Dobson*

Loving relationships are a family's best protection against the challenges of the world.

—*Bernie Wiebe*

༜

The family is the only institution in our world where the Kingdom of God can actually begin.

—*Elton Trueblood*

Traveling in the company of those we love is home in motion.

—*Leigh Hunt*

There is magic in that little word, home; it is a mystic circle that surrounds comforts and virtues never known beyond its hallowed limits.

—*Robert Southey*

Blessed is the home where each puts the other's happiness first.

—*Theodore F. Adams*

The ornaments of our house are the friends that frequent it.

—*Ralph Waldo Emerson*

A palace without affection is a poor hovel, and the meanest hut with love in it is a palace for the soul.

—*Robert Green Ingersoll*

Among the most important privileges of parents is the making of a happy home—a home where children want to be, to which they will want to return; not a place of perfection...but a place of pleasantness, of helpfulness and hospitality.

—*Richard L. Evans*

The family at its best is a nursery of love... To begin life as one who is loved and to grow up surrounded by the warmth and tenderness of family affections is to be supremely fortunate. Love flourishes in a happy home where parents, children, sisters, brothers, wives, and husbands care for each other and express affectionate interest in the well-being of all.

—*Edith Deen*

One truly affectionate soul in a family will exert a sweetening and harmonizing influence upon all its members.

—*Henry Van Dyke*

Good family life is never an accident but always an achievement by those who share it.

—*James H.S. Bossard*

❧

Religious words have value to the child only as experience in the home gives them meaning.

—*John Drescher*

The dynamic qualities of enthusiasm, excitement, energy, and faith run like golden cords through the lives of the Staffords, the Peales, the Crosbys, and the DeLaneys... How fortunate I am to be part of such a splendid family.

—*Norman Vincent Peale*

❧

My first work was done there at one dollar and twenty cents per week. It was a hard life. In winter Father and I had to rise and breakfast in the darkness, reach the factory before it was daylight, and with a short interval for lunch, work till after dark. The hours hung heavily upon me and in the work itself I took no pleasure; but the cloud had a silver lining, as it gave me the feeling that I was doing something for my world—our family. I have made millions since, but none of those millions gave me such happiness as my first week's earnings. I was now a helper of the family, a breadwinner, and no longer a total charge upon my parents.

—*Andrew Carnegie*

$\mathcal{A}$nd I *do* come home at Christmas. We all do, or we all should. We all come home, or ought to come home, for a short holiday—the longer, the better—from the great boardingschool, where we are forever working at our arithmetical slates—to take, and give a rest.

—*Charles Dickens*

$\mathcal{A}$ family is a "gallery of memories" to those who have been blessed by the presence of children.

—*James Dobson*

$\mathcal{M}$ighty are the Universities of Scotland, and they will prevail. But...the greatest of them are the poor, proud homes you come out of, which said so long ago: "There shall be education in this land."

—*Sir James M. Barrie*

$\mathcal{O}$ne of the best things in our life is when a young man has earned his own living, and when he becomes engaged to some lovely young woman, and makes up his mind to have a home of his own. Then with that same love comes also that divine inspiration toward better things, and he begins to save his money...and when he takes his bride over the threshold of that door for the first time he says in words of eloquence... "I have earned this home myself. It is all mine, and I divide with thee." That is the grandest moment a human heart may ever know.

—*Russell H. Conwell*

$\mathcal{T}$he best educational institution in the world is the home.

—*Tim LaHaye*

$\mathcal{T}$he nearest thing to heaven on this earth is...the home where husband and wife, and parents and children, live in love and peace.

—*Dr. M.R. DeHoon*

$\mathcal{T}$hey had a lovely, happy time. It used to strike me as heavenly. 'Twas a home just like you'd make for yourself—like a dream house, don't you know, that you would like more than anything else in the world. There was always fun and excitement—especially when Mr. [Samuel] Clemens was around.

—*Katy Leary*

You are a king by your own fireside as much as any monarch in his throne.

—*Cervantes*

The midnight train is slow and old,
But of it let this thing be told,
To its high honor be it said,
It carries people home to bed.
My cottage lamp shines white and clear.
God bless the train that brought me here.

—*Joyce Kilmer*

Continue to write about all your todays until the end of your life. Put the words on paper which will prevent your life and the lives of other members of your family from slipping into oblivion.

—*Lois Daniel*

Once more she [Mother] set herself to making a home. Clean whitewashed walls...wide windows opened in the walls and fresh ruffled curtains, clean matting on the floors, the court planted with grass, flowers again, chrysanthemums bought from flower vendors and gay little single roses of red and pink and yellow. Then when the beloved organ and table were in their places and beds and a few reed chairs and a kitchen made, there was home again. Outside the noisy street ran east and west through the city and was the great thoroughfare for business, and there was the roar of the city... But inside the wall and the gate there was this spot of peace and cleanliness.

—*Pearl S. Buck*

Honor your own stories and tell them too. The tales may not seem very important, but they are what binds families and makes each of us who we are.

—*Madeleine L'Engle*

Go abroad with the majesty and dignity of your home about you... Let the modest graces of the fireside adorn you...[as] one who shall carry the blessed spirit of home wherever she goes, a spirit of rest, of healing, of reconciliation and good will.

—*Julia Ward Howe*

38

The family is the nucleus of civilization.

—*Will Durant*

I will consider my earthly existence to have been wasted unless I can recall a loving family.

—*James Dobson*

Author Alex Haley once said that whenever an old person dies, it's as if a book had been removed from a library.

—*Emilie Barnes*

It was the policy of the good old gentleman to make his children feel that home was the happiest place in the world; and I value this delicious home-feeling as one of the choicest gifts a parent can bestow.

—*Washington Irving*

A family composed of a husband and wife who love each other and of children conceived in their love, is the first and oldest as well as the holiest and greatest human institution. It is the most enduring of civilization's bulwarks.

—*Edith Deen*

If we can believe that a home is potentially as much a sanctuary as any ecclesiastical building can ever be, we are well on the way to the recovery of family life which our generation sorely needs.

—*Pauline & Elton Trueblood*

The most vivid memories of Christmases past are usually not of gifts given or received, but of the spirit of love...the cherished little habits of the home.

—*Lois Rand*

When the candles were brought, all was quiet immediately, for he [Grandfather Thomas Jefferson] took up his book to read; and we would not speak out of a whisper lest we should disturb him, and generally we followed his example and took a book; and I have seen him raise his eyes from his own book, and look round on the little circle of readers, and smile and make some remark to Mamma about it.

—*Virginia J. Trist*

I, the new owner of this ancient house,
  Take over more than walls and hearths and stairs;
There has been sorrow here and human pride,
  And I am taking over things like prayers.

—*Robert Peter Tristram Coffin*

*H*ome is where one starts from.

—*T.S. Eliot*

*Y*ou never really leave a place you love. Part of it you take with you,
leaving a part of yourself behind.

—*Anonymous*

*B*road-streeted Richmond...
  The trees in the streets are old trees
Used to living with people,
Family trees that remember your grandfather's name.

—*Stephen Vincent Benet*

*I*n Istanbul I learned that Mother and my little sister Alene were safe in
Scutari. Everybody but Mother was sure I was dead. She had faithfuly
continued to light the *gantegh*, the little lamp in the niche beside the front
door... A lighted *gantegh* means that the people in the house are awaiting
the return of a loved one who is far away.
  One day I returned to stand beside the little lamp and rap on the
door. Late into that night Mother, Alene and I talked.

—*George Mardikian*

*N*o social institution is more fateful for the human race than the home.
In it the primary shaping of character takes place.

—*H.A. Overstreet*

*I*f there is righteousness in the heart there will be beauty in the
character. If there is beauty in the character there will be harmony in the
home. If there is harmony in the home there will be order in the nation. If
there is order in the nation there will be peace in the world.

—*Chinese Proverb*

40

$\mathscr{I}$ would like to know whatever happened to the rocking chair... How good it is to sit after dinner, the mother in one and the father in another, rocking away gently while reading, vigorously while talking. That used to be the standard way of putting a child to sleep. The mother would sit at her spinning wheel, or in her rocking chair, giving the cradle a gentle push with her foot.

—*Gayelord Hauser*

$\mathscr{T}$here is beauty all around
When there's love at home;
There is joy in ev'ry sound
When there's love at home.
Peace and plenty here abide,
Smiling sweet on ev'ry side.
Time doth softly, sweetly glide
When there's love at home...

In the cottage there is joy
When there's love at home;
Hate and envy ne'er annoy
When there's love at home.
Roses bloom beneath our feet;
All the earth's a garden sweet,
Making life a bliss complete
When there's love at home...

Kindly heaven smiles above
When there's love at home;
All the world is filled with love
When there's love at home.
Sweeter sings the brooklet by;
Brighter beams the azure sky.
Oh, there's One who smiles on high
When there's love at home.

—*John Hugh McNaughton*

The home is the basic unit of our society and the foundation of our way of life. A nation is only so strong as its families. And it is good mothers now, as always, who are the real heart of the home, giving families their goodness.

—*Rawley Meyers*

❦

In family life children are coming to believe they do not have to take care of the old folks. But old-age pensions do not relieve children of their duties.

—*Albert Schweitzer*

❦

I love those dear hearts and gentle people
Who live in my hometown,
Because those dear hearts and gentle people
Will never ever let you down.

They read the Good Book from "Fri." till Monday.
That's how the weekend goes.
I've got a dream house I'll build there one day
With picket fence and rambling rose.

—*Bob Hilliard*

❦

Let not him who is houseless pull down the house of another, but let him work diligently and build one for himself, thus by example assuring that his own shall be safe from violence when built.

—*Abraham Lincoln*

❦

Our only hope as a nation is in a return to the Scriptural underpinnings on which the institution of the family is based.

—*James Dobson*

As long as the family is a unit, as long as it is held together by its sense of continuity, it is better able to help its children steer their course through these ever-increasing perils of modern time. And one of the foundations of togetherness is the manifestation of nature itself and the way in which its miracles are performed. When other and older children in the family can be witness, unashamed and unembarrassed, to one of the greatest of these miracles, the feeding of a brother or sister from the person of its mother, they will have come a long way in winning protection from the miserable so-called "freedoms" which, in our times, are being imposed upon the young.

—Princess Grace of Monaco

[Being with their parents] is where the children of honest poverty have the most precious advantages of those of wealth. The mother, nurse, cook, governess, teacher, saint, all in one; the father, exemplar, guide, counselor, and friend. Thus were my brother and I brought up. What has the child of millionaire or nobleman that counts compared to such a heritage?

—Andrew Carnegie

I do think that families are the most beautiful things in all the world.

—Louisa May Alcott

To build a happy fireside clime
    for weans and for wife,
That's the true pathos and sublime
    o' human life.

—Robert Burns

❦

Some of the very principles on which the family and therefore the health of the nation is founded are in danger. We live in an age of growing self-indulgence, of hardening materialism, of falling moral standards... When we see around us the havoc which has been wrought—above all among children—by the break-up of homes, we can have no doubt that divorce and separation are responsible for some of the darkest evils in our society today.

—Queen Elizabeth II

43

People will not look forward to posterity who never look backward to their ancestors.

—*Edmund Burke*

If there's a heaven upon the earth,
   a fellow knows it when
He's been away from home a week,
   and then gets back again.

—*Will Carleton*

A house is infinitely communicative and tells many things besides the figure of its master's income. There are houses that confess intellectual penury, and houses that reek of enlightenment.

—*Robert William Chapman*

We shall fight [for our homeland] on the beaches, we shall fight on the landing grounds, we shall fight in the fields and in the streets, we shall fight in the hills; we shall never surrender.

—*Winston Churchill*

Except the Lord build the house, they labour in vain that build it.

—*Psalm 127:1*

The greatest of all arts is the art of living together!

—*William Lyon Phelps*

❧

In families well ordered there is always one firm, sweet temper, which controls without seeming to dictate.

—*Bulwer-Lytton*

Happiness is a homemade article.

—*English Proverb*

A family without a government is like a house without a roof, exposed to every wind that blows.

—*Matthew Henry*

*N*athaniel and Sophia Peabody Hawthorne spent the first years of their married life in The Old Manse, at the edge of Concord, a few steps away from the famous bridge where the first shots of the American Revolution were fired. They were poor but very much in love... But money in the Hawthorne home was something to be spent, enjoyed, given to those who needed it, and forgotten. Love, bestowed freely, and an atmosphere of cultural interests and intellectual curiosity were the heritage of the children.

—*Robin McKown*

*T*he memory of home becomes a past, an experience, an ideal we seek to re-create in our later lives, and in the new lives we shepherd into the world. We build our own homes, offer our own lessons, nurture our own children in the strength and knowledge once gained beside the first warm hearth of home.

—*William J. Bennett*

*H*elp thy brother's boat across, and lo! thine own has reached the shore.

—*Hindu Proverb*

*T*he first home was made when a woman, cradling in her loving arms a baby, crooned a lullaby.

—*Elbert Hubbard*

I recommend to parents to make your home a place of warm hospitality. You might not realize it at the time, but you may truly be entertaining angels unaware.

—*Evelyn LeTourneau*

*H*ome is the definition of God.

—*Emily Dickinson*

*L*et me be glad the kettle gently sings, let me be glad for little things.

—*Edna Jaques*

*N*ever part without loving words to think of during your absence. It may be that you will not meet again in life.

—*Jean Paul Richtery*

*M*y hope is that, when I am gone, my son will remember me not from battle, but in the home, repeating with him one simple prayer, "Our Father which art in heaven."

—*General Douglas MacArthur*

❧

*Y*ou can't appreciate home till you've left it, money till it's spent, your wife till she's joined a woman's club, nor Old Glory till you see it hanging on a broomstick on the shanty of a consul in a foreign town.

—*O. Henry*

A man cannot leave a better legacy to the world than a well-educated family.

—*Thomas Scott*

❧

A dining room table with children's eager, hungry faces around it ceases to be a mere dining room table, and becomes an altar.

—*Simeon Strunsky*

*W*hom God loves, his house is sweet to him.

—*Cervantes*

❧

*N*o one has so big a house that he does not need a good neighbor.

—*Swedish Proverb*

A life without love in it is like a heap of ashes upon a deserted hearth—with the fire dead, the laughter stilled and the light extinguished.

—*Frank P. Tebbetts*

*H*ome interprets heaven. Home is heaven for beginners.

—*Charles H. Parkhurst*

Way down upon the Swanee river,
   Far, far away,
There's where my heart is turning ever,
There's where the old folks stay.
All up and down the whole creation,
   Sadly I roam,
Still longing for the old plantation,
And for the old folks at home.

—Stephen C. Foster

Only that traveling is good which reveals to me the value of home, and enables me to enjoy it better.

—Henry David Thoreau

A father's heart is tender, though the man's is made of stone.

—Owen D. Young

The presidency is temporary—but the family is permanent.

—Yvonne de Gaulle

We Americans have lost something out of our lives and thought of late years. Something our forefathers had, something our fathers possessed. They were always aware of the uncertainty of life. They lived among hills and by streams; they lived with the simple animals of the fields. They saw the processes of life and death, of nature unfolding before their eyes. They saw planting time and harvest. They saw the passing of the seasons. And they were always thoughtful. In the terminology of a brooding sense of the ephemeral, they learned the deeper quality of life and of the eternity that underlies it.

—Norman Vincent Peale

Always reward your long hours of labor and toil in the very best way, surrounded by your family... And even if you have failed at all else in the eyes of the world, if you have a loving family, you are a success.

—Og Mandino

We often dream of the splendors of faraway places, but on inspection those attractions are seldom as precious as home.

—William J. Bennett

In ancient countries, where the social unit is the big family, where grandparents and parents, uncles and aunts and cousins all live together within one surrounding wall and function as a community, the children belong to all. The family community is itself the stream of life, leading into nation and world. But two people struggling to make a living in our highly competitive society in a fluctuating era cannot at the same time feed, clothe, educate, train and inspire a family of restless and lively children.

—Pearl S. Buck

Behold, how good and how pleasant it is for brethren to dwell together in unity!

—Psalm 133:1

Where is home? Home is where the heart can laugh without shyness. Home is where the heart's tears can dry at their own pace.

—Vernon G. Baker

Other things may change us, but we start and end with family.

—Anthony Brandt

It is impossible to overstate the need for prayer in the fabric of family life.

—James Dobson

The horrid prospect that television has opened of nobody speaking and nobody reading suggests that a bleak and torpid epoch may lie ahead. If it lasts long enough, it will gradually, according to the principles of evolution, produce a population indistinguishable from the lower forms of plant life.

Astronomers once detected something on Mars that looked like moss growing. I am convinced that Mars used to be inhabited by rational human beings like ourselves, who had the misfortune, some thousands of years ago, to invent television.

—Robert Hutchins

And having food and raiment let us be therewith content.

—I Timothy 6:8

48

*H*ome should be a place of mutual responsibility and respect, of encouragement and cooperation and counsel, of integrity, of willingness to work, of discipline when necessary, with the tempering quality of love added to it.

—Richard L. Evans

*T*oday, one can sit in the comfort of his own home and explore any part of the world or even outer space through books. They are all around us, offering such riches as can scarcely be believed. Also, I might add, having done both, it is better to sit in comfort with a cold drink at hand and read the tale than to actually walk out on the Mojave Desert.

—Louis L'Amour

*T*he thirteen members of the family Gilbreth [of *Cheaper By The Dozen* fame]...were a kind of living laboratory. Mother Lillian and Father Frank were both industrial engineers and partners, who specialized in time-and-motion studies and applied their rules for production-line efficiency to the way they ran their home.

—Life

*W*here, after all, do universal human rights begin? In small places, close to home—so close and so small that they cannot be seen on any map of the world. Yet they are the world of the individual person: the neighborhood he lives in; the school or college he attends; the factory, farm or office where he works. Such are the places where every man, woman and child seeks equal justice, equal opportunity, equal dignity without discrimination. Unless these rights have meaning there, they have little meaning anywhere. Without concerted citizen action to uphold them close to home, we shall look in vain for progress in the larger world.

—Eleanor Roosevelt

*P*art of the weariness of modern life may be that we are entertained and fed too regularly. Once we were separated by hunger from food and families, and then we learned to value both.

—Andre Deutsch

*F*amily faces are magic mirrors. Looking at people who belong to us, we see the past, present and future. We make discoveries about ourselves.

—Gail Lumet Buckley

Set thine house in order.

—*II Kings 1:20*

All happy families resemble one another.

—*Leo Tolstoy*

The family is the place to learn Jesus. God sent the family—together as husband and wife and children—to be His love.

—*Mother Teresa*

≈

In my parental home and later in my own home, we never asked if we were going to go to Sunday school. Nor was the general feeling that we *had* to go. You see, we always attended. It had always been accepted as a fact—all of us always went. None of the family stayed at home. It was important to be at Sunday school. We were never *taken* there by our parents; they came with us.

—*Evelyn LeTourneau*

No society has ever survived after its family life deteriorated.

—*Dr. Paul Popenoe*

The stable home background with its balanced parent-complex is as vital as the placental link in pregnancy. Without it the child cannot prosper or profit, however good the available facilities.

—*Dr. Louisa Eickhoff*

My precept to all who build is, that the owner should be an ornament to the house, and not the house to the owner.

—*Cicero*

Perhaps something deep within us realizes the family is the foundation of civilization. Perhaps we instinctively know that when we come to the bottom line in life it's not money, career, fame, a fine house, land or material possessions that are important—it is the people in our lives who love and care for us.

—*Awake!*

A family is a mobile strung together with invisible threads—delicate, easily broken at first, growing stronger through the years, in danger of being worn thin at times, but strengthened again with special care. A family—blended, balanced, growing, changing, never static, moving with a breath of wind—babies, children, young people, mothers, fathers, grandparents, aunts, uncles—held in a balanced framework by the invisible threads of love, memories, trust, loyalty, compassion, kindness, in honor preferring each other, depending on each other, looking to each other for help, giving each other help, picking each other up, suffering long with each other's faults, understanding each other more and more, hoping all things, enduring all things, never failing...knowing always that if a thread wears thin and sags, there is help to be had from the Expert—the Father—"Of whom the whole family in heaven and earth is named."

—Edith Schaeffer

*M*ultiply your influence by raising up God-fearing patriots at your own fireside. We need more than one generation of patriots in a family line. We need more like John Adams, who took time amid all the demands of the Revolution in the building of this republic to teach and train a future president, his own son, John Quincy Adams. Stay close to your children.

—Ezra Taft Benson

❧

*T*he ultimate survival of our society depends on the quality of our families.

—Walter Barlowe

*H*abits we learn in the home are the habits we carry with us into the world.

—William J. Bennett

*N*one but a mule denies his family.

—Anonymous

*T*he family is one of nature's masterpieces.

—George Santayana

51

$\mathcal{I}$ had rather be shut up in a very modest cottage with my books, my family, and a few old friends, dining on simple bacon and letting the world roll on as it liked, than to occupy the most splendid post which any human power can give.

—Thomas Jefferson

$\mathcal{T}$he real housewife...loves her home. Her house is only part of home. Home is the total environment and atmosphere in which the family lives. It includes the yard, the garden, the flowers on the table, the books in the living room, the music in the air, good talk as well as television, family excursions as well as indoor games on a winter's evening. The life shared by every member of the family with every other makes the atmosphere of home.

—Pearl S. Buck

$\mathcal{G}$od setteth the solitary in families.

—Psalm 68:6

$\mathcal{T}$he family you came from is important, but not as important as the family you will leave behind.

—Gary Rosberg

$\mathcal{C}$hristmas morning arrived, and Bob and I crept downstairs just after dawn... We had a glorious time as we opened the gifts that were under the tree... Mother said, "Let's all go down to meet the morning train from Cincinnati. Maybe Santa Claus forgot to send something and it will come on the train."

So we rode the horse-drawn sleigh through the snow to the railroad station and waited until the train pulled in... There it was—a red bicycle. It was a secondhand bicycle, to be sure, and two brothers had to share it, but Bob and I were ecstatic... Years later I learned that Mother made do with her old coat for another season and Dad wore the same blue suit so that we might have our dream.

—Norman Vincent Peale

$\mathcal{H}$e that raises a large family does, indeed, while he lives to observe them, stand a broader mark for sorrow; but then he stands a broader mark for pleasure, too.

—Benjamin Franklin

52

We need to help our children understand that we adults are not against sex; we're against the misuse of God's gift of sex.

—*Bob DeMoss*

A little house well fill'd, a little land well till'd, and a little wife well will'd, are great riches.

—*John Ray*

Our family life was free from parental quarreling and filled with genuine, if not demonstrated love.

—*Dwight D. Eisenhower*

Monarchs, we envy not your state.
We look with pity on the great
And bless our humbler lot.

—*Elizabeth Speer Buchanan*

Almighty and everlasting God, be Thou present with us in all our duties, and grant the protection of Thy presence to all that dwell in this house, that Thou mayest be known to be the Defender of this household and the Inhabitant of this dwelling; through Jesus Christ our Lord. Amen.

—*Gelasian Sacramentary*

Revere the religion of home. Keep its altar flame bright in your heart... In every time, the home conserves the sacred flame of life, and the destiny of the nation rests on those who keep it.

—*Julia Ward Howe*

There is no substitute for the home. Its foundation is as ancient as the world, and its mission has been ordained of God from the earliest times. From Abraham sprang two ancient races represented in Isaac and Ishmael. The one built stable homes and prized its land as a divine inheritance. The other became children of the desert, and as restless as its ever-shifting sands upon which their tents were pitched. From that day to the present, the home has been the chief characteristic of superior over inferior nations. The home then is more than a habitation, it is an institution which stands for stability and love in individuals as well as nations.

—*Joseph F. Smith*

$\mathcal{B}$y the rivers of Babylon, there we sat down, yea, we wept, when we remembered Zion... For they that carried us away captive required of us a song; and they that wasted us required of us mirth, saying, Sing us one of the songs of Zion... How shall we sing the Lord's song in a strange land?

—*Psalm 137:1,3,4*

$\mathcal{S}$ome homes are unhappy homes because of a wrong concept of success. The measure of success is often too limited; it is based on accomplishments in one area of life only... It is natural to desire a reasonable living; food, clothing, and a home are necessary. But so often our appetite grows faster than our income, and there is that tendency to become discontented.

—*Evelyn LeTourneau*

$\mathcal{I}$do not fear the might and power of the Persian army from without as much as I fear the spiritual and moral decline of our homes from within.

—*Pericles*

$\mathcal{T}$he home was the center for everything really important. The best eating place in town was at home. There were close ties to the church and the school... There were few divorces because of economic dependence on each other. In a farming community the man needed a good wife. A wife depended on her husband for support. Children needed their parents and parents needed large families to do all the work on the farm. Economically they were dependent on each other.

—*Leslie Parrott*

❧

$\mathcal{T}$here are as many pleasant things, as many
  pleasant tones
For those who dwell by cottage hearths as those
  who sit on thrones.

—*Phoebe Cary*

$\mathcal{O}$h, to have a little house!
To own the hearth and stool and all!

—*Padraic Colum*

54

There's a magical tie to the land of our home,
Which the heart cannot break, though the footsteps may roam.

—*Eliza Cook*

If solid happiness we prize,
Within our breasts this jewel lies,
    And they are fools who roam.
The world has nothing to bestow;
From our own selves our joys must flow,
    And that dear hut, our home.

—*Nathaniel Cotton*

The domestic hearth. There only is real happiness.

—*Anatole France*

Such is the patriot's boast where'er we roam,
His first, best country ever is at home.

—*Oliver Goldsmith*

Bless the four corners of this house,
    And be the lintel blest;
And bless the hearth and bless the board
    And bless each place of rest.

—*Arthur Guiterman*

My house, my house, though thou art small, thou art to me the
Escurial.

—*George Herbert*

Home is where the heart is.

—*Pliny the Elder*

Little I ask; my wants are few,
    I only wish a hut of stone,
(A very plain brown stone will do,)
    That I may call my own.

—*Oliver Wendell Holmes*

*T*here can be no freedom or beauty about a home life that depends on borrowing and debt.

—*Henrik Ibsen*

I want to go home
To the dull old town,
With the shaded street
And the open square;
And the hill
And the flats
And the house I love,
And the paths I know—
I want to go home.

—*Paul Kester*

*B*ut we who inherit the primal curse, and labour for our bread,
Have yet, thank God, the gift of Home, though Eden's gate is barred.

—*Joyce Kilmer*

ਵ

I came home forever!

—*Charles Lamb*

*K*indness is contagious. The spirit of harmony trickles down by a thousand secret channels into the inmost recesses of the household life.

—*Henry Van Dyke*

*A*fter the Exile, synagogues became centers for teaching and studying the Law. Today when Jewish families attend the synagogue they hear the Law read to them from sacred scrolls kept in an ark over which burns a perpetual light. Their faithful love and observance of the law during thousands of years is largely responsible for the unity of Jewish families.

—*Edith Deen*

*I*f the world's a wilderness,
Go, build houses in it!

—*Lucy Larcom*

56

*F*amily must be the individual's stronghold, his safety and his shelter, and there is no welfare agency or state institution or public organization which will do so well for the needy child, or adult for that matter, as the concerned family. Somehow the American family must be taught responsibility for its own again.

—*Pearl S. Buck*

*F*or there's nae luck about the house,
  There's nae luck at a';
There's little pleasure in the house
  When our gudeman's awa.

—*William Julius Mickle*

A man travels the world over in search of what he needs and returns home to find it.

—*George Moore*

*W*e go into the world wisely, go through the world bravely, and go out of the world peacefully when we start with the great fortification that is home.

—*William J. Bennett*

*T*he little Road says, Go;
The little House says, Stay;
And oh, it's bonny here at home,
But I must go away.

—*Josephine Preston Peabody*

A man of worth
In his own household will appear upright
In the state also.

—*Sophocles*

*J*est a-wearyin' for you—
All the time a-feelin' blue;
Wishin' fer you—wonderin' when
You'll be comin' home again.

—*Frank Lebby Stanton*

The sun shines bright in the old Kentucky home.
'Tis summer, the darkeys are gay.
The corn top's ripe and the meadow's in the bloom,
While the birds make music all the day.
The young folks roll on the little cabin floor.
All merry, all happy and bright:
By'n by Hard Times come a-knocking at the door,
Then my Old Kentucky Home, good night!

Weep no more, my lady, Oh! weep no more today!
We will sing one song for the old Kentucky Home,
For the old Kentucky Home, far away.

—*Stephen C. Foster*

No man but feels more of a man in the world if he have a bit of ground that he can call his own. However small it is on the surface, it is four thousand miles deep; and that is a very handsome property.

—*Charles Dudley Warner*

Family ties remain the strongest in the homes where discipline and self-control have been a way of life.

—*James Dobson*

Have I ever really told you anything about our family?... My father's parents were very rich. His father had worked himself right up and his mother came from a prominent family, who were also rich. So in his youth Daddy had a real little rich boy's upbringing, parties every week, balls, festivities, beautiful girls, dinners, a large home, etc.

After Grandpa's death all the money was lost during the World War and the inflation that followed. Daddy was therefore extremely well brought up and he laughed very much yesterday when, for the first time in his fifty-five years, he scraped out the frying pan at table.

Mummy's parents were rich too and we often listen openmouthed to stories of engagement parties of two hundred and fifty people, private balls and dinners. One certainly could not call us rich now, but all my hopes are pinned on after the war.

—*Anne Frank*

$\mathcal{I}$t ought, therefore, to enter into the domestic policy of every parent to make her children feel that home is the happiest place in the world... This delicious home-feeling is one of the choicest gifts a parent can bestow.

—Beetons's Book of Household Management

$\mathcal{B}$ut what on earth is half so dear—so longed for—as the hearth of home?

—Emily Bronte

$\mathcal{G}$od oft hath a great share in a little house.

—George Herbert

❦

$\mathcal{L}$et us pity those who haven't ancestors of whom they can be proud, dukes or duchesses though they be.

—Andrew Carnegie

$\mathcal{I}$ knew by the smoke, that so gracefully curl'd
    Above the green elms, that a cottage was near;
And I said, "If there's peace to be found in the world,
    A heart that was humble might hope for it here!"

—Thomas Moore

❦

$\mathcal{F}$or me, a house without children cannot be a home. I do not know why people who love children are so often prevented by accident from having them but, God be thanked, there are many who have children and leave them, for one reason or another, and then others can take them for love's sake... We approached our one adopted child, then eleven years old, and asked her what she thought of our adopting two little boys, and then, a year or so later, a girl and a boy. She reflected for some weeks and months, and only when she decided it would be "nice" to have babies did we adopt our three boys and a girl... That was eighteen years ago... The years...have been rich with living, with the writing of many books, and with a quiet, steady background of farming and home and children and work.

—Pearl S. Buck

As a nurse no female ever had more tenderness nor anxiety. He [Father, Thomas Jefferson] nursed my poor mother...sitting up with her and administering her medicines and drink to the last. For four months that she lingered, he was never out of calling; when not at her bedside, he was writing in a small room which opened immediately at the head of her bed.

—Martha Jefferson Randolph

To be happy at home is the ultimate result of all ambition, the end to which every enterprise and labor tends, and of which every desire prompts the prosecution.

—Samuel Johnson

Peace of mind may transform a cottage into a spacious manor hall; the want of it can make a regal park an imprisoning nutshell.

—Joshua Loth Liebman

Good-bye proud world! I'm going home.
I am going to my own hearth-stone,
Bosomed in yon green hills alone,—
A spot that is sacred to thought and God.

—Ralph Waldo Emerson

A happy family is but an earlier heaven.

—John Bowring

He is the happiest, be he king or peasant, who finds peace in his home.
—Johann Wolfgang von Goethe

Possessions, outward success, publicity, luxury—to me these have always been contemptible. I believe that a simple and unassuming manner of life is best for everyone, best for both the body and the mind.

—Albert Einstein

The end of all our exploring
Will be to arrive where we started
And know the place for the first time.

—T.S. Eliot

60

It was written of John Ruskin that "the home atmosphere in which [he] grew up was one of utter peace and complete order. The relation between his father and mother was a beautiful one. There were no quarrels, no mysterious undercurrents of trouble or unhappiness so depressing to a sensitive child; and...the domestic machinery ran in well-ordered grooves."

—*Mabel B. Peyton & Lucia Kinley*

The home is the empire! There is no peace more delightful than one's own fireplace.

—*Cicero*

Two persons who love each other are in a place more holy than the interior of a church.

—*William Lyon Phelps*

Often love of one's own summons the most miraculous human strengths.

—*William J. Bennett*

❦

Many years I lost happiness... And then one day, at a little station out on a wooded cliff near the sea, I saw a woman waiting in a tiny car, with a child asleep in her arms. A man alighted from a train, walked to her quickly, embraced her, and kissed the child gently, careful lest he should awaken it. They drove off together to some modest home among the fields; and it seemed to me that happiness was with them.

—*Will Durant*

History teaches us that there is no substitute for the family if we are to have a society that stands for human beings at their best.

—*Ray Lyman Wilbur*

Among the conditions of life or the laws of Nature, some of which seem to us faulty, some apparently unjust and merciless, there are many that amaze us by their beauty and sweetness. Love of home, regardless of its character or location, certainly is one of these.

—*Andrew Carnegie*

61

*T*is sweet to hear the watch-dog's honest bark
Bay deep-mouth'd welcome as we draw near home;
'Tis sweet to know there is an eye will mark
Our coming, and look brighter when we come.

—Lord Byron

*T*he domestic affections are the principal source of human happiness and well-being. The mutual loves of husband and wife, of parents and children, of brothers and sisters, are not only the chief sources of happiness, but the chief springs of action, and the chief safeguards from evil.

—Charles W. Eliot

*W*ithout the fireside there is no human advancement; without the family relation there is no life worth living.

—Robert Ingersoll

*H*appiness grows at our own firesides, and is not to be picked in stranger's gardens.

—Douglas Jerrold

*P*eace and rest at length have come,
   All the day's long toil is past,
And each heart is whispering, "Home,
   Home at last."

—Thomas Hood

*H*ow dear to this heart are the scenes of my childhood,
When fond recollection presents them to view:—
The orchard, the meadow, the deep-tangled wildwood,
And every lov'd spot which my infancy knew.

—Samuel Woodworth

*G*od gives all men all earth to love,
But since man's heart is small,
Ordains for each one spot should prove
Beloved over all.

—Rudyard Kipling

$\mathcal{I}$ was privileged in the spring to visit in a home that was to me—and I am sure to the occupants—a little bit of Heaven.

There was beauty there. There was a keen appreciation of the finer things of life, and an atmosphere in which it was impossible to keep from thinking of God.

The room was bright and white and clean, as well as cozy. There were many windows. Flowers were blooming in pots and vases, adding their fragrance and beauty.

Hyacinths and lilies of the valley had been placed gracefully and lovingly before a little shrine where the family could worship.

Books lined one wall—good books—good friends. Three bird cages hung in the brightness and colour of this beautiful sanctuary, and the songsters voiced their appreciation by singing as if their little throats would burst.

Nature's music, nature's beauty—nature's peace... It seemed to me a kind of Paradise that had wandered down, an enchanted oasis—home.

—*Peter Marshall*

$\mathcal{T}$ he home is the citadel of American life. If the home is lost, all is lost.

—*J. Edgar Hoover*

$\mathcal{L}$ ord, grant that our time together may be steeped in serenity, sweetened by sharing, and surrounded by the warm fragrance of your love. Amen.

—*Teatime Blessing*

$\mathcal{L}$ earn some of the old hymns and sing them together... Sunday nights before supper is a good time.

—*Norman Vincent Peale*

$\mathcal{H}$ ome and religion are kindred words, home, because it is the seat of religion; religion because it is the sacred element of home... A house without a roof would scarcely be a more indifferent home than a family without religion.

—*Horace Bushnell*

$\mathcal{T}$ he nation rests on the cottage.

—*John Bright*

Mid pleasures and palaces though we may roam,
Be it ever so humble, there's no place like home;
A charm from the sky seems to hallow us there,
Which, seek through the world, is ne'er met with elsewhere.
    Home, home, sweet, sweet home!
There no place like home, there's no place like home!

An exile from home, splendor dazzles in vain;
Oh, give me my lowly thatched cottage again!
The birds singing gaily, that came at my call—
Give me them—and the peace of mind, dearer than all!
    Home, home, sweet, sweet home!
There's no place like home, there's no place like home!

I gaze on the moon as I tread the drear wild,
And feel that my mother now thinks of her child,
As she looks on that moon from our own cottage door
Thro' the woodbine, whose fragrance shall cheer me no more.
    Home, home, sweet, sweet home!
There's no place like home, there's no place like home!

How sweet 'tis to sit 'neath a fond father's smile,
And the cares of a mother to soothe and beguile!
Let others delight 'mid new pleasures to roam,
But give me, oh, give me, the pleasures of home,
    Home, home, sweet, sweet home,
There's no place like home, there's no place like home!

To thee I'll return, overburdened with care;
The heart's dearest solace will smile on me there;
No more from that cottage again will I roam,
Be it ever so humble, there's no place like home.
    Home, home, sweet, sweet home!
There's no place like home, there's no place like home!

—*John Howard Payne*

There is little less trouble in governing a private family than a whole kingdom.

—*Michel De Montaigne*

There is probably no greater blessing in life than the blessing of a happy home.

—*Evelyn LeTourneau*

A good laugh is sunshine in a house.

—*William Makepeace Thackeray*

When Mother Teresa received her Nobel Prize, she was asked, "What can we do to promote world peace?" She replied, "Go home and love your family."

—*W.B. Freeman Concepts*

But if any provide not for his own, and specially for those of his own house, he hath denied the faith, and is worse than an infidel.

—*I Timothy 5:8*

Home is the place to build strength and resolve before going out into the world... We find that lessons we've learned and loved at home stay with us and sustain us. Virtues travel well.

—*William J. Bennett*

A house without books is like a room without windows.

—*Horace Mann*

A home is the first necessity of every family; it is indispensable to the education and qualification of every citizen.

—*Seward*

I have never seen a vagabond who really liked to roam
All up and down the streets of the world and have not a home.
The tramp who slept in your barn last night
And left at break of day
Will wander only until he finds another place to stay.

—*Joyce Kilmer*

The house of the righteous shall stand.

—Proverbs 12:7

When the going gets tough at home, get on your knees before the Lord and ask for His strength and wisdom. Finish the job to which He has called you!

—James Dobson

ॐ

You'll find, where'er you roam,
   That marble floors and gilded wall
Can never make a home.

But every house where Love abides,
   And friendship is a guest,
Is surely home, and home-sweet-home:
   For there the heart can rest.

—Henry Van Dyke

Father in Heaven, we thank Thee!
   For mother-love and father-care,
For brothers strong and sisters fair;
   For love at home and here each day;
For guidance lest we go astray,
   Father in Heaven, we thank Thee!

—Ralph Waldo Emerson

And where we love is home,
Home that our feet may leave, but not our hearts.
The chain may lengthen, but it never parts.

—Oliver Wendell Holmes

A house is built of logs and stone,
   Of tiles and posts and piers;
A home is built of loving deeds
   That stand a thousand years.

—Victor Hugo

$\mathcal{I}$ lived with Love; all she possest
  Was but a tent beside a stream.
She warmed my cold hands with her breast,
  She wove around my sleep a dream.
And One there was with face divine
  Who softly came, when day was spent,
And turned our water into wine,
  And made our life a sacrament.

—William J. Dawson

$\mathcal{W}$hat house is there so established or what state so firmly settled, that may not utterly be overthrown by hatred and dissension?

—Cicero

$\mathcal{B}$etter than gold is a peaceful home
Where all the fireside characters come,
The shrine of love, the heaven of life,
Hallowed by mother, or sister, or wife.
However humble the home may be,
Or tried with sorrow by heaven's decree,
The blessings that never were bought or sold,
And center there, are better than gold.

—Abram J. Ryan

$\mathcal{A}$s the bird that wandereth from her nest, so is a man that wandereth from his place.

—Proverbs 27:8

$\mathcal{W}$ho loves the rain
  And loves his home,
And looks on life with quiet eyes,
  Him will I follow through the storm;
  And at his hearth-fire keep me warm;
Nor hell nor heaven shall that soul surprise,
  Who loves the rain,
  And loves his home,
And looks on life with quiet eyes.

—Frances Wills Shaw

67

There's a blessing on the hearth,
A special providence for fatherhood.

—*Robert Browning*

In the days of slavery not very much attention was given to family history and family records—that is, black family records. My mother, I suppose attracted the attention of a purchaser who was afterward my owner and hers. Her addition to the slave family attracted about as much attention as the purchase of a new horse or cow. Of my father I know even less than of my mother. I do not even know his name. I have heard reports to the effect that he was a white man who lived on one of the near-by plantations. Whoever he was, I never heard of his taking the least interest in me or providing in any way for my rearing. But I do not find especial fault with him. He was simply another unfortunate victim of the institution which the Nation unhappily had engrafted upon it at that time.

—*Booker T. Washington*

Home is the one place in all this world where hearts are sure of each other. It is a place of confidence. It is the place where we tear off the mask of guarded suspiciousness and coldness which the world forces us to wear in self-defense, and where we pour out the unreserved communications of full and confiding hearts. It is the spot where expressions of tenderness flow without any sensation of awkwardness and without any dread of ridicule.

—*F.W. Robertson*

A hometown is a place where every second person you meet on Main Street is some kind of cousin.

—*Josh Billings*

But they shall sit every man under his vine and under his fig tree; and none shall make them afraid.

—*Micah 4:4*

The American West would still be an unfenced wilderness if the pioneers had left their wives at home.

—*Zane Grey*

68

The family is more sacred than the state.

—*Pope Pius XI*

I like to see a man proud of the land he lives on. I like to see a man live so his land will be proud of him.

—*Abraham Lincoln*

Happy are the families where the government of parents is the reign of affection.

—*Francis Bacon*

It is the peculiarity of man, in comparison with the rest of the animal world, that he alone possesses a perception of good and evil, of just and unjust, and of other similar qualities; and it is association in these things which makes a family.

—*Aristotle*

[Alone for more than two months at the Bolling Advance Weather Base near the South Pole:] My first need was warmth and food. The fire had been out 12 hours; I had not eaten in 36... It wasn't the fear of suffering or of death itself, but a terrible anxiety over the consequences to those at home if I failed to return... I saw my whole life pass in review. I realized how wrong my sense of values had been and how I had failed to see that the simple, homely things of life are the most important...

The only conscious resolve left was to write a message to my wife... But I was too weak to write sitting up... After I finished this letter I rested a long time and then wrote messages to my mother, my children and the expedition at Little America. I secured them all with a string to the nail from which the lantern hung.

—*Richard E. Byrd*

Not only should you have a strong spiritual home, but you should have a strong temporal home. Avoid financial bondage by getting out of debt as soon as you can. Pay as you go and live within your income.

—*Ezra Taft Benson*

Where shall a man find sweetness to surpass his own home and parents?

—*Homer*

Camp Clark,
Washington
July 14, 1861

My very dear Sarah,

The indications are very strong that we shall move in a few days—perhaps tomorrow... I feel impelled to write a few lines that may fall under your eye when I shall be no more...

I have no misgivings about, or lack of confidence in, the cause in which I am engaged, and my courage does not halt or falter... Sarah, my love for you is deathless. It seems to bind me with mighty cables that nothing but Omnipotence could break; and yet my love of country comes over me like a strong wind and burns me unresistibly on with all these chains to the battlefield.

The memories of the blissful moments I have spent with you come creeping over me, and I feel most gratified to God and to you that I have enjoyed them so long... Sarah, never forget how much I love you, and when my last breath escapes me on the battlefield, it will whisper your name.

But, O Sarah! If the dead can come back to this earth and flit unseen around those they loved, I shall always be near you in the gladdest days and in the darkest nights... Sarah, do not mourn me dead; think I am gone and wait for thee, for we shall meet again.

As for my little boys—they will grow up as I have done, and never know a father's love and care... Sarah, I have unlimited confidence in your maternal care...and feel that God will bless you in your holy work.

Tell my two Mothers I call God's blessings upon them. O! Sarah. I wait for you there; come to me and lead thither my children.
　　　　　—Sullivan Ballou [a week before being killed at Bull Run]

❦

Blessings of the home often last longer when we remember to be grateful for them.

　　　　　—William J. Bennett

70

*Y*et setteth he the poor on high from affliction, and maketh him families like a flock.

—*Psalm 107:41*

*M*ake your home a place where criticism is seldom heard but where praise is a common thing.

—*Evelyn LeTourneau*

[*U*pon Washington's return home, after being gone eight years during the Revolution:] The General and I feel like children just released from school or from a hard taskmaster, and believe that nothing can tempt us to leave the sacred roof-tree again... We are loath to share it with anyone but dear friends.

—*Martha Washington*

*S*tay, stay at home, my heart and rest;
Home-keeping hearts are happiest,
For those that wander they know not where
Are full of trouble and full of care;
　To stay at home is best...

Then stay at home, my heart, and rest;
The bird is safest in its nest,
Over all that flutter their wings and fly
A hawk is hovering in the sky;
　To stay at home is best.

—*Henry Wadsworth Longfellow*

*F*athers grow old faster than people... [Fathers can't cry] while mothers can cry where it shows... Fathers are what give daughters away to other men who are not nearly good enough...so they can have grandchildren that are smarter than anybody's.

—*Paul Harvey*

I have seven grandchildren by my daughter [Sarah], who play with and amuse me, and she is a kind, attentive nurse to me when I am at any time indisposed.

—*Benjamin Franklin*

*H*ome is the most popular, and will be the most enduring of all earthly establishments.

—*Channing Pollock*

*H*e that has...no such connecting interests...as a home and a family...is exposed to temptation, to idleness, and in danger of becoming useless, if not a burden and a nuisance in society.

—*Samuel Johnson*

I am a family face;
Flesh perished, I live on,
Projecting trait and trace
Through time to times anon,
And leaping from place to place
Over oblivion.

—*Thomas Hardy*

*S*o much of what is great...has sprung from the closeness of the family ties.

—*Sir James M. Barrie*

*I*f thou wouldst be happy and easie in thy Family, above all things observe Discipline. Every one in it should know their Duty...and whatever else is done or omitted, be sure to begin and end with God.

—*William Penn*

*T*he home, a stable and pure home, is the highest guaranty of social stability and permanence in government.

—*Joseph F. Smith*

*T*he home where happiness securely dwells
Was never wrought by charms or magic spells.
A mother made it beautiful, but knew
No magic save what toiling hands can do.

—*Arthur Wallace Peach*

I am as happy nowhere else, and in no other society, and all my wishes end, where I hope my days will end, at Monticello.

—*Thomas Jefferson*

I'll take you home Kathleen,
Across the ocean wild and wide.
To where your heart has ever been,
Since first I won you for my bride...

O I'll take you home Kathleen,
To where your heart will feel no pain;
And when the fields are fresh and green,
I will take you to your home again.

—Alfred M. Durham

I lost [daughter] Susy 13 years ago; I lost her mother—her incomparable mother!—five and a half years ago; Clara has gone away to live in Europe; and now I have lost Jean. How poor I am who was once so rich!

—Mark Twain

Lord, behold our family here assembled. We thank Thee for this place in which we dwell; for the love that unites us; for the peace accorded us this day; for the hope with which we expect the morrow; for the health, the work, the food, and the bright skies that make our lives delightful; for our friends in all parts of the earth, and our friendly helpers in this foreign isle...

Give us courage, gaiety, and the quiet mind. Spare to us our friends, soften to us our enemies. Bless us, if it may be, in all our innocent endeavors. If it may not, give us the strength to encounter that which is to come, that we be brave in peril, constant in tribulation, temperate in wrath, and in all changes of fortune and down to the gates of death, loyal and loving one to another. Amen.

—Robert Louis Stevenson

We want our children in the years ahead to remember the calm voices of fathers and mothers who loved God and faced the future with intelligence and confidence. We want them to remember also that the destiny set before the Christian is a home. God is our Father. In the Father's house are many abiding places, and in his house we shall find a warm welcome, a glorious fellowship, and peace at last.

—David & Virginia Edens

*B*ut what is material success, physical comfort and exterior elegance, without happiness of the heart and the mind and the spiritual peace of soul? I have found happiness of heart in the companionship of the girl I married. I have found peace of soul in right living and in the memory of my mother and my father who are now blessed with the peace of eternal rest.

—Max Winkler

*O*ften we do not fully recognize some of the important lessons of home and hearth until those who have taught us are gone.

—William J. Bennett

*T*here is no fireside that does not have an empty chair.

—Spanish Proverb

*W*e give them back to you, dear Lord,
   who gavest them to us.
Yet as thou didst not lose them in giving,
   so we have not lost them by their return.
For what is thine is ours always
   if we are thine.
And life is eternal and love is immortal,
   and death is only a horizon,
   and a horizon is nothing more
   than the limit of our sight.

—Quaker Prayer

Marriage

Love, Courtship, and Commitment

Chapter Three
Marriage
Love, Courtship, and Commitment

And the Lord God said, It is not good that man should be alone; I will make him an help meet...and Adam said, This is now bone of my bones, and flesh of my flesh; she shall be called Woman, because she was taken out of Man. Therefore shall a man leave his father and his mother, and shall cleave unto his wife: and they shall be one Flesh.

—*Genesis 2:18,23-24*

Marriage is the most important part of any individual's life. It is far more than an event. It is the maturity toward which life shapes from the moment of birth.

—*Pearl S. Buck*

The first symptom of love in a young man is timidity, in a girl it is boldness. The two sexes have a tendency to approach, and each assumes the qualities of the other.

—*Victor Hugo*

Woman's natural mission is to love, to love but one, to love always.

—*Jules Michelet*

&

My heart is like a singing bird
    Whose nest is in a watered shoot:
My heart is like an apple tree
    Whose boughs are bent with thickset fruit;
My heart is like a rainbow shell
    That paddles in a halcyon sea;
My heart is gladder than all these
    Because my love is come to me.

—*Christina Rossetti*

When a man meets his fitting mate society begins.

—*Ralph Waldo Emerson*

O my luve is like a red, red rose,
    That's newly sprung in June:
O my luve is like the melodie,
    That's sweetly played in tune...

And fare thee weel, my only luve!
    And fare the weel a while!
And I will come again, my luve,
    Tho' it were ten thousand mile.

—*Robert Burns*

See, how she leans her cheek upon her hand.
O! that I were a glove upon that hand,
That I might touch that cheek.

—*William Shakespeare*

If thou must love me, let it be for naught
Except to love's sake only. Do not say,
"I love her for her smile—her look—her way
Of speaking gently—for a trick of thought
That falls in well with mine, and certes brought
A sense of pleasant ease on such a day"—
For these things in themselves, beloved, may
Be changed, or change for thee—and love, so wrought,
May be unwrought so. Neither love me for
Thine own dear pity's wiping my cheeks dry:
A creature might forget to weep, who bore
Thy comfort long, and lose thy love thereby!
But love me for love's sake, that evermore
Thou mayest love on, through love's eternity.

—*Elizabeth Barrett Browning*

Life is a sweet and joyful thing for one who has some one to love and
a pure conscience.

—*Leo Tolstoy*

*Y*oung love is a flame—very pretty—often very hot and fierce, but still only light and flickering. The love of the older and disciplined heart is as coals, deep-burning, unquenchable.

—Henry Ward Beecher

*B*y all means marry. If you get a good wife, you will become very happy; if you get a bad one, you will become a philosopher—and that is good for every man.

—Socrates

*I*ndeed, from the matches that have fallen under my observation, I am rather inclined to think that early ones stand the best chance for happiness...by early marriage, youth is sooner formed to regular and useful life; and possibly some of those accidents, habits, or connections that might have injured either the constitution or the reputation, or both, are thereby happily prevented.

—Benjamin Franklin

*W*e are foolish, and without excuse foolish, in speaking of the "superiority" of one sex to the other, as if they could be compared in similar things. Each has what the other has not: each completes the other, and is completed by the other: they are in nothing alike, and the happiness and perfection of both depends on each asking and receiving from the other what the other only can give.

—John Ruskin

*S*ome enchanted evening
You may see a stranger,
Across a crowded room
And somehow you know,
You know even then
That somewhere you'll
See her again and again.

Who can explain it?
Who can tell you why?
Fools give you reasons,
Wise men never try.

—Oscar Hammerstein II

*Y*oung men and women will do well if, long before marriage, they train themselves mentally and physically to be successful husbands and wives. It is worth it; for they are training for the highest prize obtainable on earth, and yet open to and won by millions.

—William Lyon Phelps

*N*ever marry but for love; but see that thou lovest what is lovely.

—William Penn

*F*or a wife take the daughter of a good mother.

—Thomas Fuller

*T*here be three things which are too wonderful for me, yea, four which I know not: The way of an eagle in the air; the way of a serpent upon a rock; the way of a ship in the midst of the sea; and the way of a man with a maid.

—Proverbs 30:18,19

*M*arriage is a step by which two imperfect individuals unite their forces in the struggle for happiness. They establish their own small social unit in order that they may better cope with society at large. Marriage is a step in the normal development of the individual, psychologically as well as biologically. It is an opportunity for happiness, not a gift. We cannot demand success in marriage any more than in any phase of life; we must achieve it. The finality of marriage and its vows, as expressed by the rituals of the churches, rightly emphasizes the fact that marriage is an obligation to create a better life, not an experiment in compatibility.

—Dr. Henry C. Link

*G*od help the man who won't marry until he finds a perfect woman, and God help him still more if he finds her.

—Ben Tillett

*T*he first run of maple syrup, John Burroughs says, is like first love, "always the best, always the fullest, always the sweetest, while there is a purity and delicacy of flavor about the sugar that far surpasses any subsequent yield."

—Pearl S. Buck

I am not one of those who do not believe in love at first sight, but I do believe in taking a second look.

—Henry Vincent

N ow is the hour when we must say goodbye.
Soon you'll be sailing far across the sea.
While you're away, oh, then remember me.
When you return, you'll find me waiting here.

—Dorothy Stewart

T here is no sorrow like a love denied
Nor any joy like love that has its will.

—Richard Hovey

I n the choice of a horse and a wife, a man must please himself, ignoring the opinion and advice of friends.

—George John Whyte-Melville

❧

O , inexpressible as sweet,
    Love takes my voice away;
I cannot tell thee when we meet
    What most I long to say.

—George Edward Woodberry

M y bounty is as boundless as the sea,
My love is as deep; the more I give thee
The more I have, for both are infinite.

—William Shakespeare

T ying her bonnet under her chin,
She tied her raven ringlets in;
But not alone in the silken snare
Did she catch her lovely floating hair,
For, tying her bonnet under her chin,
She tied a young man's heart within.

—Nora Perry

83

Love consists in this, that two solitudes protect and touch and greet each other.

—*Rainer Maria Rilke*

To win that wonder of the world,
    A smile from her bright eyes,
I fought my King and would have hurled
    The gods out of their skies.

—*Francois de la Lochefoucauld*

Life has taught us that love does not consist in gazing at each other but in looking outward together in the same direction.

—*Saint-Exupery*

The light of love, the purity of grace,
The mind, the music breathing from her face,
The heart whose softness harmonized the whole,—
And oh, that eye was in itself a soul!

—*Lord Byron*

He gave her a look you could have poured on a waffle.

—*Ring Lardner*

Because you come to me with naught save love,
And hold my hand and lift mine eyes above,
A wider world of hope and joy I see,
Because you come to me.

Because you speak to me in accents sweet,
I find the roses waking round my feet,
And I am led through tears of joy to see,
Because you speak to me.

Because God made thee mine I'll cherish thee
Through light and darkness, through all time to be,
And pray His love may make our lives divine.
Because God made thee mine.

—*Edward Teschemacher*

Down by the old mill stream,
Where I first met you,
With your eyes of blue,
Dressed in gingham too.

It was there I knew
That you loved me true.
You were sixteen,
My village queen,
Down by the old mill stream.

—Tell Taylor

It was some time in the early spring that Stephen [Foster] discovered Jane McDowell. Young men sometimes have a strange way with them. They see a pretty girl every day for months—at church, at concerts, at dancing parties. Then all of a sudden they discover she exists. They go about telling every one and wonder why no one else saw her before. It was so with Stephen.

—Claire Lee Purdy

Drink to me only with thine eyes,
    And I will pledge with mine;
Or leave a kiss but in the cup
    And I'll not ask for wine.
The thirst that from the soul doth rise
    Doth ask a drink divine;
But might I of Jove's nectar sup,
    I would not change for thine.

I sent thee late a rosy wreath,
    Not so much honoring thee
As giving it a hope that there
    It could not withered be;
But thou thereon dids't only breathe
    And send'st it back to me;
Since when it grows, and smells, I swear,
    Not of itself but thee.

—Ben Jonson

85

There were the days of so called free love...but it didn't take long to discover that love is not free. Sooner or later it exacts its price.

—*Flora Lewis*

I shall draw no characters nor give any enumeration of my youthful flames...they were all modest and virtuous girls and always maintained this character through life. No virgin or matron ever had cause to blush at the sight of me, or to regret her acquaintance with me. No father, brother, son, or friend ever had any cause of grief or resentment for any intercourse between me and any daughter, sister, mother, or any other relation of the female sex. My children may be assured that no illegitimate brother or sister exists or ever existed. These reflections, to me consolatory beyond all expression, I am able to make with truth and sincerity and I presume I am indebted for this blessing to my education. My parents held every species of libertinage in such contempt and horror... Happiness is lost forever if innocence is lost, at least until a repentance is undergone so severe as to be an overbalance to all the gratifications of licentiousness. Repentance itself cannot restore the happiness of innocence, at least in this life.

—*John Adams*

But love is blind, and lovers cannot see
The petty follies that themselves commit.

—*William Shakespeare*

It is a truth universally acknowledged, that a single man in possession of a good fortune, must be in want of a wife.

However little known the feelings or views of such a man may be on his first entering a neighbourhood, this truth is so well fixed in the minds of the surrounding families, that he is considered as the rightful property of some one or other of their daughters.

—*Jane Austen*

My strength is the strength of ten, because my heart is pure.

—*Alfred, Lord Tennyson*

Nothing is more difficult to choose than a good husband, unless it be to choose a good wife.

—*Jean-Jacques Rousseau*

A single man has not nearly the value he would have in a state of union. He is an incomplete animal.

—*Benjamin Franklin*

*T*he sunlight clasps the earth,
   And the moonbeams kiss the sea;—
What are all these kissings worth,
   If thou kiss not me?

—*Percy Bysshe Shelley*

*W*e poor common people must take wives whom we love and who love us.

—*Wolfgang Amadeus Mozart*

*A*nd if a man entice a maid that is not betrothed, and lie with her, he shall surely endow her to be his wife.

—*Exodus 22:16*

*H*ow ironic that one of God's greatest gifts to man [the union of the sexes] should be so deadly and destructive when misused.

—*Norman Vincent Peale*

❦

*M*aid of Athens, ere we part.
Give, oh! give me back my heart.

—*Lord Byron*

*H*e that would the daughter win,
Must with the mother first begin.

—*John Ray*

*A*nd what is a kiss, when all is done?
A promise given under seal—a vow
Taken before the shrine of memory—
A signature acknowledged—a rosy dot
Over the *i* of Loving.

—*Edmond Rostand*

$\mathcal{I}$f you wish to ruin yourself, marry a rich wife.

—*Jules Michelet*

$\mathcal{I}$n marriage, being the right person is as important as finding the right person.

—*Wilbert Donald Gough*

"$\mathcal{F}$orget thee?"—If to dream by night and muse on thee by
    day,
If all the worship, deep and wild, a poet's heart can pay,
If prayers in absence breathed for thee to Heaven's
    protecting power,
If winged thoughts that flit to thee—a thousand in an hour,
If busy fancy, blending thee with all my future lot—
If this thou call'st "forgetting," thou, indeed, shall be forgot!

—*John Moultrie*

$\mathcal{W}$ere beauty under twenty locks kept fast,
Yet love breaks through and picks them all at last.

—*William Shakespeare*

                     ॐ

$\mathcal{T}$here is nothing holier in this life of ours than the first consciousness of love—the first flutterings of its silken wings.

—*Henry Wadsworth Longfellow*

$\mathcal{T}$he perfect marriage must be a perfect blend of the spiritual, the physical, the social, and the intellectual... We are souls living in bodies. Therefore, when we really fall in love, it isn't just a physical attraction. If it's just that, it won't last. Ideally, it's also a spiritual attraction. God has opened our eyes and let us see into someone's soul. We have fallen in love with the inner person, the person who's going to live forever. That's why God is the greatest asset to romance. He thought it up in the first place. Include Him in every part of your marriage, and He will lift it above the level of the mundane to something rare and beautiful and lasting.

—*Peter Marshall*

I met Charlie at a party. He walked over to me, offered me a dish of peanuts, and said, "I wish they were emeralds."

—*Helen Hayes*

My love for you is mixed throughout my body.

—*Ancient Egyptian Love Song*

What I do and what I dream include thee, as the wine must taste of its own grapes.

—*Elizabeth Barrett Browning*

Where true love has found a home, every new year forms one more ring around the hearts of those who love each other, so that in the end they cannot love apart.

—*Julius Stinde*

Be ye not unequally yoked together with unbelievers...for ye are the temple of the living God.

—*II Corinthians 6:14,16*

❧

How can there be sexual freedom between man and woman without producing the homeless, unwanted child?

—*Pearl S. Buck*

The most important characteristic for a woman who will make a good marriage partner is a continuing regard for kindness. She doesn't have to be good-looking to be a good marriage partner, but she does need to be kind.

—*Leslie Parrott*

You can predict a good marriage with a woman who (1) is kind to everyone, (2) expects kindness from others, (3) is not easily offended, (4) is not unduly concerned over the impression she makes on others, and (5) does not see social relationships as rivalry situations. This kind of woman has the habit of happiness.

—*Dr. Termane*

She smiled, and the shadows departed;
   She shone, and the snows were rain;
And he who was frozen-hearted
   Bloomed up into love again.

                     —John Addington Symonds

I could not love thee, dear, so much,
Loved I not honor more.

                     —Richard Lovelace

Some pray to marry the man they love,
   My prayer will somewhat vary:
I humbly pray to Heaven above
   That I love the man I marry.

                     —Rose Pastor Stokes

The guy who marries the boss's daughter just winds up with two bosses.
                     —Ethel Merman

A prudent wife is from the Lord.

                     —Proverbs 19:14

A woman's best accessory is a well-dressed man.

                     —Albert Capraro

I am convinced that one of the reasons young married couples divorce so readily today is because the wife is not economically dependent upon her husband; whenever difficulties and pressures arise she can say, as one young lady said to me, "I don't have to take that kind of thing; I can live by myself." ...Marriage is a joint venture between two people who live as one. It is not two distinct corporations doing business under the same roof.
                     —Tim LaHaye

Remember if you marry for beauty, thou bindest thyself all thy life for that which, perchance, will neither last nor please thee one year.
                     —Sir Walter Raleigh

$\mathcal{W}$hatever woman may cast her lot with mine, should any ever do so, it is my intention to do all in my power to make her happy and contented; and there is nothing I can imagine that would make me more unhappy than to fail in the effort.

—Abraham Lincoln

$\mathcal{B}$eautiful dreamer, wake unto me,
Starlight and dew-drops are waiting for thee;
Sounds of the rude world heard in the day,
Lull'd by the moonlight have all pass'd away!
Beautiful dreamer, queen of my song,
List while I woo thee with soft melody;
Gone are the cares of life's busy throng,
Beautiful dreamer, awake unto me!
Beautiful dreamer, awake unto me!

—Stephen C. Foster

$\mathcal{I}$n the spring a young man's fancy lightly turns to thoughts of love.

—Alfred, Lord Tennyson

$\mathcal{N}$ot from the whole wide world I chose thee,
    Sweetheart, light of the land and the sea!
The wide, wide world could not enclose thee,
    For thou art the whole wide world to me.

—Richard Watson Gilder

$\mathcal{W}$hoso findeth a wife findeth a good thing.

—Proverbs 18:22

$\mathcal{C}$ome live with me, and be my love;
And we will all the pleasures prove
That hills and valleys, dales and fields,
Woods or steepy mountain yields.

—Christopher Marlowe

$\mathcal{G}$ood night, good night! parting is such sweet sorrow
That I shall say good night till it be morrow.

—William Shakespeare

She whom I love is hard to catch and conquer,
Hard, but O the glory of the winning were she won!

—*George Meredith*

ĕ

[To his fiancee Martha Custis, as he was leaving upon a campaign to oust the French:] We have begun our march for the Ohio...and I embrace the opportunity to send a few words to one whose life is now inseparable from mine. Since that happy hour when we made our pledges to each other, my thoughts have been continually going to you as to another self. That an all-powerful Providence may keep us in safety is the prayer of your ever faithful and affectionate friend.

—*George Washington*

Since we parted yester eve,
I do love thee, love, believe,
Twelve times dearer, twelve hours longer—
One dream deeper, one night stronger,
One sun surer—thus much more
Than I loved thee, love, before.

—*Edward Robert Bulwer Lytton*

Somewhere there waiteth in this world of ours
  For one lone soul, another lonely soul—
Each chasing each through all the weary hours,
  And meeting strangely at one sudden goal;
Then blend they—like green leaves with golden flowers,
  Into one beautiful and perfect whole—
And life's long night is ended, and the way
  Lies open onward to eternal day.

—*Sir Edwin Arnold*

Holy Matrimony...is an honorable estate, instituted of God in the time of innocency, signifying unto us the mystical union that is betwixt Christ and his Church.

—*The Book of Common Prayer*

92

She is coming, my own, my sweet;
  Were it ever so airy a tread...
My dust would hear her and beat,
  Had I lain for a century dead.

—*Alfred, Lord Tennyson*

I suppose the reason I long so much for you to love one who can truly love you is because your father and I have been utterly happy together. I have never loved another man, nor had he loved another woman before me. It is old-fashioned, I know. It is quite the thing, I hear, to say that one must experiment in love. Perhaps that is true for the shallow-hearted. But it is not true for the deep in heart. Your father and I are among those few. It made our love complete when we knew that what we gave each to the other was new and never given before. I assure you it did.

—*Pearl S. Buck*

[Peter]...made it clear to me in words that admitted of no duplicity that he had practiced the continence for the unmarried which he had preached.

—*Catherine Marshall*

The...key that guarantees a happy marriage is love. Probably no other word is more misunderstood in the English language than this one. Most people today do not know what love is. They often confuse physical attraction, lust, personal desire, sympathy, or compassion with love. Love is one of the most common experiences of man and one of the most difficult to define.

—*Tim LaHaye*

❧

An Undutiful Daughter will prove
An Unmanageable Wife.

—*Benjamin Franklin*

Marriage is like a three-speed gearbox: affection, friendship, love. It is not advisable to crash your gears and go right through to love straightway. You need to ease your way through. The basis of love is respect, and that needs to be learned from affection and friendship.

—*Peter Ustinov*

True love's the gift which God has given
To man alone beneath heaven.
It is not fantasy's hot fire,
Whose wishes soon as granted fly.
It liveth not in fierce desire...
With dead desire, it doth not die.
It is the secret sympathy,
The silver link, the silken ties,
Which heart to heart and mind to mind
In body and soul can bind.

—*Sir Walter Scott*

A wise young man will do well to rate ability to work in a prospective wife higher than beauty or wealth.

—*Dr. John A. Schindler*

To be a man in a true sense is, in the first place and above all things, to have a wife.

—*Jules Michelet*

Trust me—with women worth the being won,
The softest lover ever best succeeds.

—*Hill*

It warms me, it charms me,
   to mention but her name;

—*Robert Burns*

For oh! so wildly do I love him
That paradise itself were dim
And joyless, if not shared with him.

—*Thomas Moore*

My heart is heavy at the remembrance of all the miles that lie between us; and I can scarcely believe that you are so distant from me. We are parted; and every parting is a form of death, as every reunion is a type of heaven.

—*Edwards*

94

[The day of his wedding George Washington was]...so tall, so straight! And then he sat [upon] a horse and rode with such an air! Ah, sir, he was like no one else! Many of the grandest gentleman in their gold lace were at the wedding, but none looked like the man himself!

—*A Servant*

Why don't you speak for yourself, John?

—*Priscilla Mullins [Alden]*

The holy estate of matrimony...[is] to have and to hold from this day forward, for better for worse, for richer for poorer, in sickness and in health, to love and to cherish, till death do us part.

—*The Book of Common Prayer*

May He who has admitted these young people into the halls of highest human happiness richly bless them in their new life.

—*Peter Marshall*

❧

Let all thy joys be as the month of May,
And all thy days be as a marriage day:
Let sorrow, sickness, and a troubled mind
Be stranger to thee, let them never find
Thy heart at home.

—*Francis Quarles*

Music rose with its voluptuous swell—
Soft eyes looked love to eyes which spoke again
And all went merry as a marriage bell.

—*Lord Byron*

Under this window in stormy weather
I marry this man and woman together;
Let none but Him who rules the thunder
Put this man and woman asunder.

—*Jonathan Swift*

To most grooms the womanhood of his wife has almost a sacred quality. He views her in the double halo of a mystic mother-wife. She arouses his finest sensitivity, tenderness, and awareness of the things which are precious. She rings every bell there is in him, she turns on all the lights he has. If he could write poetry, he would. If he were a musician, he would compose his masterpiece.

—*Dr. John A. Schindler*

What therefore God hath joined together, let not man put asunder.

—*Matthew 19:6*

Hear the mellow wedding bells,
    Golden bells!
What a world of happiness their harmony foretells!
    Through the balmy air of night
    How they ring out their delight!

—*Edgar Allan Poe*

Look, how my ring encompasseth thy finger,
Even so thy breast encloseth my poor heart;
Wear both of them, for both of them are thine.

—*William Shakespeare*

Two persons who have chosen each other out of all the species, with the design to be each other's mutual comfort and entertainment, have, in that action, bound themselves to be good-humored, affable, discreet, forgiving, patient, and joyful, with respect to each other's frailties and perfections, to the end of their lives.

—*Joseph Addison*

The contract 'twixt Hannah, God and me,
Was not for one or twenty years, but for eternity.

—*David Ross Locke*

The details are different, but weddings are alike, and all of them have the same high hopes. So do we, the wedding guests. Hopes for them, for ourselves, for our children and for the persistence of so rash, romantic and brave a ceremony.

—*New York Times*

96

[*W*edding sermon written in a Nazi prison:] Just as it is the crown, and not merely the will to rule, that makes the king, so it is marriage, and not merely your love for each other, that joins you together in the sight of God and man. As high as God is above man, so high are the sanctity, the rights, and the promise of marriage above the sanctity, the rights and the promise of love. It is not your love that sustains marriage, but from now on, the marriage that sustains your love.

—Dietrich Bonhoeffer

*A*nd Isaac brought her into his mother Sarah's tent, and took Rebekah, and she became his wife; and he loved her: and Isaac was comforted after his mother's death.

—Genesis 24:67

*M*arriage ceremonies are more meaningful at the time for many parents than they are for the children who are getting married. Why? For one thing, parents have probably seen more weddings, are more familiar with that ceremonial genre. More important, they know more about what the event signifies, about the power to which it refers. In their own marriages they have lived it out, for better and for worse. They know what marriage is, with all its transcendent meanings and associations.

—William P. Harman

č

*T*he woman was not taken
    From Adam's head, you know,
So she must not command him,
    'Tis evidently so;
The woman was not taken
    From Adam's feet, you see,
So he must not abuse her—
    The meaning seems to be.
The woman she was taken
    From under Adam's arm,
Which shows he must protect her
    From injury and harm.

—Old Scottish Nuptial Song

97

*T*he marriage vows are intended as a lifetime commitment and that's the way it works best.

—*James Dobson*

*I*t takes about twenty minutes for a simple wedding ceremony, but it takes years to develop the maturity needed for making the step into a marriage commitment—and years more to let the marriage unfold into a beautiful, secure relationship.

—*Leslie Parrott*

*H*ail, wedded love, mysterious law, true source
Of human offspring.

—*John Milton*

*W*hen it is not only the husband and wife who say Yes to each other, but God says His great Yes to their marriage, then within their marriage things become possible which would be impossible without it.

—*Theodore Bonet*

*W*ith all my worldly goods I thee endow.

—*Book of Common Prayer*

A happy marriage is a new beginning of life, a new starting point for happiness and usefulness.

—*A.P. Stanley*

*T*he only thing that can hallow marriage is love, and the only genuine marriage is that which is hallowed by love.

—*Leo Tolstoy*

*H*ow does it feel to waken in the morning with one of the most beautiful people in the world?

—*Peter R. Stone*

*M*arriage is a natural thing in life and to consider it derogatory in any sense is wholly wrong... The ideal is to look upon marriage as a sacrament and therefore to lead a life of self restraint in the married state.

—*Mohandas Gandhi*

98

My duty is to keep close to her steps, to surround her existence with mine, to serve as a barrier against all dangers; to offer my head as a stepping stone, to place myself unceasingly between her and all sorrows...if she but consent to lean upon me at times amidst the difficulties of life.

—*Victor Hugo*

What is there in the vale of life
Half so delightful as a wife,
When friendship, love, and peace combine
To stamp the marriage bond divine?

—*William Cowper*

Marriage, or a union of the sexes, though it be in itself one of the smallest societies, is the original fountain from whence the greatest and most extensive governments have derived their beings.

—*Benjamin Franklin*

Though thirty-three years of age, Winston Churchill...had shown very little interest in women. There were no romances in his career up to that time. But now he had fallen in love with Miss Clementine Hozier... He and Miss Hozier were married in St. Margaret's Church, Westminster, London. All the bluebloods of England and all the notables of the political world turned out for the ceremony. The couple's wedding presents included gifts from the King and Queen and every member of the Cabinet. Some said that Churchill was so unpredictable and individualistic that the marriage would not last six months.

—*Leonard Wibberly*

I married and lived happily ever afterwards.

—*Winston Churchill*

Beautiful before God and men are a man and wife who agree together.

—*Anonymous*

[Three weeks after her wedding to Mark Twain:] We are two as happy people as you ever saw. Our days seem to be made up of only bright sunlight, with no shadow in them.

—*Olivia Langdon Clemens*

Accept your womanhood, my daughter, and rejoice in it. It is your glory that you are a woman, for this is why he loves you, he whom you love. Be gentle, be wise, as a woman is gentle and wise. Be ardent and love with a woman's ardor. Through your love, teach him what it means to be a man, a noble man, a strong man. Believe in him, for only through your belief can he believe in himself. In our secret hearts, man and woman, we long above all else to know that the other, the one we love, knows what we are and believes in what we can be...

I say nothing of your duties of housewifery or motherhood or care of your person or even of the preservation of your beauty and charm. All such duties are easy enough to perform if you have this knowledge of yourself as woman. For if you know yourself as woman, you will comprehend your own need of him, your primary and profound need. Without him, you are only half a woman, as without you he is less than a man. Stay together, you two—never let him go, and never leave him, once your love is established and alive. Stay together, cling hand in hand, walk step in step, sleep close, so that you know forever that you are not alone!

—*Pearl S. Buck*

Give a husband a bed that is comfortable, food that's hot, a flagon of ale beside the fire, let him talk about himself—and he'll love you forever.

—*Old Wives' Saying*

Yesterday Tom Lincoln had arrived on horseback, all the way from his Indiana farm, at her house in Elizabethtown. He had come straight to the point: "Miss Sally, I have no wife and you no husband. I came a-purpose to marry you. I knowed you from a girl and you knowed me from a boy. I've no time to lose. If you're willin', let it be done straight off."

The preacher wrote down that she, Sarah Bush Johnston, had been three years a widow and Tom's wife had died last winter. The horses and wagon Tom had borrowed waited outside. The wagon was piled high with her household goods, so that there was scarcely room for her three children. Tom had two children of his own; he hadn't told them he was bringing back a new mother. There was a shadow in her blue-gray eyes when she thought about that. Maybe they'd feel she didn't belong.

—*Bernadine Bailey & Dorothy Walworth*

100

And when Clara and I were married...its dreariness was completely transformed. The house was Clara. Everything I did radiated from her. Going from her, coming to her, thinking of her, working for her. I am old today, but my heart feels young again when I turn back the pages of my life and remember our first year in that little house.

—*Max Winkler*

ॐ

If all of one's married days are as happy as these new ones have been to me, I have deliberately fooled away 30 years of my life. If I were to do it all over again I would marry in early infancy instead of wasting time cutting teeth and breaking crockery.

—*Mark Twain*

When he took his wife, he [Chiang Kai-shek] entered upon an entirely new phase of the spiritual world. Love had made a shrewd and momentous choice. Companionship with Mayling had transformed him from a great soldier into a great man.

—*Henry & Dana Lee Thomas*

Marriages do not, like dropped chinaware, smash as a result of that first quarrel which the newly married hope is unthinkable. Marriage is a rooted thing, a growing and flowering thing that must be tended faithfully.

Daily watering with the little gracious affectionate acts we all welcome, with mutual concern for the other's contentment, with self-watchfulness here and self-forgetfulness there, brings forth ever new blossoms.

—*Donald Culross Peattie*

I do not think you can perform any finer service than to help maintain the Christian doctrine that the relation of husband and wife is a permanent one, not to be lightly broken because of difficulties or quarrels.

—*Queen Elizabeth II*

Unto the woman he said, I will greatly multiply thy sorrow and thy conception; in sorrow thou shalt bring forth children; and thy desire shall be to thy husband, and he shall rule over thee.

—*Genesis 3:16*

Plant two lips today.

—*Peter R. Stone*

Don't get into the habit of sweeping your problems under the rug. Face them and resolve them... Actually, there is nothing wrong with having a conflict of interest between husband and wife. In fact, every such case is a test of your maturity.

—*Tim LaHaye*

❦

In my estimation, more permanent and genuine happiness is to be found in the sequestered walks of connubial life than in the giddy rounds of promiscuous pleasure, or the more tumultuous and imposing scenes of successful ambition.

—*George Washington*

❦

There is a primary need for openness and honesty between husband and wife.

—*James Dobson*

My Katie is in all things so obliging and pleasing to me that I would not exchange my poverty for the riches of Croesus.

—*Martin Luther*

❦

A successful marriage is not a gift; it is an achievement.

—*Ann Landers*

All other goods by fortune's hand are given.
A wife is the peculiar gift of heaven.

—*Alexander Pope*

102

The highest civilizations—the longest to last and I believe the most successful in human terms—are those which have come the closest to achieving real understanding and mutual appreciation between men and women.

—*Pearl S. Buck*

Music I heard with you was more than music,
And bread I broke with you was more than bread.

—*Conrad Aiken*

I shall never forget how I awoke from the deep sleep of exhaustion on my second night in Auschwitz—roused by music... Suddenly there was a silence and into the night a violin sang a desperately sad tango, an unusual tune... The violin wept and a part of me wept with it, for on that same day someone had a twenty-fourth birthday. That someone lay in another part of the Auschwitz camp, possibly only a few hundred or thousand yards away, and yet completely out of reach. That someone was my wife.

—*Viktor E. Frankl*

❧

Man's best possession is a sympathetic wife.

—*Euripides*

How much the wife is dearer than the bride.

—*George, Lord Lyttelton*

Never a lip is curved with pain
That can't be kissed into smiles again.

—*Francis Bret Harte*

Let there be spaces in your togetherness.

—*Kahlil Gibran*

Ye have heard that it was said by them of old time, Thou shalt not commit adultery: But I say unto you, That whosoever looketh on a woman to lust after her hath committed adultery with her already in his heart.

—*Matthew 5:27,28*

He is the half part of a blessed man,
Left to be finished by such as she;
And she a fair divided excellence,
Whose fulness of perfection lies in him.

—*William Shakespeare*

Be to her vitues very kind;
Be to her faults a little blind.

—*Matthew Prior*

The hours I spent with thee, dear heart,
    Are as a string of pearls to me;
I counted them over, every one apart,
    My rosary, my rosary.

—*Robert Cameron Rogers*

Can you find within yourself sunshine enough for two?

—*Peter R. Stone*

The test of a man or woman's breeding is how they behave in a quarrel.

—*George Bernard Shaw*

Keep not your kisses for my dead, cold brow;
The way is lonely, let me feel them now...
When dreamless rest is mine, I shall not need
The tenderness for which I long to-night.

—*Arabella Eugenia Smith*

Marriage resembles a pair of shears, so joined that they cannot be separated; often moving in opposite directions, yet always punishing anyone who comes between them.

—*Sydney Smith*

Marriage is honorable in all, and the bed undefiled: but whoremongers and adulterers God will judge.

—*Hebrews 13:4*

$\mathcal{G}$od intended man to be the head of his home. If he is not, he will not have a sense of responsibility but will subconsciously feel he is married to a second mother. His children will soon detect who is boss, and as teenagers they will lose the natural respect for their father that is necessary for their adjustment to life.

Usually a wife-dominated home is a quarrelsome home until the husband finally "gives up." He then crawls into his shell of introversion and degenerates into a sub-par human being. The sad thing is, a wife will eventually grow to despise the husband she dominates.

—*Tim LaHaye*

$\mathcal{T}$he finest woman in nature should not detain me an hour from you; but you must sometimes suffer the rivalship of the wisest men.

—*Sir Richard Steele*

$\mathcal{A}$ good wife is heaven's last, best gift to man—his gem of many virtues, his casket of jewels; her voice is sweet music, her smiles his brightest day, her kiss the guardian of his innocence, her arms the pale of his safety, her industry his surest wealth, her economy his safest steward, her lips his faithful counsellors, her bosom the softest pillow of his cares.

—*Jeremy Taylor*

ॐ

$\mathcal{C}$onsider...the promiscuous man and woman. They move from one bed to another, yet all beds are only beds, unless love attends—not casual love but faithful, mutual love, deeply rooted in all of life. The sex act is the most intimate communication possible between two human beings, the one man, the other woman... [When it] is carelessly and casually bestowed, the degradation is profound. I have not seen a promiscuous man or woman who did not show the open effects of this degradation.

—*Pearl S. Buck*

$\mathcal{W}$ith thee goes thy husband, him to follow thou art bound. Where he abides, think there thy native soil.

—*John Milton*

$\mathcal{A}$ good husband makes a good wife.

—*Robert Burton*

*M*any have tried to demonstrate the illusion of female-directed families where the male assumes a nurturing role in housekeeping and child care, while the wife by virtue of her giftedness and special abilities goes off into the world to earn the family's income... The attempt to succeed at it just brings frustration.

—*James Walker*

*A*n ideal wife is any woman who has an ideal husband.

—*Booth Tarkington*

*T*reat your wife always with respect; it will procure respect to you, not from her only but from all that observe it. Never use a slighting expression to her, even in jest, for slights in jest, after frequent bandying, are apt to end in angry earnest.

—*Benjamin Franklin*

A man is in general better pleased when he has a good dinner upon his table, than when his wife talks Greek.

—*Samuel Johnson*

*E*very wise man loves the wife he has chosen.

—*Homer*

*H*e knew whose gentle hand was at the latch,
Before the door had given her to his eyes.

—*John Keats*

*T*he kindest and the happiest pair,
  Will find occasion to forbear;
Find something every day they live,
  To pity, and perhaps forgive.

—*William Cowper*

[*M*arried life]...must be watered by the showers of tender affection, expanded by the cheering glow of kindness, and guarded by the impregnable barrier of unshaken confidence. Thus matured, it will bloom with fragrance in every season of life, and sweeten even the loneliness of declining years.

—*Thomas Sprat*

*W*hen a man dwells in love, then the breasts of his wife are pleasant... Her eyes are fair as the light of Heaven, she is a fountain sealed, and he can quench his thirst, and ease his cares, and lay his sorrow down upon her lap, and can retire home as to his sanctuary and refectory, and his garden of sweetness and chaste refreshment.

—*Jeremy Taylor*

*S*he who ne'er answers till a husband cools,
Or, if she rules him, never shows she rules;
Charms by accepting, by submitting sways,
Yet has her humor most when she obeys.

—*Alexander Pope*

A good wife and health are man's best wealth.

—*John Ray*

*C*aresses, expressions of one sort or another, are necessary to the life of the affections as leaves are to the life of a tree.

—*Nathaniel Hawthorne*

*L*et the husband render unto the wife due benevolence: and likewise also the wife unto the husband. The wife hath not power of her own body, but the husband: and likewise also the husband hath not power of his own body, but the wife. Defraud ye not one the other, except it be with consent for a time, that ye may give yourselves to fasting and prayer; and come together again, that Satan tempt you not for your incontinency.

—*I Corinthians 7:3-5*

A woman is usually comfortable in following masculine leadership if her man is loving, gentle, and worthy of her respect.

—*James Dobson*

A successful marriage is an edifice that must be rebuilt every day.

—*Andre Maurois*

*I*n lover's quarrels, the party that loves most is always most willing to acknowledge the greater fault.

—*Sir Walter Scott*

107

*P*rayer to their heavenly Father is the best means of communication between two people. Many a marriage has been completely transformed by initiating a practice of regular prayer.

—*Tim LaHaye*

*T*he most wonderful of all things in life, I believe, is the discovery of another human being with whom one's relationship has a glowing depth, beauty, and joy as the years increase. This inner progressiveness of love between two human beings is a most marvelous thing, it cannot be found by looking for it or by passionately wishing for it. It is a sort of Divine accident.

—*Sir Hugh Walpole*

*H*e that would thrive, must ask his wife.

—*English Proverb*

*W*hen, in disgrace with fortune and men's eyes,
I all alone beweep my outcast state,
And trouble deaf heaven with my bootless cries,
And look upon myself, and curse my fate,
Wishing me like to one more rich in hope,
Featured like him, like him with friends possessed,
Desiring this man's art and that man's scope,
With what I most enjoy contented least;
Yet in these thoughts myself almost despising,
Haply I think on thee, and then my state,
Like to the lark at break of day arising
From sullen earth, sings hymns at heaven's gate;
For thy sweet love remembered such wealth brings
That then I scorn to change my state with kings.

—*William Shakespeare*

*C*aring is taking the moment to share.

—*Peter R. Stone*

*C*an two walk together, except they be agreed?

—*Amos 3:3*

108

*N*o happiness is like unto it, no love so great as that of man and wife, no such comfort as a sweet wife.

—*Robert Burton*

*L*ove built on beauty, soon as beauty, dies.

—*John Donne*

[*W*hile away from his wife:]
I dream of Jeanie with the light brown hair,
Borne, like a vapor, on the summer air;
I see her tripping where the bright streams play,
Happy as the daisies that dance on her way...
Oh! I dream of Jeanie with the light brown hair,
Floating, like a vapor, on the soft summer air.

—*Stephen C. Foster*

*T*hou shalt not commit adultery.

—*Exodus 20:14*

*B*ut whoso committeth adultery with a woman lacketh understanding: he that doeth it destroyeth his own soul.

—*Proverbs 6:32*

A spirited spat is good for most marriages... Arguments are inevitable in a marriage and probably offer one of the best ways couples have to work out touchy problems. When most of the frustrations have been talked out or discharged in some vicarious way, the fight can be ended. Those marriages that exist without any type of fighting are generally frozen or inflexible marriages in which other aspects of the relationship are compromised in order to maintain the facade of peace and harmony.

—*Dr. Alfred B. Messer*

I know that the only completely happy life for man and for woman is their life, first together, and then with their children. I am a firm believer that no marriage can be really happy, and no home a happy one for the children as well, unless man puts woman first and woman puts man first, each for the other the giver of every good gift. Children are the fruit of this total love.

—*Pearl S. Buck*

109

*M*arriage is not a federation of two sovereign states...
It is a fusion of two hearts—
   the union of two lives—
      the coming together of two tributaries,
which, after being joined in marriage, will flow in the same
   channel in the same direction...
      carrying the same burdens of responsibility and obligation...

The average woman, if she gives her full time to her home
   her husband
      her children...

If she provides in the home a proper atmosphere of culture
   of love of music
      of beautiful furniture
         and of a garden...

If she can do all this, she will be engaged in a life work that will demand
   every ounce of her strength
      every bit of her patience
         every talent God has given her
            the utmost sacrifice of her love.

It will demand everything she has and more
   And she will find that for which she was created.
      She will know that she is carrying out the plan of God.
      She will be a partner with the Sovereign Ruler of the universe.

And so, today's daughters need to think twice before they seek to make a
   place for themselves
      by themselves
         in our world today.

—Peter Marshall

ॐ

There is an irrelevant and erroneous saying about marriage that has somehow become popular: Marriage is a fifty-fifty proposition. Nothing could be further from the truth! Marriage, under God, should be a one hundred percent to nothing proposition.

—Tim LaHaye

❧

Marriage is a heavy cross because so many couples quarrel. It is the grace of God when they agree. The Holy Spirit declares there are three wonders: when brothers agree, when neighbors love each other, and when a man and a wife are at one. When I see a pair like that, I am as glad as if I were in a garden of roses.

—Martin Luther

❧

I should enjoy more real happiness in one month with you [wife Martha] at home, than I have the most distant prospect of finding abroad, if my stay were to be seven times seven years.

—George Washington

❧

My mind still clung to the image of my wife... I didn't even know if she were still alive. I knew only one thing... Love goes very far beyond the physical person of the beloved. It finds its deepest meaning in his spiritual being, his inner self. Whether or not he is actually present, whether or not he is still alive at all, ceases somehow to be of importance... Nothing could touch the strength of my love, my thoughts, and the image of my beloved.

—Viktor E. Frankl

Above all things I dislike family quarrels, and, when they happen among my relations, nothing gives me more pain... What can I say between you, but that I wish you were reconciled, and that I will love that side best that is most ready to forgive and oblige the other?

—Benjamin Franklin

When married people tell me their love has died, I sometimes think it might be more accurate to say that they have killed it. I am not thinking of violent, brutal acts of dark betrayal. I mean that the flame of love has gradually waned and guttered out from sheer neglect.

—David Mace

The most important single ingredient in a marriage is the ability to communicate... Most marital problems stem from the inability of two people to talk to each other. How precious is the ability to communicate!... The mature man and woman recognize that there is a unity in love, but at the same time there must be freedom for both individuals... The couples who are secure in marriage can be honest about all kinds of feelings... The man and wife who can air their differences, get the hostility out of their system, then kiss and make up have an excellent chance of growing old together.

—Ann Landers

You'll never see perfection in your mate, nor will he or she find it in you.

—James Dobson

A bachelor never quite gets over the idea that he is a thing of beauty and a boy forever.

—Helen Rowland

He who marries a wife reared on the land marries strength and purity and compassion.

—Beecher

Wives, submit yourselves unto your own husbands, as unto the Lord. For the husband is the head of the wife, even as Christ is the head of the church; and he is the saviour of the body. Therefore as the church is subject unto Christ, so let the wives be to their own husbands in every thing. Husbands, love your wives, even as Christ also loved the church, and gave himself for it.

—Ephesians 5:22-25

*S*tolen goods can be returned, or compensated for, lies can be retracted and corrected, covetousness can be overcome. Even idolatry can be undone and forgiven. But the sex act once committed with another person cannot be undone. The interpersonal relationship has undergone a radical change, and the couple concerned can never return to where they were before. Something indelible has stamped them both.

—William Graham Cole

*T*here is nothing upon this earth that can be compared to the faithful attachment of a wife.

—Daniel Webster

❧

[*W*ritten to his wife who, renowned for her beauty and charm, had survived the ravages of smallpox, only to remain horribly disfigured for life by its scars:]
Believe me, if all those endearing young charms,
    Which I gaze on so fondly today,
Were to change by tomorrow, and fleet in my arms,
    Like fairy-gifts fading away,
Thou wouldst still be adored, as this moment thou art,
    Let thy loveliness fade as it will,
And around the dear ruin each wish of my heart
    Would entwine itself verdantly still.

It is not while beauty and youth are thine own,
    and thy cheeks unprofaned by a tear,
That the fervour and faith of a soul can be known,
    To which time will but make thee more dear:
No, the heart that has truly loved never forgets,
    But as truly loves on to the close,
As the sunflower turns on her god, when he sets,
    The same look which she turned when he rose.

—Thomas Moore

*T*o love is to place our happiness in the care of another.

—Spanish Proverb

Of all the home remedies, a good wife is the best.

—*Kin Hubbard*

A good wife makes the cares of the world sit easy.

—*L.M. Stretch*

Of earthly goods, the best is a good wife; a bad, the bitterest curse of human life.

—*Simonides*

The great Russian novelist, Turgenev, said he would give all his fame and all his genius if there were only one woman who cared whether he came home late to dinner.

—*William Lyon Phelps*

A soft answer turneth away wrath; but grievous words stir up anger.

—*Proverbs 15:1*

[He said he had] lost the cherished companion of my life, in whose affections...I had lived the last ten years in uncheckered happiness.

—*Thomas Jefferson*

If you deal as much with people as I do, you become convinced—not through some high-flown theory, but from plain, everyday observation—that life is so arranged that morality and happiness go hand in hand.

—*Norman Vincent Peale*

It was in this miserable old shed that the best and happiest years of our life were spent, entirely consecrated to work.

—*Marie Curie*

If the husband says one thing and the wife another, life becomes unbearable.

—*Mohandas Gandhi*

Marriages are made in Heaven.

—*Alfred, Lord Tennyson*

114

*A*lmost no one is foolish enough to imagine that he automatically deserves great success in any field of activity; yet almost everyone believes that he automatically deserves success in marriage.

—*Sidney J. Harris*

*W*e walked, that winter evening, in the fields together; and the blessed calm within us seemed to be partaken by the frosty air. The early stars began to shine while we were lingering on, and looking up to them, we thanked God for having guided us to this tranquillity.

—*Charles Dickens*

*B*uilding a good marriage and building a good log fire are similar in many ways. You build a fire with paper and kindling, and all at once it goes up in a brilliantly burning blaze. Then the primary blaze burns down and you wonder if the fire will fizzle out and leave you in the dark. You blow on it and fan it for all you are worth. Sometimes smoke billows out and almost chokes you, but if the materials are good and if you invest enough energy and interest in maintaining it, soon the big solid logs catch, and your fire takes on new qualities.

—*Josephine Lowman*

*M*ost arts require long study and application, but the most useful of all, that of pleasing, requires only the desire.

—*Lord Chesterfield*

A marriage without conflicts is almost as inconceivable as a nation without crises.

—*Andre Maurios*

*S*he [wife Alice] was beautiful in face and form and lovelier still in spirit. Her life had been always in the sunshine... Fair, pure, and joyous as a maiden; loving, tender and happy as a young wife; when she had become a mother, when her life seemed to be but begun—then, by a strange and terrible fate, death came to her. And when my heart's dearest died, the light went from my life forever.

—*Theodore Roosevelt*

*L*ove, honor and negotiate.

—*Alan Loy McGinnis*

Story writers say that love is concerned only with young people, and the excitement and glamour of romance end at the altar. How blind they are. The best romance is inside marriage; the finest love stories come after the wedding, not before.

—Irving Stone

In a successful marriage, there is no such thing as one's way. There is only the way of both, only the bumpy, dusty, difficult, but always mutual path.

—Phyllis McGinley

The greatest of all arts is the art of living together.

—William Lyon Phelps

Write injuries in sand, kindnesses in marble.

—French Proverb

ॐ

A successful marriage requires falling in love many times, always with the same person.

—Mignon McLaughlin

Let not the sun go down upon your wrath.

—Ephesians 4:26

The middle years of marriage are the most crucial. In the early years spouses want each other and in later years they need each other.

—Rebecca Tilly

When two people love each other deeply...they share countless private memories unknown to the rest of the world.

—James Dobson

One advantage of marriage is that, when you fall out of love with him or he falls out of love with you, it keeps you together until you fall in again.

—Judith Viorst

One of the important things about marriage is to be accepted. Love is the basis of marriage, but there are many married people who have never felt accepted. Marriage is not a reformatory, and spouses need to reach out to each other without criticism or reservations. To live with a wife or a husband who does not accept you is a dark valley to walk through.

—*Charles L. Allen*

When you love someone, you do not love him or her in exactly the same way, from moment to moment. It is an impossibility. And yet this is exactly what most of us demand. We have so little faith in the ebb and flow of life, of love, of relationships. We leap at the flow of the tide and resist in terror its ebb. We are afraid it will never return. We insist on permanency, on continuity, when the only continuity possible is in growth, in freedom, in the sense that the dancers are free, barely touching as they pass but partners in the same pattern. The only real security in a relationship lies neither in looking back in nostalgia, nor forward in dread or anticipation, but living in the present relationship and, accepting it as it is now.

—*Anne Morrow Lindbergh*

ॐ

Marriages break up because so few people have been educated—*truly educated*—to the very purpose and meaning of marriage.

—*Garner Ted Armstrong*

I have learned that it isn't money, diamonds, furs, houses or other things that make a woman happy, but just plain love. Not lovemaking, but the treatment that produces lovemaking—kindness, thoughtfulness, understanding, acceptance or approval, and the recognition on the part of the husband that he is just not complete without her. Happy is the wife whose husband knows and tells her that if given the chance to marry all over again, he would choose the same bride.

—*Tim LaHaye*

You are my true and honourable wife,
As dear to me as are the ruddy drops
That visit my sad heart.

—*William Shakespeare*

As unto the bow the cord is,
So unto the man is woman;
Though she bends him, she obeys him,
Though she draws him, yet she follows;
Useless each without the other!

—Henry Wadsworth Longfellow

It takes a loose rein to keep a marriage tight.

—John Stevenson

The understanding of the marriage relation is the work of a lifetime.

—Ellen G. White

My marriage was much the most fortunate and joyous event which happened to me in my whole life.

—Winston Churchill

I can wish the women of our country no greater blessing than that their home and lives be as happy, and their husbands may be as kind, attentive and considerate and affectionate as mine [Grover Cleveland].

—Frances Cleveland

The married state is, after all our jokes, the happiest, being comfortable to our natures. Man and woman have each of them qualities and tempers in which the other is deficient, and which in union contribute to the common felicity. Single and separate, they are not the complete human being; they are like the odd halves of scissors; they cannot answer the end of their formation.

—Benjamin Franklin

Woman knows the better she obeys the surer she is to rule.

—Jules Michelet

Some marriages are still made in heaven, but all have to be lived out on earth, and heaven comes only as we work for it.

—Catherine Marshall

*M*arriage is not a union, merely between two creatures—it is a union between two spirits; and the intention of that bond is to perfect the nature of both, by supplementing their deficiencies with the force of contrast, giving to each sex those excellencies in which it is naturally deficient; to the one strength of character and firmness of moral will; to the other sympathy, meekness, tenderness, and just so solemn and glorious as these ends are for which the union was intended, just so terrible are the consequences if it be perverted and abused; for there is no earthy relationship which has so much power to ennoble and to exalt. There are two rocks, in this world of ours, on which the soul must either anchor or be wrecked—the one is God, and the other is the opposite sex.

—*Fredrick W. Robertson*

*M*arriage hath more of safety than the single life; it hath not more ease, but less danger; it is more merry and more sad; it is fuller of sorrows and fuller of joys; it lies under more burdens, but is supported by all the strength of love and charity, and those burdens are delightful. Marriage is the mother of the world, and preserves kingdoms, fills cities and churches, and peoples heaven itself.

—*Jeremy Taylor*

*W*hen souls that should agree to will the same,
To have one common object for their wishes,
Look different ways, regardless of each other,
Think what a train of wretchedness ensues!

—*Nicholas Rowe*

*T*he small courtesies sweeten life; the greater ennoble it.

—*Bovee*

A West German magazine reported the results of a study conducted by a life insurance company... Husbands who kiss their wives every morning:
    —live an average of five years longer.
    —are involved in fewer automobile accidents.
    —are ill 50 percent less, as noted by sick days, and
    —earn 20 to 30 percent more money.

—*W.B. Freeman Concepts*

*S*peak the truth in love—in kind words say exactly what is on your heart. Make sure that your love is equal to your truth.

—*Tim LaHaye*

I had a notion it was her duty to obey me, her lord and master, in everything. I literally made life hell for her, changed my residence, prescribed her dress, forced her, brought up in an orthodox family where Untouchability was practiced, to accept Moslems and Untouchables in her husband's home. And I made her serve them, regardless of her abhorrence... Her unresisting meekness opened my eyes. It began slowly to dawn on me that I had no such prescriptive rights over her, and if I wanted her obedience, I had to persuade her by patient argument, and she thus became my teacher in *Satyagraha,* non-violence.

—*Mohandas Gandhi*

❧

*W*here'er I roam, whatever realms to see...
My heart, untravelled, fondly turns to thee.

—*Oliver Goldsmith*

*W*e could not know, my dear, we could not guess
How years augment the miracle of love;
How autumn brings a depth of tenderness
That is beyond young April's dreaming of!
How there would burn a richer flame some day
Than that which first threw glory on our way.

—*A. Warren*

*T*he question is asked, "Is there anything more beautiful in life than a boy and girl clasping clean hands and pure hearts in the path of marriage?" And the answer is given, "Yes—there is a more beautiful thing; it is the spectacle of an old man and an old woman finishing their journey together on that path. Their hands are gnarled but still clasped; their faces are seamed but still radiant; their hearts are tired and bowed down but still strong. They have proved the happiness of marriage and have vindicated it from the jeers of cynics."

—*A.L. Anderson*

[To his wife on her 40th birthday:] We have reached another milestone, my darling, and a very, very remote one from the place whence we started...We have company on the journey—ah, such precious company, such inspiring, such lovely, and gracious company!... Our faces are toward the sunset...and our old love grows and never diminishes... Our march shall still be through flowers and green fields, and the evening light as pleasant as that old soft morning glow yonder behind. Your Husband.

—*Mark Twain*

The happiest and most meaningful moments in marriage are those that are the most intimate. But if these most intimate acts have already been used elsewhere and have lost their meaning as profound communication, then even the marriage is robbed of its full meaning.

—*Pearl S. Buck*

I've been married eighteen years
And still adore my wife.

—*Henrik Ibsen*

If a woman is to have the contentment and self-satisfaction necessary to produce a successful family, she needs the constant support and respect of the man she loves.

—*James Dobson*

❧

I am a little different from some people in Hollywood, for I have lived with the same wife for thirty years—and what's more, I like it.

—*Will Rogers*

The ring, so worn as you behold,
So thin, so pale, is yet of gold.

—*George Crabbe*

Were he [a widower] not to marry again, it might be concluded that his first wife had given him a disgust to marriage; but by taking a second wife he pays the highest compliment to the first, by showing that she made him so happy as a married man, that he wishes to be so a second time.

—*Samuel Johnson*

In the gloaming, oh, my darling,
When the lights are dim and low,
And the quiet shadows falling,
Softly come, and softly go:
When the winds are sobbing faintly,
With a gentle, unknown woe;
Will you think of me and love me?
As you did once long ago?

—*Meta Orred*

Methought I saw my late espoused Saint
Brought to me like Alcestis from the grave...
Came vested all in white, pure as her mind:
Her face was veiled, yet to my fancied sight,
Love, sweetness, goodness, in her person shined
So clear, as in no face with more delight.
But O as to embrace me she inclined
I waked, she fled, and day brought back my night.

—*John Milton*

Grow old along with me;
The best is yet to be,
The last of life,
For which the first was made.

—*Robert Browning*

ॐ

With death, marriage is one of life's two greatest adventures... I would keep it an adventure—an adventure in happiness.

—*Frances Starr*

[A letter sent to Otis Skinner upon the death of his wife:] Dear Otis: You lucky bum! You had 40 blissful years together, you and that enchanting woman. How I envy you.

—*Alexander Woollcott*

Say I'm weary, say I'm sad,
Say that health and wealth have missed me,
Say I'm growing old, but add,
　　Jenny kissed me.

—Leigh Hunt

✿

I wander'd today to the hill, Maggie,
To watch the scene below,
The creek and the creaking old mill, Maggie,
As we used to long ago.
The green grass is gone from the hill, Maggie,
Where first the daisies sprung;
The creaking old mill is still, Maggie,
Since you and I were young...

They say I am feeble with age, Maggie,
My steps are less sprightly than then,
My face is a well written page, Maggie,
But time alone was the pen.
They say we are aged and gray, Maggie,
As sprays by the white breaker's flung;
But to me you're as fair as you were, Maggie,
When you and I were young.

—George W. Johnson

✿

She [Olivia] was my life, and she is gone; she was my riches, and I am a pauper.

—Mark Twain

The happy married man dies in good style at home, surrounded by his weeping wife and children. The old bachelor doesn't die at all. He sort of rots away, like a pollywog's tail.

—Artemus Ward

A couple [were] at their golden wedding anniversary celebration. Surrounded by her children, grandchildren, and great grandchildren, the wife was asked the secret to a long and happy marriage. With a loving glance toward her husband, she answered, "On my wedding day, I decided to make a list of ten of my husband's faults which, for the sake of our marriage, I would overlook. I figured I could live with at least ten faults."

A guest asked her to identify some of the faults she had chosen to overlook... [The] wife sweetly replied. "To tell you the truth, dear, I never did get around to listing them. Instead, every time my husband did something that made me hopping mad, I would simply say to myself, *Lucky for him, that's one of the ten!*"

—W.B. Freeman Concepts

The most perfect compliment I've ever heard of was given by Joseph Choate, one-time U.S. ambassador to Great Britain. When asked who he would like to be if he could come back to earth again after he died, he replied without an instant's hesitation: "Mrs. Choate's second husband."

—Doris Ann Krupinski

❦

Two are better than one; because they have a good reward for their labour. For if they fall, the one will lift up his fellow: but woe to him that is alone when he falleth; for he hath not another to help him up.

—Ecclesiastes 4:9,10

A man and woman should choose each other for life. A long life is barely enough for a man and woman to understand each other; and to understand is to love. The man who understands one woman is qualified to understand pretty well everything.

—J.B. Yeats

An archaeologist is the best husband any woman can have. The older she gets the more interested he is in her.

—Agatha Christie

Heaven will not be heaven to me if I do not meet my wife there.

—Andrew Jackson

124

A happy marriage is a long conversation that seems all too short.
—Andre Maurois

*M*arried life is a marathon... It is not enough to make a great start toward long-term marriage. You will need the determination to keep plugging... Only then will you make it to the end.
—James Dobson

*T*here's a bliss beyond all that the minstrel has told,
When two, that are link'd in one heavenly tie,
With heart never changing, and brow never cold,
Love on thro' all ills, and love on till they die.
One hour of passion so sacred is worth
Whole ages of heartless and wandering bliss;
And oh! if there be an Elysium on earth,
It is this—it is this!
—Thomas Moore

*W*e are grown old together, and if she has any faults, I am so used to them that I don't perceive them.
—Benjamin Franklin

*D*arling I am growing old,
Silver threads among the gold,
Shine upon my brow today;
Life is fading fast away.
But my darling you will be, will be,
Always young and fair to me.
—Alfred M. Durham

*T*he highest happiness on earth is in marriage. Every man who is happily married is a successful man even if he has failed in everything else.
—William Lyon Phelps

It must be true that marriage, if entered into with due consideration and with deep love, is still the most fulfilling and rewarding of human relationships.

—*Pearl S. Buck*

Man and Woman may only enter Paradise hand in hand. Together, the myth tells us, they left it and together must they return.

—*Richard Garnet*

Feminine Qualities

Woman and Her Role

Chapter Four
Feminine Qualities
Woman and Her Role

*W*ho can find a virtuous woman? for her price is far above rubies. The heart of her husband doth safely trust in her, so that he shall have no need of spoil. She will do him good and not evil all the days of her life. She seeketh wool, and flax, and worketh willingly with her hands. She is like the merchants' ships; she bringeth her food from afar. She riseth also while it is yet night, and giveth meat to her household, and a portion to her maidens.

She considereth a field, and buyeth it: With the fruit of her hands she planteth a vineyard. She girdeth her loins with strength, and strengtheneth her arms. She percieveth that her merchandise is good: her candle goeth not out by night. She layeth her hands to the spindle, and her hands hold the distaff. She stretcheth out her hands to the poor; yea, she reacheth forth her hands to the needy. She is not afraid of the snow for her household: for all her household are clothed with scarlet. She maketh herself coverings of tapestry; her clothing is silk and purple. Her husband is known in the gates, when he sitteth among the elders of the land.

She maketh fine linen, and selleth it; and delivereth girdles unto the merchant. Strength and honour are her clothing; and she shall rejoice in time to come. She openeth her mouth with wisdom; and in her tongue is the law of kindness. She looketh well to the ways of her household, and eateth not the bread of idleness. Her children arise up, and call her blessed; her husband also, and he praiseth her.

Many daughters have done virtuously, but thou excellest them all. Favour is deceitful, and beauty is vain: but a woman that feareth the Lord, she shall be praised. Give her of the fruit of her hands; and let her own works praise her in the gates.

—*Proverbs 31:10-31*

*L*ove is the whole history of a woman's life, it is but an episode in a man's.

—*Madame de Stael*

131

The fact that God did not give man dominion until he had woman standing beside him is evidence enough of her exalted place in the creation.

—Edith Deen

Her voice was ever soft,
Gentle, and low; an excellent thing in woman.

—William Shakespeare

Virtue shows quite as well in rags and patches as she does in purple and fine linen.

—Charles Dickens

℧

Beautiful faces are they that wear
The light of a pleasant spirit there;
Beautiful hands are they that do
Deeds that are noble, good and true;
Beautiful feet are they that go
Swiftly to lighten another's woe.

—McGuffey's Second Reader

Behold Rebekah came out...with her pitcher upon her shoulder. And the damsel was very fair to look upon, a virgin, neither had any man known her: and she went down to the well, and filled her pitcher...and the servant ran to meet her, and said, Let me, I pray thee, drink a little water of thy pitcher.

And she said, Drink, my lord: and she hasted and let down her pitcher upon her hand, and gave him drink. And when she had done giving him drink, she said, I will draw water for thy camels also, until they have done drinking.

—Genesis 24:15-20

Love is a great beautifier.

—Louisa May Alcott

132

$\mathcal{O}$f all the things you wear, your expression is the most important.

—*Janet Lane*

$\mathcal{B}$ut there is a beauty every girl has—a gift from God, as pure as the sunlight, and as sacred as life. It is a beauty that all men love, a virtue that wins all men's souls. That beauty is chastity...

The flower by the roadside that catches the dust of every traveler is not the one to be admired and is seldom if ever plucked; but the one blooming away up on the hillside, protected by a perpendicular cliff is the flower with the virgin perfume, the one the boy will almost risk his life to possess.

—*David O. McKay*

$\mathcal{I}$ like the quiet reflective moments after a meal, my hands in the hot soapy water and the view from the kitchen window before my eyes. Then, too, I love my dishes. Some I brought with me from the house in Peking, and the rest are my Mother's and the ones that I used as a child. I do not understand women who complain about their houses and their children and their husbands. This is our dear daily work.

—*Pearl S. Buck*

❧

$\mathcal{T}$he fulness of maternity is the blossoming of beauty. There is no beauty in the world comparable to that of a fully developed woman.

—*Gayelord Hauser*

$\mathcal{M}$ake two homes for thyself, my daughter. One actual home...and the other a spiritual home, which thou art to carry with thee always.

—*Catherine of Sienna*

$\mathcal{N}$othing makes a woman more beautiful than the belief that she is beautiful.

—*Sophia Loren*

$\mathcal{S}$miles are the soul's kisses.

—*Minna Antrim*

133

*T*he buckling on of the knight's armor by his lady's hand was not a mere caprice of romantic fashion. It is the type of an eternal truth that the soul's armor is never well set to the heart unless a woman's hand has braced it, and it is only when she braces it loosely, that the honor of mankind fails.

—*John Ruskin*

~

*T*he challenge to twentieth century womanhood is as old as motherhood itself.
Although the average American mother has advantages that pioneer women never knew—material advantages
    education
    culture
   advances made by science and medicine;
although the modern mother knows a great deal more about sterilization, diets, health, calories, germs, drugs, medicines, and vitamins, than her mother did, there is one subject about which she does not know as much—and that is God.

The modern challenge to motherhood is the eternal challenge—
that of being godly women.
The very phrase sounds strange to our ears. We never hear it now.

We hear about every other kind of women—
 beautiful women,
  smart women,
   sophisticated women,
    career women,
     talented women,
      divorced women,
but so seldom do we hear of a godly woman—or of a godly man either, for that matter.

—*Peter Marshall*

134

In winter and summer in all kinds of weather, the [Frontier Nurses, under Mary Breckinridge]...rode out to visit the sick in their cabin homes. And time and time again they were awakened by a call from some worried mountaineer... Within minutes one of the nurse-midwives would be dressed and headed out to saddle her horse, her 30-pound saddle bag on her shoulder. A three-hour ride in inky darkness, through chilly waters...or across snow and ice...to reach the bedside of a patient—that was part of the life of a Frontier Nurse.

—Robin McKown

We can make no greater mistake as a nation than to continue the pervasive disrespect shown to women who have devoted their lives to the welfare of their families.

—James Dobson

A word spoken in due season, how good it is.

—Proverbs, 15;23

The duty of motherhood, which the vast majority of women will always undertake, requires qualities which man need not possess. She is passive, he is active. She is essentially mistress of the house. He is the bread winner. She is the keeper and distributor of the bread. She is the caretaker in every sense of the term. The art of bringing up the infants of the race is her special and sole prerogative. Without her care the race must become extinct.

—Mohandas Gandhi

No one knows like a woman how to say things that are at once gentle and deep.

—Victor Hugo

When you educate a man you educate an individual; when you educate a woman you educate a whole family.

—R.W. MacIver

*B*eing a full-time mother is one of the highest-salaried jobs in my field since the payment is pure love.

—*Mildred B. Vermont*

A hundred men may make an encampment, but it takes a woman to make a home.

—*Chinese Proverb*

*T*rue strength is delicate.

—*Louis Nevelson*

*W*omen make us poets, children make us philosophers.

—*Malcolm De Chazal*

*N*ature meant woman to be her masterpiece.

—*Gotthold E. Lessing*

ॐ

*I*f the instinct of daughter, sister, wife, or mother dies out of a college-bred woman, even in the course of a most brilliant career otherwise, the world will forget to love her; it will scorn her, and justly. If she does not make her surroundings homelike wherever she is, whether she be teacher, artist, musician, doctor, writer, daughter at home, or a mother in her household, and if she herself is not cheery and loving, dainty in dress, gentle in manner, and beautiful in soul as every true woman ought to be, the world will feel that the one thing needful is lacking—vivid, tender womanliness... It is better for a woman to fill a simple human part lovingly, better for her to be sympathetic in trouble and to whisper a comforting message into but one grieving ear, than that she should make a path to Egypt and lecture to thousands on ancient Thebes.

—*Anna R. Brown Lindsay*

*T*here is a light which is not the sudden blaze of torches, but the quiet shining of a lamp. This is what women at their best have been and are. They have possessed within themselves the quality and spirit from which the great ideals of courage and of sacrifice have been kindled in our human race.

—*Walter Russell Bowie*

136

*W*here there are no women there are no good manners.
—*Johann Wolfgang von Goethe*

*T*here is always a different, more kindly look, in the eyes of women who live on the land.
—*Swedish Proverb*

A caress is better than a career.
—*Elisabeth Marbury*

A gentle heart is tied with an easy thread.
—*George Herbert*

"*S*he made home happy!"—these
few words I read
Within a churchyard, written
on a stone;
No name, no date, the simple
words alone,
Told me the story of
the unknown dead.
—*Henry Coyle*

I am the last person in the world to insist upon a spotless house. Our living room can be thoroughly disorderly in the process of play or work, but when such periods are ended, I have always restored order. It is my duty to do so, as a woman. Children have been taught to help, but when...they do not help, then I restore order alone. It is my responsibility as homemaker, I believe, to keep our home as beautiful as I can without pressure on anyone, and there is no beauty without order.
—*Pearl S. Buck*

*T*o form women with all the qualifications required by their necessary and lofty mission is to form the fertile seed of social regeneration and improvement.
—*Benito Juarez*

*T*he bearing and the training of a child is woman's wisdom.
—*Alfred, Lord Tennyson*

137

As the daughter of Nathaniel Hawthorne, she was a child of culture. She could quickly create a poem or a sketch and enliven any salon with her wisdom and radiance. Yet in 1896, at 44, Rose Lathrop moved into a grimy hovel in the New York slums and became a ministering "angel" to cancer victims, insisting only that her patients be both destitute and incurable. Joining the Dominican order as Mother Alphonsa, she offered patients peace, comfort and her dedication to the creed "I am for God and the poor."

—*Life*

A bride should begin one ritual immediately after her honeymoon: the last thirty minutes before her husband returns from work she should spend on her appearance. His homecoming should be the high point of her day, and if she plans toward it she will always appear at first sight after his day's work the way she did when they were courting... Even after you have children, avoid using them as an excuse for shoddy or careless appearance—maintain your attractiveness to your companion.

—*Tim LaHaye*

*E*verybody knows that women's minds are cleaner than men's—they change them more often!

—*Traditional*

*T*o me, fair friend, you never can be old,
For as you were when first your eye I eyed,
Such seems your beauty still.

—*William Shakespeare*

*H*ast thou virtue? Acquire also the graces and beauties of virtue.
—*Benjamin Franklin*

*W*hat is civilization? I answer, the power of good women.
—*Ralph Waldo Emerson*

*H*er plants, her books...her writing desk...were all within her reach...she could scarcely see an object in that room which had not an interesting remembrance connected with it.

—*Jane Austen*

The aged women...[should] be in behaviour as becometh holiness...that they may teach the young women to be sober, to love their husbands, to love their children. To be discreet, chaste, keepers at home, good, obedient to their own husbands.

—*Titus 2:3-5*

The humorist Will Rogers did an article about the service [of Frontier Nurses], appealing for funds. "I have read more about you than I have Mahatma Gandhi," he wrote Mrs. Breckinridge. "I can't be a midwife but I can sure hold the nurse's horse."

—*Robin McKown*

A woman is like a teabag. It's only when she's in hot water that you realize how strong she is.

—*Nancy Reagan*

❧

You can almost trace light and darkness in the Bible by the women themselves.

—*Edith Deen*

The home is a temple of the woman, the education of children her divine service, and the family her congregation.

—*Talmud*

Hardly anything can be of greater value to a man of theory and speculation...than to carry on his speculations in the companionship and under the criticism of a really superior woman.

—*John Stuart Mill*

❧

The holier a woman is, the more she is a woman.

—*Leon Bloy*

Have a heart that never hardens, a temper that never tires, and a touch that never hurts.

—*Charles Dickens*

Place the sexes in right relations of mutual respect, and a severe morality gives that essential charm to a woman which educates all that is delicate, poetic and self-sacrificing; breeds courtesy and learning, conversation and wit in her rough mate; so that I have thought a sufficient measure of civilization is the influence of good women.

—*Ralph Waldo Emerson*

The nice, calm, cold thought, which in women shapes itself so rapidly that they hardly know it as thought, should always travel to the lips by way of the heart. It does so in those women whom we love and admire.

—*Oliver Wendell Holmes*

She walks in beauty, like the night
Of cloudless climes and starry skies;
And all that's best of dark and bright
Meet in her aspect and her eyes:
Thus mellow'd to that tender light
Which heaven to gaudy day denies.

—*Lord Byron*

No finer compliment can be paid to womanhood than a recitation of the Biblical facts that women were among the last at the Cross, the first at the tomb on the day of our Lord's resurrection, and the first to greet the resurrected Savior. This bears witness of a loyalty which cannot be excelled.

—*LeRoy Brownlow*

Many a raw wilderness of a man has been fashioned into something worthwhile by a woman without whom he would have floundered all his life.

—*John A. Schindler*

If a woman is reasonable, she will go along with his ideas, though she may share an opposite viewpoint—unless his policies are wicked. And if a man becomes wicked—would teach his children to lie, or cheat or steal—she should take them out of his household. But as long as she remains under his roof she should honor his authority to rule.

—*Helen B. Andelin*

140

*H*as woman, the true inspirer of man in all that is good and true, forgotten how to cast her gaze Godward?

—*Edith Deen*

*T*here is no land so sacred, no air so pure and wholesome as is the air she breathes, and the soil that is pressed by her footsteps. Here for her sake will I stay, and like an invisible presence, hover around her forever, protecting, supporting her weakness.

—*Henry Wadsworth Longfellow*

*F*or after this manner in the old time the holy women...[were] in subjection to their own husbands: Even as Sara obeyed Abraham, calling him lord: whose daughters ye are, as long as ye do well.

—*I Peter 3:5,6*

*I*f you get simple beauty and naught else, you get about the best thing God invents.

—*Robert Browning*

A man succeeds and reaps honors of public applause when in truth, a quiet little woman has made it all possible—has by her tact and encouragement held him to his best; has had faith in him when his own faith has languished, has cheered him on with unfailing assurance: "You can, you must, you will."

—*Jack Appleton*

I had no reason to doubt that brains were suitable for a woman.

—*Margaret Mead*

*T*here is as much bravery in keeping one's home in good order and condition as there is in defending it against attack from without.

—*Mohandas Gandhi*

*Y*our personality is your most precious possession. What you wear, and how you wear it, can be a beautiful expression of your own personality or an unbeautiful imitation of another's. You can be a creative artist in terms of your own personality, and translate the ideal image of yourself into reality.

—*Gayelord Hauser*

*W*omen are the supreme realists of the race. Women decide the larger questions of life correctly and quickly. They see at a glance what most men could not see with searchlights and telescopes... Apparently illogical, they are the possessors of a rare and subtle super-logic.

—*H.L. Mencken*

*S*he [Miss Dove] thought of all the children she had pruned and polished and kept in line, and to whom she had explained, by precept and example, the hard, the true, the simple and beautiful meaning of the human adventure. She thought of their faces lighting up with fresh wonder when they conceived, for the first time, the roundness of the earth.

She knew, with a passion of yearning, exactly where she wished to go. Not to old Cathay. Not to London or Paris or to the country with the golden light. She wanted to walk down to Oakwood, across Lafayette, up Maple, over to Grant...and into the portals of Cedar Grove School. She wanted to go into the geography room. To put her hat and gloves and bag in the cupboard. To unroll the big map of the world. To mount her platform and to stand there waiting for the first-graders to file in.

—*Frances Gray Patton*

*S*arah [Bush Lincoln] had what folks called "faculty"; she worked hard and she could make other people work, too. Even Tom, who meant well but was likely to let things slide. She never said he must do thus and so; she was too wise and too gentle. But somehow Tom found himself making a real door for the cabin and cutting a window, like she wanted. He put down a floor, chinked up the cracks between the logs, whitewashed the inside walls. Abe couldn't get over how sightly it was. And she wove Abe shirts out of homespun cloth, coloring them with dye she steeped out of roots and barks. She made him deerskin breeches that really fitted, and moccasins, and a coonskin cap. She had a mirror and she rubbed it bright and held it up so's he could see himself—it was the first time he had ever seen himself—and he said, "Land o'Goshen, is that me?"

—*Bernadine Bailey & Dorothy Walworth*

*M*en have sight; women insight.

—*Victor Hugo*

142

A woman is made physically, emotionally, and spiritually for the central task of nurturing... It is part of the feminine nature to be a receiver and a responder. One of the great pressures placed on women today is the notion that it is not all right to be feminine in this way. The "new and improved" model of femininity is aggressive, self-reliant, rock-solid emotionally. The attempt to live up to this legend causes some women to deny their basic inner nature, which is that of a responder...the innermost yearnings of a woman's nature are touched when she responds to her husband's leadership. To deny this is to deny nature.

—*James Walker*

ॐ

*L*egions of American women have heeded the call to serve as missionaries overseas, but none more fervently than Southern Baptist Lottie Moon...[who] left her native Virginia for Shantung Province, China. Known as the "Heavenly Book Visitor," she set up a girls' school and taught the Gospel to village women. When famine struck in 1911, Moon gave away her rations and died of starvation.

—*Life*

*H*ow far may a girl run after a man? Cat-like, she can do a little stalking, but run? Not a step. The freedom of today allows her to meet him halfway, but the girl who runs, runs after a man who runs faster.

—*Emily Post*

*W*hen she attempts to play a part not intended for her she sacrifices her own special beauty and grace. The moon, when it moves from its sphere of night into day, loses its lustre, its charm, its very poetry. And so it is with woman, when she attempts to play a part not intended for her.

—*Helen B. Andelin*

I never cease to marvel at the endurance of a woman's love... Men would never put up with some of the things that most women are forced to endure. It must be a carryover of a mother's love which we tend to think of as the greatest illustration of human love. Whatever the cause, I am convinced that a woman has a far greater capacity to love a man than a man has to love a woman. I have yet to see a woman who will not respond to love.

—*Tim LaHaye*

The greatest opportunity to better the world which can come to any woman is through the experience of maternity.

—*Ella Wheeler Wilcox*

Make all your dreams portable. Women should learn to be happy anywhere, in any circumstance—on a mountain top, or on burning desert, in poverty's vale or abounding in wealth.

—*Helen B. Andelin*

The wonderful generosity of her sentiments raises her at times into heroical and godlike regions...and by the firmness with which she treads her upward path, she convinces the coarsest calculators that another road exists than that which their feet know.

—*Ralph Waldo Emerson*

[Clara Barton] gave first aid to the wounded. The very sick received bread soaked in wine. She cooked up soup and applesauce for others, and passed out fresh shirts. Grateful for these small comforts, the men called her the Angel of the Battlefield.

—*Robin McKown*

Kindness in women, not their beauteous looks, shall win my love.

—*William Shakespeare*

Men have recognized that womanhood is a sacred and a noble thing, that women are of a finer clay, are more in touch with the angels of God and have the noblest function that life affords.

—*Peter Marshall*

And a certain woman named Lydia, a seller of purple...which worshipped God, heard us...and when she was baptized, and her household, she besought us, saying...come into my house and abide there.

—*Acts 16:14,15*

There is no better time for a woman to think than in the hours when she sweeps and dusts and makes beds. The physical activity sends blood coursing through her frame and the brain awakes.

—*Pearl S. Buck*

*L*et thy mind's sweetness have its operation upon thy body, thy clothes and thy habitation.

—*George Herbert*

*I*f thy husband is foolish, be thou discreet.

—*American Indian Maxim*

*T*he most beautiful object in the world, it will be allowed, is a beautiful woman.

—*Macaulay*

*C*heerfulness and content are great beautifiers and are famous preservers of youthful looks.

—*Charles Dickens*

A man is a great thing upon the earth and through eternity; but every jot of the greatness of man is unfolded out of woman.

—*Walt Whitman*

*T*here is one type of woman rarely seen in a psychiatrist's office. That is the woman who is glad she is a woman...she honestly enjoys homemaking, and more than anything in the world she wants to raise a family of healthy, normal youngsters.

—*Dr. Marynia F. Farnham*

*T*he first nurse was the first mother who instinctively cared for her child. But it is from compassion, rather than instinct, that the desire to care for the sick and needy stranger arose.

—*Frontispiece, Heroic Nurses*

A lady's imagination is very rapid; it jumps from admiration to love, from love to matrimony in a moment.

—*Jane Austen*

'*T*s strange what a man may do, and a woman yet think him an angel.

—*William Makepeace Thackeray*

145

Her heart is always doing lovely things,
Filling my wintry mind with simple flowers;
Playing sweet tunes on my untuned strings,
Delighting all my undelightful hours.

—John Masefield

Every man who is high up loves to think that he has done it all himself;
and the wife smiles, and lets it go at that.

—Sir James M. Barrie

ॐ

What makes men tick—and women tock?

—James Walker

A woman's life is a history of the affections.

—Washington Irving

There is no cosmetic for beauty like happiness.

—Countess of Blessington

When a girl ceases to blush, she has lost the most powerful charm of
her beauty.

—Gregory I

A really plain woman is one who, however beautiful, neglects
to charm.

—Edgar Saltus

Gracefulness has been defined to be the outward expression of the
inward harmony of the soul.

—William Hazlitt

The hair is the richest ornament of women.

—Martin Luther

There is no instinct like that of the heart.

—Lord Byron

There is nothing enduring in life for a woman except that she builds in a man's heart.

—Judith Anderson

She is not made to be the admiration of all, but the happiness of one.

—Edmund Burke

ॐ

By the banks of the Nile that day when she found the baby, the daughter of Pharaoh could not have known or imagined that destinies were at stake, but those destinies depended in that moment on the emotions in her heart... What she saw was the helplessness to which her instinctive womanhood responded. Her instant pity was stronger than any cautious thought she might have had as to what was safe and prudent, and so she acted as she did... But whatever in the Book of Exodus account may be historic and what portion a beautiful tradition, the story of it reflects a recognition of that which has been true since human life existed. It is the woman who cherishes the weaknesses, which through her, may grow into strength. All that a man in his career goes on to accomplish may trace back, as did the career of Moses, to the protectiveness which in some critical moment a woman gave.

—Walter Russell Bowie

ॐ

Being a woman is a terribly difficult task since it consists principally in dealing with men.

—Joseph Conrad

A woman's guess is much more accurate than a man's certainty.

—Rudyard Kipling

Despite woman's so-called emancipated place, and her many added opportunities, there are some things she should continue to be, whatever else she is: the mother, the wife, the helpmate and homemaker, the true and virtuous teacher of children, the symbol of service, of purity and compassion, and of the living of a good and gracious life.

—Richard L. Evans

147

I have wept in the night
For the shortness of sight
That to somebody's need made me blind;
But I never have yet
Felt a tinge of regret
For being a little too kind.

—*Anonymous*

A beautiful lady is an accident of nature. A beautiful old lady is a work of art.

—*Louis Nizer*

The ideal which the wife and mother makes for herself, the manner in which she understands duty and life, contain the fate of the community. Her faith becomes the star of the conjugal ship, and her love the animating principle that fashions the future of all belonging to her. Woman is the salvation or destruction of the family. She carries its destinies in the folds of her mantle.

—*Henri F. Amiel*

The Girl of the Period...seems sorrowfully ignorant or ashamed of the good old fashions which make woman truly beautiful and honored, and, through her, render home what it should be—a happy place, where parents and children, brothers and sisters, learn to love and know and help one another.

—*Louisa May Alcott*

D orothy Day has taken to the barricades in a range of causes from disarmament to civil rights to prison reform. She has been shot at, pelted with eggs and jailed eight times... A co-founder of the Catholic Worker movement and editor of its penny-a-copy paper, she's spent much of her life on New York's Bowery, where her 44-year-old "House of Hospitality" offers food and shelter, with dignity, to the down-and-out. "The best thing to do with the best things in life," she believes, "is to give them up."

—*Life*

W hat manly eloquence can produce such an effect as woman's silence?

—*Jules Michelet*

148

If women are going to walk, and they should, then they must have equipment that does not torture them. The day of the bound Chinese foot has gone. A walking woman will have more beautiful legs, stronger abdomen, better carriage, happier mind, and will probably give birth to healthier children, and do so with less danger to herself and her child.

—Gayelord Hauser

Inner happiness is not a voluntary quality which can be put on as a smile, but must be earned by personal victory over our weaknesses and an upward reach for perfection.

—Helen B. Andelin

O Woman, in our hours of ease,
Uncertain, coy, and hard to please,
And variable as the shade
By the light quivering aspen made;
When pain and anguish wring the brow
A ministering angel thou!

—Sir Walter Scott

One of Clara Barton's many good deeds was to write letters home for her wounded soldiers. Sometimes their families wrote back to thank her and forwarded her gifts for the other soldiers. When a New Englander was reported missing, she was invariably asked for news of his whereabouts. By the time the war was over, there were thousands of families who had no way of knowing whether their loved ones were living or dead.

Clara Barton, with the aid of young Jules Golay, turned herself into a missing persons bureau. They circulated 20,000 copies of lists of missing men, arranged by states, asking information about them. The response was tremendous. On March 11, 1865, Abraham Lincoln gave her a note which made her job official: "To the Friends of Missing Persons: Miss Clara Barton has kindly offered to search for missing prisoners of war. Please address her at Annapolis, giving her the name, regiment, and company of any missing prisoners."

—Robin McKown

Her lips are roses over-washed with dew.

—Green

Disguise our bondage as we will,
'Tis woman, woman rules us still.

—*Thomas Moore*

He's a fool, who thinks by force, or skill,
To turn the current of a woman's will.

—*Samuel Tuke*

Women have more strength in their looks than we have in our laws, and more power by their tears than we have by our arguments.

—*Saville*

Just about everything significant in my life happened after I passed forty. I was a housewife and mother, but yearned to be a writer. I worked at my writing whenever I could snatch a moment, and I assembled several manuscripts.

I was just about forty when my first novel, *East Wind, West Wind,* was published. Then a few months later came *The Good Earth.* My career was launched at last, and it has given me the richest possible satisfaction.

—*Pearl S. Buck*

And when the woman saw that the tree was good for food, and that it was pleasant to the eyes, and a tree desired to make one wise, she took the fruit thereof, and did eat, and gave also unto her husband with her; and he did eat.

—*Genesis 3:6*

Women are special custodians of all that is pure and religious in life. Conservative by nature, if they are slow to shed superstitious habits, they are also slow to give up all that is pure and noble in life.

—*Mohandas Gandhi*

When woman has a fair chance, her work will vie creditably with that of the ages. Don't fear that she will become too masculine. When she learns to use her intellect, she will show that the use of it need not absorb or weaken, but rather refine and invigorate her affections.

—*Margaret Fuller*

So dear to heaven is saintly chastity,
That when a soul is found sincerely so
A thousand liveried angels lacky her.

—*John Milton*

Next to God we are indebted to women, first for life itself, and then for making it worth having.

—*Christian Bovee*

It was lucky for me that I had one as much disposed to industry and frugality as myself. She assisted me cheerfully in my business, folding and stitching pamphlets, tending shop, purchasing old linen rags for the paper makers... We kept no idle servants, our table was plain and simple, our furniture of the cheapest. For instance, my breakfast was for a long time bread and milk (no tea), and I ate it out of a two penny earthen porringer with a pewter spoon.

But mark how luxury will enter families, and make a progress, in spite of principle: being called one morning to breakfast, I found it in a China bowl, with a spoon of silver! They had been bought for me without my knowledge by my wife, and had cost her the enormous sum of three-and-twenty shillings, for which she had no other excuse or apology to make, but that she thought *her* husband deserved a silver spoon and China bowl as well as any of his neighbors.

—*Benjamin Franklin*

The world has enough women who know how to be smart.
　　It needs women who are willing to be simple.
The world has enough women who know how to be brilliant.
　　It needs women who will be brave.
The world has enough women who are popular.
　　It needs women who are pure.

—*Peter Marshall*

The bosom can ache beneath diamond brooches; and many a blithe heart dances under coarse cloth.

—*Edwin H. Chapin*

151

$\mathcal{D}$on't agonize. Organize.

—Flarynce Kennedy

$\mathcal{T}$he laughter of girls is, and ever was, among the delightful sounds of earth.

—Thomas De Quincey

$\mathcal{A}$ woman can become a constant joy to herself, to her children, to her husband, to the world, by being glad she is alive and by showing it... Such a woman is one of those magnificent people for whom everyone is glad, because the corner of the world she occupies becomes a mighty pleasant estate.

—Dr. John A. Schindler

$\mathcal{A}$ge cannot wither her, nor custom stale
Her infinite variety.

—William Shakespeare

$\mathcal{H}$er modest looks the cottage might adorn,
Sweet as the primrose peeps beneath the thorn.

—Oliver Goldsmith

$\mathcal{A}$ good and true woman is said to resemble a Cremona fiddle—age but increases its worth and sweetens its tone.

—Oliver Wendell Holmes

$\mathcal{S}$he who studies her mirror neglects her heart.

—John Casper Lavater

$\mathcal{A}$ simple maiden in her flower
Is worth a hundred coats-of-arms.

—Alfred, Lord Tennyson

$\mathcal{T}$here is an inner radiance to the eyes. There will be a dignity about her bearing—an optimism, hope and faith in her attitude. She smiles easily, and suggests a feeling of contentment. She is slow to criticize. She is trustful and patient, and her spirit radiates tranquility, serenity and peace. Her appearance and influence are uplifting.

—Helen B. Andelin

$\mathcal{W}$omen can give you an exact and circumstantial account of some quite insignificant conversation with a friend years before; and what is worse, they do.

—*William Somerset Maugham*

$\mathcal{I}$f you are a womanly woman, you cherish the manliness of your man. You want to build up that ego, not break it down. You will quickly realize that what he needs from you is not talking...but doing...

If you have been trying to change his ways with words, give it up. Slip into a new gear. Change to the gentle, artful persuasion that only a woman knows how to do. Change his ways without even letting him know it.

You have the power to do this. You are still the mistress of the home...you are the queen.

—*Gayelord Hauser*

❦

$\mathcal{I}$ would urge upon every young woman to obtain as soon as she can, by the severest economy, a restricted, serviceable, and steadily—however slowly—increasing series of books for use through life; making her little library, of all the furniture in her room, the most studied and decorative piece; every volume having its assigned place, like a little statue in its niche.

—*John Ruskin*

❦

$\mathcal{T}$he heart of a woman is never so full of affection that there does not remain a little corner for flattery and love.

—*Julien Mauveaux*

$\mathcal{E}$ven virtue is more fair when it appears in a beautiful person.

—*Virgil*

$\mathcal{A}$ woman with her hair combed up always looks as if she were going some place, either to the opera or the shower bath—depending on the woman.

—*Orson Wells*

153

If a woman is to stay in the home—where she should be if she is married and certainly if she has small children—then merchants must understand there will be a drop in business... If the people are to buy all the wonderful things that are made for them to buy...then husband and wife will both have to bring in the cash and woman cannot therefore afford to be homemaker alone. Such housekeeping as she does will have to be hasty; her husband will have to help with the dishes, the cleaning and the children. This is inescapable truth.

—*Pearl S. Buck*

The greatest piano teacher in all the world [is] Rosina Lhevinne... Rosina began playing in Russia, taking lessons at 9 from her future husband, Josef Lhevinne, then 14. Both won the prestigious Gold Medal of the Moscow Conservatory, but after they married she forsook a solo career, giving concerts with him instead... Semiretired at 96, she still hears a few students...teaching them: "Be yourself. And one must listen with the heart."

—*Life*

Were women meant to do everything—work *and* have babies?

—*Candice Bergen*

č

Be yourself—it's the one thing you can do better than anyone else.

—*Ethel Merman*

A virtuous woman is a crown to her husband.

—*Proverbs 12:4*

From a sensitive woman's heart springs the happiness of mankind, and from the kindness of her noble spirit comes mankind's affection.

—*Kahlil Gibran*

Many girls today are unwilling to make marriage a full-time job... They prefer a career to a home or try to mix both... Of course, there are many exceptions, and I am not referring to those married women who are forced by economic necessity to continue working.

—*Peter Marshall*

154

There is no garment more becoming than love, no cosmetic more glamorizing. Some say that when beauty fades, loves goes. Isn't it the other way around? Beauty fades only when love is gone.

—*Marjorie Holmes*

When I think of the countless women in this country who get up in the morning, make breakfast, see that the kids are dressed properly, send them off to school, dress, go to work, come home, make dinner, speak to the emotional needs of the children, do the wash, retire, and get up again in the morning only to do it over again, I don't know how...they manage.

—*Phil Donahue*

I have never had my face lifted. I prefer to have my spirits lifted. In my opinion, the effect is very nearly the same.

—*Helena Rubenstein*

God created man before woman, but then there's always a rough draft before the masterpiece.

—*Anonymous*

[In past times the]...ideal woman not only pressed out oil for cooking but for her lamps as well. She probably had many, for they signified the divine presence, and the woman with a lamp that did not go out by night became one who gave spiritual as well as visible light to her household.

—*Edith Deen*

It is time to leave this question up to Mother Nature—a difficult lady to fool. You have only to give women the same opportunities as men, and you will soon find out what is or is not in their nature. What is in women's nature to do they will do, and you won't be able to stop them.

But you will also find, and so will they, that what is not in their nature, even if they are given every opportunity, they will not do, and you won't be able to make them do it.

—*Clare Boothe Luce*

All through the long winter I dream of my garden. On the first warm day of spring I dig my fingers deep into the soft earth. I can feel its energy, and my spirits soar.

—*Helen Hayes*

It is possible that blondes also prefer gentlemen.

—Mamie Van Doren

There is a sacredness in tears. They are not the mark of weakness, but of power. They speak more eloquently than 10,000 tongues. They are the messengers of overwhelming grief, of deep contrition and of unspeakable love.

—Washington Irving

If I were asked the mission of the ideal woman, I would say it is to make the whole world homelike. The true woman will make every place she enters homelike—and she will enter every place in this wide world.

—Frances E. Willard

There may be times when we are powerless to prevent injustice, but there must never be a time when we fail to protest.

—Elie Wiesel

My mother was always at hand to help and advise... Indeed she became an ardent ally, furthering my plans and guarding my interests with all her influence and boundless energy. She was still, at 40, young, beautiful and fascinating.

—Winston Churchill

Compliments seem few and far between these days, sighs a gentlewoman we know. "It's too bad because they provide an element of grace in our contacts with one another."

—Doris Ann Krupinsk

I stand at the altar of the murdered men and while I live I fight their cause.

—Florence Nightingale

While we have the gift of life, it seems to me the only tragedy is to allow part of us to die—whether it is our spirit, our creativity or our glorious uniqueness.

—Gilda Radner

$\mathcal{W}$omen are meant to be loved, not to be understood.

—*Oscar Wilde*

$\mathcal{M}$oral beauty is an exceptional and very striking phenomenon—one never forgets it. This form of beauty is far more impressive than the beauty of nature. It gives to those who possess its divine gifts a strange, an inexplicable power. It increases the strength of the intellect.

—*Dr. Alexis Carrel*

$\mathcal{M}$y mother's mother, of conservative French descent and Huguenot family, had reared her daughters to be good housewives, and this included, in that generation, the making of garments for the family. The garments were decorated with embroidery and lace, and these arts were taught, too. In due course, therefore, I had my seam to sew, embroidery to make, and lace to crochet. The same combination of plain work and artistic decoration also was necessary for cooking. I was taught to make bread as well as cake, to roast and broil and fry as well as to conjure up confections. A house must be thoroughly clean and ordered before flowers could be arranged, but all was equally essential to the well-being and happiness of family life. This work and decoration, my mother declared, was woman's business.

—*Pearl S. Buck*

$\mathcal{T}$hat is the worst of those dear people who have charm; they are so terrible to do without, when once you have got accustomed to them and all their ways.

—*George Louis Palmella*

$\mathcal{N}$o one has made a better case for the competence of women than Margaret Thatcher, the Tory Party leader, who happens to be cool to feminism.

—*Time*

$\mathcal{L}$et her transfer that love to the whole of humanity...and she will occupy her proud position by the side of man as his mother, maker and silent leader. It is given to her to teach the art of peace to the warring world thirsting for that nectar.

—*Mohandas Gandhi*

$\mathcal{I}$ do know that women should no longer be ashamed to glory in being women, or to enjoy the satisfactions that are unique to women, such as motherhood. When women feel that they must divest themselves of their uniquely feminine qualities, they are not achieving equality, but losing identity. To be somebody, a woman does not have to be more like a man, but has to be more of a woman.

—*Sally E. Shaywitz*

$\mathcal{I}$ am rather proud of the fact that after nearly a quarter of a century of marriage my husband feels free to make his decisions and act on them without consulting me or giving me advance information concerning them.

—*Grace Coolidge*

$\mathcal{W}$oman's beauty is not imprisoned by her skin; it permeates her entire home, creating warmth, love and harmony, and often it radiates far beyond her own four walls.

—*Gayelord Hauser*

$\mathcal{D}$orothea Lange wanted to record a life that included the migrating Okie families of the dust bowl years she so memorably photographed, and the sharecropper faces...seamed by wind and the strain of poverty. Lange left the security of a portrait studio to cover that other world of people too poor to pay for a sitting.

—*Life*

[$\mathcal{T}$wentieth-century women have contributed to the National Cathedral in Washington.] Through the cathedral's Needlepoint Guild, a thousand women have volunteered their work for the portrayal of the Christian story in needlework. Twenty-six women in Pittsburgh embroidered the cloth covering the steps to the cathedral's main altar. Women in all fifty states wove the seals of their states and territories into tapestry for the War Memorial Chapel. Hundreds of others, including the late Queen Mary of England, did the needlework for the nine hundred and sixty kneeling pads.

—*Edith Deen*

$\mathcal{A}$ gentleman makes no noise; a lady is serene.

—*Ralph Waldo Emerson*

158

Beauty and grace command the world.

—*Park Benjamin*

So sweet the blush of bashfulness
Even pity scarce can wish it less.

—*Lord Byron*

O she is all perfection,
All that the blooming earth can send forth fair,
All that the gaudy heavens could drop down glorious.

—*Lee*

Do not think you can make a girl lovely, if you do not make her happy.

—*John Ruskin*

Grace was in all her steps, heav'n in her eye,
In every gesture dignity and love.

—*John Milton*

Being a loving and understanding wife, a wonderful mother and a devoted and successful homemaker are key requirements to her happiness. Success in the feminine role is her real glory, and brings her an inner peace and satisfaction that cannot be met otherwise. It is impossible for a woman who neglects these sacred duties to experience real joy. She may gain satisfaction from activities and success elsewhere, but they cannot compensate for her failure as a woman.

—*Helen B. Andelin*

Her eyes, her lips, her cheeks, her shape, her features,
Seem to be drawn by love's own hand; by love
Himself in love.

—*John Dryden*

The criterion of true beauty is that it increases on examination; of false, that it lessens. There is something, therefore, in true beauty that corresponds with the right reason, and it is not merely the creature of fancy.

—*Sir Fulke Greville*

159

That is the best part of beauty which a picture cannot express.

—*Francis Bacon*

Beauty is truth, truth beauty—that is all
Ye know on earth, and all ye need to know.

—*John Keats*

All orators are dumb when beauty pleadeth.

—*William Shakespeare*

I believe women come nearer fulfilling their God-given function in the home than anywhere else. It is a much nobler thing to be a good wife than to be Miss America.

—*Peter Marshall*

Beauty, without virtue, is like a flower without perfume.

—*French Proverb*

The person whose clothes are extremely fine I am too apt to consider as not being possessed of any superiority of fortune, but resembling those Indians who are found to wear all the gold they have in the world in a bob at the nose.

—*Oliver Goldsmith*

I can't imagine that I would have to lead the same sort of life as...all the women who do their work and are then forgotten... I want to go on living even after my death! And therefore I am grateful to God for giving me this gift, this possibility of developing myself and of writing, of expressing all that is in me.

—*Anne Frank*

What is becoming is honest, and whatever is honest must be becoming.

—*Cicero*

Nothing lovelier can be found
In woman, than to study household good,
And good works in her husband to promote.

—*John Milton*

160

A child no more! a maiden now—
A graceful maiden, with a gentle brow;
A cheek tinged lightly and a dove-like eye;
And all hearts bless her as she passes by.

—Mary Howitt

&

We must realize that homemaking, in the full sense of the word and the deed, takes time. It takes time, not only to do the actual work of keeping a house clean and beautiful on limited means, but it takes time to think about each member of the family in relation to the home and to the whole. A woman cannot be hurried and harried every moment of the day, struggling to earn money and at the same time to be a real homemaker. She knows she is not succeeding and she will, to silence her own conscience, glorify the pleasure of having money to spend. Then the homemaker, the woman who does not earn wages in cash, listens and wonders in discontent whether she is choosing the right way. She is, she feels, nothing but a housewife... It takes real self-discipline to be a good housewife.

—Pearl S. Buck

&

Woman knows that the better she obeys the surer she is to rule.
—Jules Michelet

She hugged the offender and forgave the offense.
—John Dryden

[Edith Cavell] told her young cousin, Eddy Cavell, "I don't know what I am going to do, but some day, somehow, I am going to do something useful..." [She nursed] her father to health...and it was likely this experience that showed her where her true vocation lay. In 1895, at the age of thirty, she entered London's Fountain Hospital as a nurse. The hospital had no training school. For three months she worked from six in the morning until ten at night with hardly a breathing spell, scrubbing floors, emptying slop pails, making bandages.

—Robin McKown

As early as fourteen centuries before Christ, women engaged in construction work. Sherah, an ancestress of Joshua, was one of these. She designed and supervised the building of three ancient towns... When the walls of Jerusalem were restored during Ezra's and Nehemiah's time, the daughters of Shallum were among the workers.

—*Edith Deen*

The special genius of woman has always been that of nurture, for which men have no talent whatever.

—*Dr. Marynia F. Farnham*

Of life's two chief prizes, beauty and truth, I found the first in a loving heart and the second in a laborer's hand.

—*Kahlil Gibran*

With women the heart argues, not the mind.

—*Matthew Arnold*

No matter how hard a man may labour, some woman is always in the background of his mind. She is the one reward of virtue.

—*Gertrude Franklin Atherton*

The world was sad, the garden was a wild,
And man, the hermit, sigh'd—till woman smiled.

—*Thomas Campbell*

Women know
The way to rear up children (to be just),
They know a simple, merry, tender knack
Of tying sashes, fitting baby shoes,
And stringing pretty words that make no sense.

—*Elizabeth Barrett Browning*

Auld Nature swears the lovely dears
Her noblest work she classes O.
Her 'prentice han' she tried on man,
And then she made the lasses, O!

—*Robert Burns*

162

Nothing can replace a woman at the bedside of a wounded man, not only at base hospitals, but more especially at the front... When a wounded man arrived at my field hospital, scared and in pain, he immediately found two girls dressed in white leaning over his bed. That was enough: his doubts and anxieties were over there and then. He felt he was safe the moment he saw a girl's quiet smile. After all, one has to smile back at an attractive face...pretend that there's nothing wrong even when one is ready to howl with pain. One has to show gratitude for so much gentleness and patience, for the mysterious feminine quality which appears even in the most professional actions. It acts like a charm.

—*Major Paul Grauwin*

❧

First, she [Anna Mary Robertson] bore ten children and raised the five who survived, working hard farmwife days until she was 78. Only then, in 1938, did she have leisure to hearken again to her girlhood yearning to paint. On panels of Masonite, using paints she found out in the barn, working on several pictures at once to make the pigments go further, she brought alive the warm world of the past as brightly as it lived in her mind. Skating parties in up-state New York, Christmas tree fetching, tapping maples for sugar—all were done in a style so deceptively childlike but so powerfully original as to make Grandma Moses one of the great primitives in art.

—*Life*

There are but two things that chiefly excite us to love a woman, an attractive beauty, and unspotted fame.

—*Miguel de Cervantes*

Her very frowns are fairer far
Than smiles of other maidens are.

—*Hartley Coleridge*

Women are door-mats and have been—
    The years those mats applaud—
They keep their men from going in
    With muddy feet to God.

—*Mary Carolyn Davies*

163

Grace is to the body what good sense is to the mind.

—Francois de la Rochefoucauld

Beauty does not always make one happy, but happiness always brings a kind of beauty. A bride is always beautiful. Many women are beautiful in pregnancy, and when nursing a baby. Happiness, love, the knowledge that she is nourishing life—all these shine in the loveliness of a woman at these great moments in her life.

—Gayelord Hauser

And all the women that were wise hearted did spin with their hands, and brought that which they had spun, both of blue, and of purple and of scarlet, and of fine linen.

—Exodus 35:25

ॐ

She was one of those rarely gifted beings who cannot look or speak or even stir without waking up (and satisfying) some vague longing that lies dormant in the hearts of most of us.

—George Louis Palmella

The appreciative woman will enjoy drinking water from a tin cup, while another feels she must have china dishes. One woman will enjoy sitting on an apple box in her backyard letting the warm summer sun shine down on her shoulders. Another may feel she must have patio furniture to be happy. One will enjoy the sounds of the forest or the birds and the leaves rustling while another must have grand opera. One will enjoy a simple wardrobe of cottons while another lives for the day she can buy her clothes on Fifth Avenue. One feels real joy in pushing her baby buggy in the park, while another must have the bright light and gay places. One will enjoy the simple cottage, while another must have a modern home with a view... Women who learn to enjoy these common things are never left wanting.

—Helen B. Andelin

A woman's work, grave sirs, is never done.

—Laurence Eusden

164

Mozart's sister was known to be more talented than he was, but their father would not allow her to continue her musical education lest it take her beyond her "sphere." She submitted, trained in submission, just as Chinese women in the not distant past themselves bound their daughters' feet even as their own feet had been bound, in spite of the pain and the crippling, and thought they were doing their duty.

—*Pearl S. Buck*

Woman is woman's natural ally.

—*Euripides*

[*Grandma's* Prayer:]
I pray that, risen from the dead,
I may in glory stand—
A crown, perhaps, upon my head,
But a needle in my hand.

—*Eugene Field*

I believe in the proper education of women. But I do not believe that woman will make her contribution to the world by mimicking or running a race with men. She can run the race, but she will not rise to the great heights she is capable of by mimicking man. She has to be the complement of man.

—*Mohandas Gandhi*

They talk about a woman's sphere as though it had a limit;
There's not a place in earth or heaven,
There's not a task to mankind given,
There's not a blessing or a woe,
There's not a whispered "yes" or "no,"
There's not a life, or death, or birth,
That has a feather's weight of worth
Without a woman in it.

—*Kate Field*

A child of our grandmother Eve, a female; or, for thy more sweet understanding, a woman.

—*William Shakespeare*

165

*W*oman's work is—
  I. To please people.
  II. To feed them in dainty ways.
  III. To clothe them.
  IV. To keep them orderly.
  V. To teach them.

—John Ruskin

*S*he commandeth her husband, in any equal matter, by constant obeying him.

—Thomas Fuller

A woman's hopes are woven of sunbeams; a shadow annihilates them.

—George Eliot

A modest woman, dressed out in all her finery, is the most tremendous object of the whole creation.

—Oliver Goldsmith

*W*hen a mother falls from grace, the whole family of mankind suffers, for a mother is the silent carrier of those great, historically effective talents. Man spends his talents but woman transmits them.

—Edith Deen

*L*ord of the pots and pipkins,
    since I have no time to be
A saint by doing lovely things and
    vigilling with Thee,
By watching in the twilight dawn,
    and storming Heaven's gates,
Make me a saint by getting meals
    and washing up the plates!

—Cecily R. Hallack

*S*he would have made a splendid wife, for crying only made her eyes more bright.

—O. Henry

166

Forgive you?—Oh, of course, dear,
    A dozen times a week!
We women were created
    Forgiveness but to speak.

                                                                   —Ella Higginson

There is in every true woman's heart a spark of heavenly fire, which lies dormant in the broad daylight of prosperity; but which kindles up, and beams and blazes in the dark hour of adversity.

                                                         —Washington Irving

Patience makes women beautiful in middle age.

                                                           —Elliot Paul

By the time she [Edith Cavell] reached Brussels, the Germans had already invaded Belgium, violating its neutrality... Word came that the Germans were nearing Brussels. The Belgian nurses, weeping, declared they would never tend an enemy soldier. Edith firmly reminded them that their duty as nurses was to care for the sick, no matter who they were.

                                                         —Robin McKown

I am very fond of the company of ladies. I like their beauty, I like their delicacy, I like their vivacity, and I like their silence.

                                                         —Samuel Johnson

❧

A nun hath no nation.
Wherever man suffers or woman may soothe,
There her land! there her kindred!

                                                —Edward Robert Bulwer Lytton

We were gentle among you, even as a nurse cherisheth her children.

                                                    —I Thessalonians 2:7

Learning is nothing without cultivated manners, but when the two are combined in a woman you have one of the most exquisite products of civilization.

                                                       —Andre Maurois

She walks—the lady of my delight—
   A shepherdess of sheep.
Her flocks are thoughts. She keeps them white;
   She guards them from the steep.

—Alice Meynell

She doeth little kindnesses
Which most leave undone, or despise.

—James Russell Lowell

If she seem not chaste to me,
What care I how chaste she be?

—Sir Walter Raleigh

There's a woman like a dewdrop, she's so purer than the purest.

—Robert Browning

She was good as she was fair,
None—none on earth above her!
As pure in thought as angels are:
To know her was to love her.

—Samuel Rogers

It is very certain that a well-informed woman, conscious of her nature
and dignity, is more capable of performing the relative duties of life, and
of engaging and retaining the affections of a man of understanding, than
one whose intellectual endowments rise not above the common level.

—Abigail Adams

The woman who is happy in her work brings solace and stability to the
home. Her children are warmed by her, her husband at peace, and both
admire her for the honor she brings to her feminine role.

—Helen B. Andelin

If woman lost us Eden, such
As she alone restore it.

—John Greenleaf Whittier

168

*N*ever think she loves him wholly.
Never believe her love is blind,
All his faults are locked securely
In a closet of her mind.

—*Sara Teasdale*

❦

*E*yes of pure women [are] wholesome stars of love.
—*Alfred, Lord Tennyson*

❦

*L*ove is the best of all cosmetics. Love is nature's most magical
beauty potion... A woman in love hardly needs the touch of rouge to bring
a glow to her face and a light to her eyes. Love does it for her. Love
creates her beauty from within better than any cosmetic can do it from
without.

—*Gayelord Hauser*

❦

[*A* Kitchen Prayer:]
May I have eyes to see
Beauty in this plain room
Where I am called to be.

—*Nancy Byrd Turner*

❦

*M*ightier far than strength of nerve and sinew, or the sway
Of magic potent over sun and star,
Is Love, though oft to agony distrest,
And though his favorite seat be feeble woman's breast.

—*William Wordsworth*

*M*odesty is not only an ornament, but also a guard to virtue.
—*Joseph Addison*

*T*here is no spectacle on earth more appealing than that of a beautiful woman in the act of cooking dinner for someone she loves.

—Thomas Wolfe

*Y*e must know that women have dominion over you: do ye not labour and toil, and give and bring all to the woman?

—The Apocrypha, 1 Esdras 4:22

*W*oman's happiness is in obeying. She objects to men who abdicate too much.

—Jules Michelet

*I*f I have not been absolutely feminine, then I have failed.

—Mary Cassatt

*G*od has placed the genius of women in their hearts; because the works of this genius are always works of love.

—Alphonse M.L. Lamartine

*A*mbition is, in many ways, the most deadly foe we [women] have—the most deadly foe to our character I mean. Little by little that intellectual ambition will draw us away, if we are not careful, from our true place in life, and will make cold, unloved, and unhelpful women of us, instead of the joyous, affectionate, and unselfish women we might have been.

—Anna R. Brown Lindsay

*L*ove preserves beauty, and the flesh of woman is fed with caresses as are bees with flowers.

—Anatole France

I know a woman's portion when she loves,
It's hers to give, my darling, not to take;
It isn't lockets, dear, nor pairs of gloves,
It isn't marriage bells nor wedding cake,
It's up and cook, although the belly ache;
And bear the child, and up and work again,
And count a sick man's grumble worth the pain.

—John Masefield

*N*o matter how hard a woman works on a ranch—she always looks pretty on Saturday night.

—*Old Western Saying*

*G*race has been defined, the outward expression of the inward harmony of the soul.

—*William Hazlitt*

*T*he wife is the key of the house.

—*Thomas Fuller*

*M*aids must be wives and mothers to fulfil the entire and holiest end of woman's being.

—*Frances Anne Kemble*

A pretty woman is a welcome guest.

—*Lord Byron*

A beautiful form is better than a beautiful face; a beautiful behavior is better than a beautiful form: it is the finest of the fine arts.

—*Ralph Waldo Emerson*

A thing of beauty is a joy for ever:
Its loveliness increases; it will never
Pass into nothingness; but still will keep
A bower quiet for us, and a sleep
Full of sweet dreams, and health, and quiet breathing.

—*John Keats*

*W*oman's mind, conditioned by the biological role of motherhood, has always veered toward tenderness and compassion.

—*Dr. John A. Schindler*

*F*rom women's eyes this doctrine I derive:
They sparkle still the right Promethean fire;
They are the books, the arts, the academes,
That show, contain, and nourish all the world.

—*William Shakespeare*

171

A gracious woman retaineth honour.

—*Proverbs 11:16*

I'm firmly convinced that the type of life people lead shows on their faces—especially women. By the time a woman is 40 she has the kind of face she deserves.

—*Ann Landers*

It will avail humanity very little if the women of the developed countries improve their status without being aware of the need to further the cause of the underprivileged classes in the rest of the world.

—*Luis Echeverria*

For 40 years, beginning in 1837 she [Sarah Josepha Hale] gently, crisply guided women to see their roles as important, not merely subservient. "The most important vocation on earth," she said, "is that of the Christian mother in the nursery." And, of course, that of learning how to think, which Hale was superb at, too, discerning a civil war decades away, getting women into professions, and even finding time to write, "Mary Had a Little Lamb."

—*Life*

It's the woman who keeps the family together. She is the heart of the home and thereby must be the strongest person in the family structure.

—*Princess Grace of Monaco*

[A Letter to the Editors:] I am a girl of 15 and I have been confronted with opposite views of women's liberation for quite a few years now. What I derived...is that women's lib is absurd.

My plans for the future are to serve the man that I love and provide him a happy home. I have no intention of being the household leader. I plan on doing housework and raising children, but if I'm needed to do part-time work elsewhere, I'll do it until we can get back onto our feet again.

Women have been happy in the home raising children since the beginning of man and it would be unheard of to change an old family tradition now.

—*H.J.C.*

172

*M*y home and husband come first in my life. I took care of my children myself when they were little and breast-fed them all... I taught them all to read at home [keeping them out of school until the second grade].

—*Phyllis Schlafly*

ॐ

*W*omen [should] adorn themselves in modest apparel...and sobriety; not with broided hair, or gold, or pearls, or costly array.

—*I Timothy 2:9*

*M*an endures pain as an undeserved punishment; woman accepts it as a natural heritage.

—*Anonymous*

*N*ot only her willingness to bear children, but her tender care of the children are important to a man... [She] is always conscious and concerned about the physical care of her children, to see that they are properly fed and bathed. She takes pride in the way they look and never allows them to go hungry or cold, or neglected.

She is a tender, smiling, gentle, sympathetic mother who teaches her children how to be happy and offers them praise and understanding—giving them bread for their souls as well as their bodies.

—*Helen B. Andelin*

I'm perfectly happy... I'm able to do the things that I enjoy doing within the framework of our home.

—*Nancy Thurman*

*B*eauty is essential and the foundation of beauty is order. The homemaker is responsible for beauty and therefore for order... Order is not for order's sake but for beauty's sake. Order is the shape upon which beauty depends.

—*Pearl S. Buck*

*N*o man ever lived a right life who had not been chastened by a woman's love, strengthened by her courage, and guided by her discretion.

—*John Ruskin*

173

*M*en derive self-esteem by being respected; women feel worthy when they are loved.

—*James Dobson*

I have no doubt that they can do infinitely more than men against war. Answer for yourselves what your great soldiers and generals would do, if their wives and daughters and mothers refused to countenance their participation in militarism in any shape or form.

—*Mohandas Gandhi*

I have found such joy in things that fill
My quiet days; a curtain's blowing grace,
A growing plant upon a window sill,
A rose, fresh-cut and placed within a vase;
A table cleared, a lamp beside a chair,
And books I long have loved beside me there.

Oh, I have found such joy I wish I might
Tell every woman who goes seeking far
For some elusive, feverish delight,
That very close to home the great joys are:
The fundamental things—old as the race,
Yet never, through the ages commonplace.

—*Grace Noll Crowell*

*T*he happiest women, like the happiest nations, have no history.

—*George Eliot*

*W*hat woman needs is not as a woman to act or rule, but as a nature to grow, as an intellect to discern, as a soul to live freely, and unimpeded to unfold such powers as were given to her when we left our common home.

—*Margaret Fuller*

*I*t's a good time to be a woman.

—*Kate Louchheim*

When a woman achieves full status as a person this does not mean that she ought to be admitted to all the callings of men... Each has a characteristic perfection and one perfects the other.

—*Edith Deen*

The best thing I can do for him is to try to create a pleasant little island where he can work—where he likes the food and is not constantly bothered with questions about household and family affairs, or with people who disagree with him on every issue.

—*Lady Bird Johnson*

The mere departure of women from the duties of the domestic circle, far from being a reproach to her, is a virtue of the highest order, when it is done from purity of motive, by appropriate means, and the purpose good.

—*John Quincy Adams*

As I am a woman, so I am also a mistress of a large family... I cannot but look upon every soul you leave under my care as a talent committed under a trust by the great Lord of all the families both of heaven and earth.

—*Susanna Wesley*

A woman can produce what no man can: a child.

—*Clare Boothe Luce*

A woman well bred and well taught, furnished with the additional accomplishments of knowledge and behaviour, is a creature without comparison. Her society is the emblem of sublimer enjoyments, her person is angelic, and her conversation heavenly. She is all softness and sweetness, peace, love, wit and delight. She is every way suitable to the sublimest wish, and the man that has such a one to his portion, has nothing to do but to rejoice in her, and be thankful.

—*Daniel Defoe*

My luxury shall henceforth be to minister to human misery.

—*Julia Ward Howe*

The sweetest of all sounds is that of the voice of the woman we love.

—*Jean de la Bruyere*

175

*D*uring the radiant far off yesterdays of our history, it was the sacred duty of our womanhood to kindle and sustain the fires of hearth and altar, to light the beacon lights and we are today again awake and profoundly aware of our splendid destiny.

—Sarojini Naidu

I sometimes think the arrangement is not quite as it ought to have been; that I, who had much rather be at home, should occupy a place with which a great many younger and gayer women would be prodigiously pleased... I know too much of the vanity of human affairs to expect felicity from the splendid scenes of public life. I am still determined to be cheerful and to be happy in whatever situation I may be; for I have also learned from experience that the greater part of our happiness or misery depends upon our dispositions, and not upon our circumstances.

—Martha Washington

*S*omewhere in the process of "being educated" they [women]...lost that simple and almost automatic response to the human appeal.

—Jane Addams

*I*t may be said that the most important feature in a woman's history is her maternity.

—Mrs. Trollope

*E*very wise woman buildeth her house.

—Proverbs 14:1

*D*ignity is a wonderful weapon when it is consistently used, and if never lost, it always wins.

—Pearl S. Buck

O woman! lovely woman! Nature made thee
To temper man; we had been brutes without you;
Angels are painted fair, to look like you;
There's in you all that we believe of Heaven,
Amazing brightness, purity, and truth,
Eternal joy, and everlasting love.

—Thomas Otway

176

$\mathcal{T}$hou, while thy babes around thee cling, shalt show us how divine a thing a woman may be.

—Harper

$\mathcal{W}$ith her curly locks, her dimples and her infectious grin, little Shirley Temple helped bring millions of Americans some joy during the Depression. She was the movies' No. 1 box office attraction for four straight years, and she was smart, too... After retiring from the movies in 1949 she began a new career in her 20s, starring in two successful TV series. Simultaneously, she raised three children and then, in her late 30s, began a third career. As Shirley Temple Black, she ran for Congress, served as an articulate and well-informed delegate to the United Nations and in 1974, at 46, was appointed as ambassador to Ghana. "Dr. Kissinger was surprised," she said sweetly, "that I knew where Ghana was."

—Life

$\mathcal{T}$he most beautiful women I know are not beautiful because of showy clothes or striking make-up. They are beautiful because of the force and power that emanates from within... To be beautiful, they must care for their bodies from within, which is the only place from which the spirit can be fed.

Beauty is the enhancement of one's own characteristics... Amplify yourself with the beauty of a healthy body and a happy mind. Do this and your beauty will grow and grow, and never wither and fade. This has been the eternal secret of all the great women of the world.

—Gayelord Hauser

$\mathcal{T}$here will be singing in your heart;
There will be rapture on your eyes;
You will be a woman set apart;
You will be so wonderful and wise.

—Robert Service

$\mathcal{N}$othing can compare in beauty, and wonder, and admirableness, and divinity itself, to the silent work in obscure dwellings of faithful women bringing their children to honour and virtue and piety.

—Beecher

177

A woman with her eyes and cheeks aglow,
Watching a kettle, tending a scarlet flame,
Guarding a little child—there is no name
For this great ministry. But eyes are dull
That do not see that it is beautiful.

—*Grace Noll Crowell*

❧

I remembered my experience with my new house. I could not make the living room seem homelike. I would move the chairs here and there and change the pictures on the wall, but something was lacking.

Then, as I stood in the middle of the room one day wondering what I could possibly do to improve it, it came to me that all that was needed was for someone to live in it and furnish it with the everyday pleasant thoughts of friendship and cheerfulness and hospitality.

—*Laura Ingalls Wilder*

❧

N ow it came to pass on the third day, that Esther put on her royal apparel, and stood in the inner court of the king's house...and it was so, when the king saw Esther, the queen standing in the court, that she obtained favour in his sight: and the king held out to Esther the golden scepter that was in his hand. So Esther drew near, and touched the top of the sceptre. Then said the king unto her, What wilt thou, queen Esther? and what is thy request? it shall be even given to thee to the half of the kingdom.

—*Esther 5:1-3*

❧

The best of beauty is a finer charm than skill in surfaces, in outlines, or rules of art can ever teach; namely a radiation from the work of art of human character.

—*Ralph Waldo Emerson*

178

'Tis beauty that doth oft make women proud;
'Tis virtue, that doth make them most admired;
'Tis modesty, that makes them seem divine.

—William Shakespeare

[Positive adjectives used to describe biblical women:] aged, beautiful, chaste, comely, compassionate, complacent, devout, diligent, discreet, domestic, elect, fair, faithful, glorious, godly, good, gracious, grave, great, high-principled, holy, honest, honorable, kind, loving, obedient, peaceable, prudent, reverent, righteous, sensible, serious, silent, simple, sober, steady, submissive, subtle, temperate, trustworthy, virtuous, wealthy, worthy and young.

—Edith Deen

❦

As a white candle
In a holy place,
So is the beauty
Of an aged face...

Her brood gone from her,
And her thoughts as still
As the waters
Under a ruined mill.

—Joseph Campbell

Next to being an angel, the greatest bestowment of God is to make one a woman.

—Frances E. Willard

The country girl walks, and the very earth smiles beneath her feet. Something comes with her that is more than mortal—witness the yearning welcome that stretches towards her from all. As the sunshine lights up the aspect of things, so her presence sweetens the very flowers like dew... The world yearns towards her beauty as to the flowers that are past. The loveliness of seventeen is centuries old.

—Richard Jefferies

Perfection of shape, dignity of features and smoothness of skin are all vanity. Suffering impairs them, age changes them; and death destroys them. But the woman who fears the Lord shall be praised. Her consecration to the Lord cools her temper, purifies her soul and gives her a lasting beauty, for it is within her.

—*LeRoy Brownlow*

A man's work is from sun to sun,
But a woman's work is never done.

—*Traditional*

❧

One cannot forget the partner of his [the pioneer's] sufferings and perils. Look at the young woman who is sitting on the other side of the fire with her youngest child in her lap... Like the emigrant, this woman is in the prime of her life; she also recollects an early youth of comfort. The remains of taste are still observed in her dress. But time has pressed hardly upon her; in her faded features and attenuated limbs it is easy to see that life has to her been a heavy burden... Destitution, suffering, and lassitude have weakened her delicate frame, but have not dismayed her courage...

Round this woman crowd the half-clothed children, glowing with health, careless of the morrow, true children of the wilderness. Their mother turns on them from time to time a mingled look of sadness and of joy. Judging from their strength and her weakness, it would seem as she had exhausted herself in giving them life, and without regretting the cost.

—*Alex de Tocqueville*

❧

There is nothing so strong as gentleness, and there is nothing so gentle as real strength.

—*St. Francis de Sales*

You can take no credit for beauty at sixteen. But if you are beautiful at sixty, it will be your own soul's doing.

—*Marie Carmichael Stopes*

If a woman have long hair, it is a glory to her.

—*I Corinthians 11:15*

Housework is what women do that nobody notices until they don't do it.

—*Anonymous*

Put a woman on a big ranch, and the first thing she wants to do is build a church.

—*Old Bachelor Cowhand*

ठ

To get the whole world out of bed
and washed, and dressed and
   warmed and fed,
To work, and back to bed again,
Believe me...costs worlds of pain.

—*John Masefield*

[The poet feels true poetry] in the beauty of a woman—in the grace of her step—in the lustre of her eye—in the melody of her voice—in her self laughter—in her sigh—in the harmony of the rustling of her robes. He deeply feels it in her winning endearments—in her burning enthusiasm—in her gentle charities—in her meek and devotional endurances, but above all—ah! far above all—he kneels to it—he worships it in the faith—in the purity—in the strength—in the altogether divine majesty of her *love*.

—*Edgar Allan Poe*

The outlandish theory that women can be as qualified as men to heal the sick was first proved by Elizabeth Blackwell...[who] devoted her life to fighting for the education and acceptance of women M.D.s. She herself was rejected by no fewer than 29 American medical schools before New York's Geneva College—as a lark—admitted her in 1847... Blackwell graduated at the head of her class... Due largely to her exertions, the U.S. had more than 7,000 practicing women doctors by the turn of the century.

—*Life*

For nineteen hundred years she had not been equal—she had been superior.
But now, they said, she wanted equality, and in order to obtain it, she had to step down.

And so it is, that in the name of broadminded tolerance, a man's
vices have now become a woman's...
Today they call it "progress"—
but tomorrow—oh, you Keepers of the Springs, they must be made to see
that it is not progress...

It is not progress when the moral tone is lower than it was.
It is not progress when purity is not as sweet.
It is not progress when womanhood has lost its fragrance.
Whatever else it is, it is not progress!

We need Keepers of the Springs who will realize that what is
socially correct may not be morally right.

Our country needs today women who will lead us back to
an old-fashioned morality
  to old-fashioned decency
    to old-fashioned purity and sweetness
      for the sake of the next generation, if for no other reason.

—*Peter Marshall*

ॐ

To call women the weaker sex is libel; it is man's injustice to women. If by strength is meant brute strength, then indeed, is woman less brute than man. If by strength is meant moral power, then woman is immeasurably man's superior. Has she not got greater powers of endurance, has she not greater courage? Without her man would not be. If non-violence is the law of our being, the future is with women.

—*Mohandas Gandhi*

Wheresoever she was, *there* was Eden.

—*Mark Twain*

$\mathcal{T}$he study of history is useful to the historian by teaching him his ignorance of women... The woman who is known only through a man is known wrong.

—*Henry Brooks Adams*

❦

$\mathcal{E}$very physical quality admired by men in women is in direct connection with the manifold functions of the woman for the propagation of the species.

—*James Joyce*

❦

$\mathcal{A}$ noble woman typifies love and loveliness. The eternal ideal for woman embodies grace, charm, beauty, physical and intellectual creativity, resourcefulness, courage, and honor. But, again, love is first.

The more a woman is filled with love, the more fully the life of God will possess her. Inevitably, love, which is creative, will bring forth the other fruits, all tenderly nurturing the soul.

—*Edith Deen*

❦

$\mathcal{B}$lessed is the man that hath a virtuous wife, for the number of his days shall double. A virtuous woman rejoiceth her husband and he shall fulfill the years of his life in peace. A good wife is a good portion, which shall be given in the portion of them that fear the Lord. The grace of a wife delighteth her husband, and her discretion will fatten his bones. A silent and loving woman is a gift of the Lord...

As the sun when it ariseth in the high heaven; so is the beauty of a good wife in the ordering of her house. A godly woman is given to him that feareth the Lord. An honest woman will reverence her husband. A woman that honoureth her husband shall be judged wise of all.

—*Apocrypha's Book of Ecclesiasticus 26:1-3,13-14,15-16,23-26*

The influence of woman, the homemaker, reaches indeed far beyond the walls of her house. Her reach is beyond her own comprehension. She creates the center where the world begins, the world and all its peoples... True, man is her mate and cobuilder, but for some reason, perhaps divine, it is she who is the more responsible for the creation of life in all its forms.

—*Pearl S. Buck*

Children

Chapter Five
Children

*A*nd the angel came in unto her, and said, Hail, thou that art highly favoured, the Lord is with thee: blessed art thou among women... Fear not Mary: for thou has found favour with God. And, behold, thou shalt conceive in thy womb, and bring forth a son, and shalt call his name Jesus. He shall be great, and shall be called the Son of the Highest; and the Lord God shall give unto him the throne of his father David: and he shall reign over the house of Jacob for ever; and of his kingdom there shall be no end.

—Luke 1:28-33

*F*or there is no king had any other first beginning.
For all men have one entrance into life.

—The Wisdom of Solomon, Apocrypha

*W*e are all conceived as a thought of love and desire that became bound into minute genetic matter. When we were newborns the same love nurtured us and our first conscious thoughts of ourselves were so intertwined with our mother's love that there was no awareness of separation. If love can conceive life, nurture it, and give it identity, then it must be part of the intelligence that is us.

—Deepak Chopra

*G*od loves each of us as if there were only one of us.

—St. Augustine

*T*hou has covered me in my mother's womb. I will praise thee; for I am fearfully and wonderfully made.

—Psalm 139:13,14

*G*od created man in his own image, in the image of God created he him; male and female created he them. And God blessed them, and God said unto them, Be fruitful, and multiple, and replenish the earth.

—Genesis 1:27,28

189

When you were born, you cried and the world rejoiced. Live your life in such a manner that when you die the world cries and you rejoice.

—Indian Proverb

Our birth is but a sleep and a forgetting:
The soul that rises with us, our life's star,
   Hath had elsewhere its setting,
     And cometh from afar:
Not in entire forgetfulness,
     And not in utter nakedness,
But trailing clouds of glory do we come
   From God, who is our home:
     Heaven lies about us in our infancy!

—William Wordsworth

Where did you come from, baby dear?
Out of the everywhere into the here.
Where did you get those eyes so blue?
Out of the sky as I came through.

—George MacDonald

For you know who created you and there is only one of you. Never, in all the seventy billion humans who have walked this planet since the beginning of time has there been anyone exactly like you. Never, until the end of time, will there be another such as you... From your father, in his moment of supreme love, flowed countless seeds of love, more than four hundred million in number. All of them, as they swam within your mother, gave up the ghost and died. All except one! You.

You alone persevered within the loving warmth of your mother's body, searching for your other half, a single cell from your mother so small that more than two million would be necessary to fill an acorn shell. Yet, despite impossible odds, on that vast ocean of darkness and disaster, you persevered, found that infinitesimal cell, joined with it, and began a new life. Your life.

—Og Mandino

Children bring to the world newness, regeneration, color, and vigor.

—James Dobson

190

To be someone in that true sense is the highest realization of yourself as a child of God. And a mother tries to instill in her children this longing for achievement.

—*Norman Vincent Peale & Smiley Blanton*

The first notes we hear are those cradle songs that spring from a parent's heart.

—*William J. Bennett*

There is not a child—not an infant Moses—placed, however softly, in his bulrush ark upon the sea of time, whose existence does not stir a ripple, gyrating outward and on, until it shall have moved across and spanned the whole ocean of God's eternity, stirring even the river of life, and the fountains at which the angels drink.

—*Elihu Burritt*

And she [Hannah] vowed a vow, and said, O Lord of hosts, if thou wilt indeed look on the affliction of thine handmaid, and remember me, and not forget thine handmaid, but wilt give unto thine handmaid a man child, then I will give him unto the Lord all the days of his life...and the Lord remembered her...that she bare a son, and called his name Samuel, saying, Because I have asked him of the Lord.

—*I Samuel 1:11,19,20*

Making the decision to have a child—it's momentous. It is to decide forever to have your heart go walking around outside your body.

—*Elizabeth Stone*

In due course, the baby was born. There was no fuss or noise. Everything seemed to have been carried out according to an ordered plan... I had tried to persuade my patient to let me put the mask over her face and give her some chloroform...but she refused the help, kindly yet firmly. It was the first time in my short experience that I had met opposition when offering chloroform... I asked her why it was that she would not use the mask. She did not answer at once, but looked from the old woman who had been assisting to the window through which was bursting the first light of dawn; then shyly she turned to me and said, "It didn't hurt. It wasn't meant to, was it, doctor?"

—*Grantly Dick-Read*

*W*ho takes a child by the hand, takes the mother by the heart.

—*Danish Proverb*

*B*abies are such a nice way to start people.

—*Herold*

*A*nd they came with haste, and found Mary, and Joseph, and the babe lying in a manger.

—*Luke 2:16*

A baby's feet, like sea-shells pink,
   Might tempt, should heaven see meet,
An angel's lips to kiss, we think,
   A baby's feet.

—*Algernon Charles Swinburne*

*S*weet and low, sweet and low,
   Wind of the western sea,
Low, low, breathe and blow,
   Wind of the western sea!
Over the rolling waters go,
   Come from the dying moon, and blow,
Blow him again to me;
   While my little one,
While my pretty one sleeps.

Sleep and rest, sleep and rest,
   Father will come to thee soon;
Rest, rest, on mother's breast,
   Father will come to thee soon;
Father will come to his babe in the nest,
   Silver sails all out of the west
Under the silver moon;
   Sleep, my little one,
Sleep, my pretty one, sleep.

—*Alfred, Lord Tennyson*

Hush, my dear, lie still and slumber!
   Holy angels guard thy bed!
Heavenly blessings without number
   Gently falling on thy head.

                                              —*Isaac Watts*

Babies are bits of stardust blown from the hand of God. Lucky the woman who knows the pangs of birth, for she has held a star.

                                            —*Larry Barretto*

O little town of Bethlehem,
How still we see thee lie.
Above thy deep and dreamless sleep
The silent stars go by...

For Christ is born of Mary;
And gathered all above,
While mortals sleep, the angels keep
Their watch of wondering love.

                                       —*Phillips Brooks*

The infant as soon as Nature, with great pangs of travail, hath sent him forth from the womb of its mother into region of light, lies like a sailor cast out from the waves, naked upon the earth, in utter want and helplessness.

                                       —*Francis Bacon*

When we first bend over the cradle of our own child, God throws back the temple door, and reveals to us the sacredness and mystery of a father's and a mother's love to ourselves.

                                   —*Henry Ward Beecher*

Sleep, baby, sleep.
Thy father guards the sheep;
Thy mother shakes the dreamland tree,
Down falls a little dream for thee:
   Sleep, baby, sleep.

                                       —*Traditional*

*W*eavers, weaving on break of day,
Why do you weave a garment so gay?
Blue as the wing of a halcyon wild,
We weave the robes of a new-born child.

—Sarojini Naidu

*F*or unto us a child is born, unto us a son is given: and the government shall be upon his shoulder: and his name shall be called Wonderful, Counsellor, The mighty God, The everlasting Father, The Prince of Peace.

—Isaiah 9:6

*W*ho is queen of baby land?
Mother kind and sweet,
And her love, born above,
Guides the little feet.

—Anonymous

*T*here is only one most beautiful baby in the world—every mother has it!

—Traditional

❧

A huge ball was being held at Blenheim Palace, near Woodstock, England, the home of the Dukes of Marlborough. Prominent among the guests was Lord Randolph Churchill...[with] his American-born wife, Jennie. The family had tried to dissuade Lady Churchill from attending the ball because she was expecting a child. But she was high spirited and since her baby was not due for some weeks, insisted that she would be present.

When the festivities were at their highest, however, Lady Churchill became faint and was quietly taken to a cloakroom. There, amidst mounds of ladies' wraps and feather boas, gentlemen's silk hats and opera cloaks, Winston Leonard Spencer Churchill, who was later to become twice Prime Minister of Great Britain and one of the greatest men of the twentieth century, was born.

—Leonard Wibberley

God sends children to enlarge our hearts, and to make us unselfish and full of kindly sympathies and affections.

—Mary Howitt

A little child is an uncommonly interesting object!—An immortal soul confined in such a fairy form.

—Anonymous

Here all mankind is equal: rich and poor alike, they love their children.

—Euripides

And then he saw his child—this tiny thing he and Elaine had created. Oh, dear Lord, she *was* beautiful—so unlike any other baby that had ever been born.

Carefully, reverently, he reached out toward one tiny arm that pushed up from beneath the bunting. With his finger tips Phillip touched the soft skin. His daughter's hand, no bigger than a budding rose petal, found his finger and clasped itself to him.

The strangest, strongest feeling he had ever known swept over him. His chin began to quiver, his eyes blurred...

"She loves her daddy already," Elaine whispered. It was too much. There were tears on Phillip's cheek as he buried his head in the shelter of her outstretched arms. And that was how Cassandra Templeton was born.

—Graham Porter

❦

Every person in this world is a dream of God.

—Anonymous

What feeling is so nice as a child's hand in yours? So small, so soft and warm, like a kitten huddling in the shelter of your clasp.

—Marjorie Holmes

Is nothing in life ever straight and clear, the way children see it?

—Rosie Thomas

*E*ven when freshly washed and relieved of all obvious confections, children tend to be sticky.

—*Fran Lebowitz*

*T*he potential of a child is the most intriguing thing in all creation.

—*Ray Lyman Wilbur*

*L*ook for me in the nurseries of Heaven.

—*Francis Thompson*

*F*ortunately for children, the uncertainties of the present always give way to the enchanted possibilities of the future.

—*Gelsey Kirkland*

*N*o joy in nature is so sublimely affecting as the joy of a mother at the good fortune of her child.

—*Jean Paul Ritcher*

*S*low down, parents! What's your rush, anyway? Your children will be gone so quickly.

—*James Dobson*

*A*s a small boy...I lived in the country surrounded by swamp lands. Those were days of chills and fever and malaria. When I came to the city to school, I was sallow-cheeked and hollow-chested. One of my teachers, George Warren Krall, was what we then called a health crank. We laughed at his ideas... One day he seemed to single me out personally... He looked straight at me and said, "I dare you to be the healthiest boy in the class... I dare you to chase those chills and fevers out of your system. I dare you to fill your body with fresh air, pure water, wholesome food, and daily exercise until your cheeks are rosy, you chest full, and your limbs sturdy."

...Something seemed to happen inside me. My blood was up. It answered the dare and surged through my body into tingling finger tips as though itching for battle. I chased the poisons out of my system. I built a body that has equaled the strongest boys in that class, and has outlived and outlasted most of them.

—*William H. Danforth*

What is a neglected child? He is a child not planned for, not wanted; neglect begins, therefore, before he is born.

—*Pearl S. Buck*

Once the children were in the house the air became more vivid and more heated; every object in the house grew more alive.

—*Mary Gordon*

Everything else you grow out of, but you never recover from childhood.

—*Beryl Bainbridge*

A little girl is...innocence playing in the mud, beauty standing on its head, and motherhood dragging a doll by the foot.

—*A. Beck*

Children are the anchors that hold a mother to life.

—*Sophocles*

So nigh is grandeur to our dust,
So near is God to man,
When Duty whispers low, Thou must,
The youth replies, I can.

—*Ralph Waldo Emerson*

Parents can only give good advice or put children on the right paths, but the final forming of a person's character lies in their own hands.

—*Anne Frank*

I think when I read that sweet story of old,
When Jesus was here among men,
How he called little children like lambs to his fold:
I should like to have been with him then.

I wish that his hands had been placed on my head,
That his arms had been thrown around me,
That I might have seen his kind look when he said,
Let the little ones come unto me.

—*Jemima Luke*

A mother once took her eight-year-old son to a concert by the noted pianist Paderewski... Just before Paderewski appeared, the little boy ran up onto the stage and began to pound out "Chopsticks" on the grand piano...

But when Paderewski appeared he went to the piano, sat down by the little boy and put his arms around him. Whispering to him to continue, he improvised a brilliant accompaniment to the childish tune. The listeners burst into applause.

—*Norman Vincent Peale*

As thou knowest not what is the way of the spirit, or how the bones do grow in the womb of her that is with child; even so thou knowest not the works of God who maketh all.

—*Ecclesiastes 11:5*

If I understand the nature of God...children represent His most generous gift to us.

—*James Dobson*

From father have I my stature,
My zest for earnest living.
From little mother my gay nature,
My love of story-telling.

—*Johann Wolfgang von Goethe*

This "waiting until we could afford children" concerns me because often the waiting is caused by a selfish desire for a high standard of living. The couple never finds the joy and satisfaction from material things that they would have found in having children.

—*Tim LaHaye*

Ho! All ye heavens, all ye of the earth,
I bid ye hear me!
Into your midst has come a new life;
Consent ye! Consent ye all, I implore!
Make its path smooth, then shall it travel
beyond the four hills.

—*Omaha Tribal Rite*

198

*S*uffer the little children to come unto me, and forbid them not: for of such is the kingdom of God.

—Mark 10:14

*W*hat we all know, is that every child has the right to be born into a family. Security and stability depend upon a child's being born into a family. Without family no child grows into a whole human being. This we have learned, this we know, from one generation to another.

—Pearl S. Buck

*S*leep, my babe, and peace attend thee,
   All through the night;
Guardian angels God will lend thee,
   All through the night;
Soft the drowsy hours are creeping,
Hill and vale in slumber sleeping,
Mother dear her watch is keeping
   All through the night.

—Traditional

*A*lmost from the time he could talk Little Sam [Mark Twain] was a marvelous storyteller, and some of his stories were indeed astonishing. Once, a neighbor said, "You don't believe a word that child says, I hope!" "Oh, I know his average," Jane Clemens answered. "I discount him 90 percent. The rest is pure gold."

—Readers Digest

*T*hy wife shall be as a fruitful vine by the sides of thine house; thy children like olive plants round about thy table.

—Psalm 128:3

*T*he dove says coo, coo,
   What shall I do?
I can scarce maintain two.
Pooh, pooh! says the wren,
   I've got ten,
And keep them all like gentlemen.

—Nursery Rhyme

199

Children divine those who love them; it is a gift of nature which we lose as we grow up.

—*Paul De Kock*

Before I was born out of my mother generations guided me.

—*Walt Whitman*

Princess Grace gave birth to Caroline, naturally, without anesthetic, in a room at the Palace which had been specially converted for confinement... Grace's decision to go through natural childbirth was regarded as "bold" and "brave." But what elicited mild stupefaction was her breast-feeding her babies. Women, particularly women of her social and economic station, and *particularly* young beautiful shapely women, simply did not do it...

Grace was amazed at the amazement. To her way of thinking, breast-feeding was the natural thing to do. And she and her sisters and brother had been breast-fed by Ma Kelly, so she would breast-feed Caroline and Albert. It was "wholly normal and right—I never considered anything else," she wrote later.

—*Steven Englund*

Lullaby and good night, with roses bedight,
With lilies bedecked, is baby's wee bed.
Lay thee down now and rest, may thy slumber be blest,
Lay thee down now and rest, may thy slumber be blest.

—*Johannes Brahms*

Self-interest attacks us from infancy, and we are startled to observe little heads calculate before knowing how to reflect.

—*Madame de Girardin*

The greatest thing a man can do for his Heavenly Father is to be kind to some of His other children.

—*Henry Drummond*

[At six years of age:] I don't know what I'm going to be. But I think that it will be something hard.

—*Susan Blackwell*

200

I know there are bad big families and bad small families; but take it by and large, I would assume that there is a thousand percent better chance of a great leader in a good cause from a family of ten than from a family of one.

—*Stephen L. Richards*

I n the breast of a bulb
Is the promise of spring;
In the little blue egg
Is a bird that will sing;
In the heart of a seed
Is the hope of the sod;
In the soul of a child
Is the kingdom of God.

—*W.L. Stedger*

S o Boaz took Ruth, and she was his wife...and she bare him a son. And the women said unto Naomi, Blessed be the Lord, which hath not left thee this day without a kinsman, that his name may be famous in Israel. And he shall be unto thee a restorer of thy life, and a nourisher of thine old age; for thy daughter in law, which loveth thee, which is better than seven sons, hath born him.

And Naomi took the child, and laid it in her bosom, and became nurse unto it. And the women her neighbours gave it a name, saying there is a son born to Naomi, and they called his name Obed: he is the father of Jesse, the father of David.

—*Ruth 4:13-17*

T he change to the small family pattern has serious psychological implications. Growth into maturity requires growth into self-confidence. It requires, also, growth into the arts of companionship. It requires the experience of understanding other persons—playing with them, working with them, helping them in time of need, making shared plans with them. In the one-child or two-child family, the conditions for such growth are hard to provide.

—*H.A. Overstreet*

L et me learn how to read, God. Let me learn how to read.
—*Childhood Prayer of Mary McLeod Bethune*

If there is design in the universe, and if that design is of spiritual force, then the birth of a child must be an incident of spiritual importance.

—Grantly Dick-Read

I went to China in the summer...with a second child, my first little adopted daughter, a tiny creature of three months whom the orphanage had given up because she had not gained an ounce since she was born. Nothing, they told me, agreed with her, and so I said, "Give her to me," and they did, and as soon as she felt herself with her mother she began to eat and grow fat. How easily happiness can be made, and when it is made how wonderfully it works!

—Pearl S. Buck

But whoso shall offend one of these little ones which believe in me, it were better for him that a millstone be hanged about his neck, and that he were drowned in the depths of the sea.

—Matthew 18:6

*R*aising kids is a pretty awesome task, even when the job is handled by a team of two, as intended.

—James Dobson

*G*ive a little love to a child and you get a great deal back.

—John Ruskin

*O*ur virtues are dearer to us the more we have had to suffer for them. It is the same with our children. All profound affection admits a sacrifice.

—Vauvenargues

*O*ne way in which all of us can help to combat the current wave of public indecency which threatens to undermine Western civilization is to concentrate upon and increase the solidarity of the family. This solidarity begins with a child at the mother's breast.

—Princess Grace of Monaco

*F*ellow citizens, why do you turn and scrape every stone to gather wealth and take so little care of your children, to whom one day you must relinquish it all?

—Socrates

202

I leave to children exclusively, but only for the life of their childhood, all and every, the dandelions of the fields and the daisies thereof, with the right to play among them freely.

—Williston Fish

*A*nne never spoke about hatred anywhere in her diary. She wrote that despite everything, she believed in the goodness of people. And that when the war was over, she wanted to work for the world and for people. This is the duty that I have taken over from her. I have received many thousands of letters. Young people especially always want to know how these terrible things could ever have happened. I answer them as well as I can, and I often finish by saying: "I hope that Anne's book will have an effect on the rest of your life so that insofar as it is possible in your circumstances, you will work for unity and peace."

—Otto Frank

*W*hen 12-year-old Bobby Hill, the son of a U.S. Army sergeant stationed in Italy, read a book about the work of Nobel Prize winner Albert Schweitzer, he decided to do something to help the medical missionary. He sent a bottle of aspirin to Lieutenant General Richard C. Lindsay, Commander of the Allied air forces in Southern Europe, asking if any of his airplanes could parachute the bottle of aspirin to Dr. Schweitzer's jungle hospital in Africa.

Upon hearing the letter, the Italian radio station issued an appeal, resulting in more than $400,000 worth of donated medical supplies. The French and Italian governments each supplied a plane to fly the medicines and the boy to Dr. Schweitzer. The grateful doctor responded, "I never thought a child could do so much for my hospital."

—W.B. Freeman Concepts

*T*hy daughters bright thy walks adorn,
Gay as the gilded summer sky,
Sweet as the dewy, milk-white thorn,
Dear as the raptured thrill of joy.

—Robert Burns

*D*ear Mother:
I'm all right. Stop worrying about me.

—Papyrus Letter of 17-year-old Egyptian Girl

In looking back on my life I have the satisfaction of feeling that I became useful to my parents even at the early age of ten.

—Andrew Carnegie

[*Ch*ildren are] fragile beginnings of a mighty end.

—Mrs. Norton

*H*ow sharper than a serpent's tooth it is
To have a thankless child!

—William Shakespeare

ॐ

I remember, I remember,
   How my childhood fleeted by—
The mirth of its December,
   And the warmth of its July.

—W.W. Praed

*O*nly a baby small,
   Dropt from the skies;
Small, but how dear to us,
   God knoweth best.

—Matthias Barr

*Th*e child's sob in the silence curses deeper
Than the strong man in his wrath.

—Elizabeth Barrett Browning

*Y*ou are the trip I did not take;
You are the pearls I cannot buy;
You are my blue Italian lake;
You are my piece of foreign sky.

—Anne Campbell

It is not possible for civilization to flow backwards while there is youth in the world.

—Helen Keller

There is no finer investment for any community than putting milk into babies.

—*Winston Churchill*

I wish thee all thy mother's graces,
Thy father's fortunes and his places.

—*Bishop Richard Corbet*

The purest affection the heart can hold
Is the honest love of a nine-year-old.

—*Holman Francis Day*

Mrs. Lofty keeps a carriage,
    So do I;
She has dappled grays to draw it,
    None have I;
She's no prouder with her coachman
    Than am I
With my blue-eyed, laughing baby
    Trundling by.

—*Mrs. C. Gildersleeve*

Child, you are like a flower,
So sweet and pure and fair.

—*Heinrich Heine*

The God who made your children will hear your petitions. He has promised to do so. After all, He loves them more than you do.

—*James Dobson*

No calamity so touches the common heart of humanity as does the straying of a little child. Their feet are so uncertain and feeble; the ways are so steep and strange.

—*O. Henry*

Who can tell what a baby thinks?

—*Josiah Gilbert Holland*

*W*here shall the baby's dimple be,
Cheek, chin, knuckle or knee?

—Josiah Gilbert Holland

*Y*ou hear that boy laughing?
 —You think he's all fun;
But the angels laugh, too,
At the good he has done.

—Oliver Wendell Holmes

*T*he sublimest song to be heard on earth is the lisping of the human soul
on the lips of children.

—Victor Hugo

*T*hose who have lost an infant are never, as it were, without an infant
child. They are the only persons who, in one sense, retain it always.

—Leigh Hunt

*F*orasmuch as it hath pleased Almighty God of his goodness to entrust
to your care and keeping this child and to have raised you to the holy
estate of motherhood, you shall give hearty thanks unto God.

—Grantly Dick-Read

*D*eborah danced, when she was two,
As buttercups and daffodils do.

—Aline [Mrs. Joyce] Kilmer

A lady with her daughters or her nieces
Shines like a guinea and seven-shilling pieces.

—Lord Byron

*W*e find delight in the beauty and happiness of children that makes the
heart too big for the body.

—Ralph Waldo Emerson

*T*hou straggler into loving arms,
Young climber-up of knees...

—Mary Lamb

$\mathcal{I}$n my school days I had no aversion to slavery... We had a little slave boy whom we had hired from someone... [He] had been brought away from his family and his friends halfway across the American continent and sold. He was a cheery spirit, innocent and gentle, and the noisiest creature that ever was, perhaps. All day long he was singing, whistling, yelling, whooping, laughing... One day, I lost my temper and went raging to my mother and said Sandy had been singing for an hour without a single break and I couldn't stand it and wouldn't she please shut him up. The tears came into her eyes and her lip trembled and she said...

"Poor thing, when he sings it shows that he is not remembering and that comforts me... He will never see his mother again; if he can sing I must not hinder it, but be thankful for it. If you were older you would understand me; then that friendless child's noise would make you glad."

—*Mark Twain*

$\mathcal{O}$ften while he was writing [five volumes of *The World Crisis*, Churchill] would be distracted by his children playing in the garden. If the play sounded exciting, he would dismiss his secretary and join in the fun.

—*Leonard Wibberly*

$\mathbf{\tilde{e}}$

$\mathcal{B}$ut Jesus said, Suffer little children, and forbid them not, to come unto me: for of such is the kingdom of heaven.

—*Matthew 19:14*

$\mathcal{A}$nd the king of Egypt spake to the Hebrew midwives... And he said, When ye do the office of a midwife to the Hebrew women...if it be a son, then ye shall kill him; but if it be a daughter, then she shall live. But the midwives feared God, and did not as the king of Egypt commanded them, but saved the men children alive.

And the king of Egypt called for the midwives, and said unto them, why have ye done this thing, and have saved the men children alive? And the midwives said unto Pharaoh, Because the Hebrew women are not as the Egyptian women; for they are lively and are delivered ere the midwives come in unto them. Therefore God dealt well with the midwives: and the people multiplied, and waxed very mighty.

—*Exodus 1:15-20*

Old men have need to touch sometimes with their lips the brow of a woman or the cheek of a child, that they may believe again in the freshness of life.

—Maurice Maeterlinck

Children are unpredictable. You never know what inconsistency they're going to catch you in next.

—Henry Ward Beecher

Men are generally more careful of the breed of their horses and dogs than of their children.

—William Penn

[Thank you] for the laughter of children who tumble barefooted and bareheaded in the summer grass.

—Carl Sandburg

Hath she not then for pains and fears,
    The day of woe, the watchful night,
For all her sorrow, all her tears,
    An over-payment of delight?

—Robert Southey

It is good to be children sometimes, and never better than at Christmas, when its mighty Founder was a child Himself.

—Charles Dickens

"My son!" What simple, beautiful words!
    "My boy!" What a wonderful phrase!
With double my virtues and half of my faults,
    You can't be a stranger to me!

—Cyril Morton Thorne

A babe in a house is a well-spring of pleasure.

—Martin Farquhar Tupper

[Children are] the keystone of the arch of matrimonial happiness.

—Thomas Jefferson

Upon the profound discontent of the young in every country do I set my faith. I beg you, the young, to be discontented. I pray that you may rebel against what is wrong, not with feeble negative complaining but with strong positive assertion of what is right for all humanity.

—Pearl S. Buck

We haven't all had the good fortune to be ladies; we haven't all been generals, or poets, or statesmen; but when the toast works down to the babies, we stand on common ground.

—Mark Twain

We shall never get our happy, joyous, peaceful world until we learn to love and understand and share and become brothers to one another, because we are children of a common Father.

—Rufus M. Jones

In praise of little children I will say
God first made man, then found a better way
For woman, but his third way was the best.
Of all created things, the loveliest
And most divine are children.

—William Canton

One laugh of a child will make the holiest day more sacred still.

—Robert G. Ingersoll

If there is anything that will endure
The eye of God, because it still is pure,
It is the spirit of a little child,
Fresh from his hand, and therefore undefiled.

—Richard Henry Stoddard

Children think not of what is past, nor what is to come, but enjoy the present time, which few of us do.

—La Bruyere

A rose with all its sweetest leaves yet folded...

—Lord Byron

Children are God's apostles, day by day sent forth to preach of love and hope and peace.

—James Russell Lowell

God bless all little boys who look like Puck,
  With wide eyes, wider mouths and stick-out ears,
Rash little boys who stay alive by luck
  And Heaven's favor in this world of tears.

—Arthur Guiterman

Call not that man wretched, who, whatever else he suffers as to pain inflicted or pleasure denied, has a child for whom he hopes and on whom he dotes.

—Samuel Taylor Coleridge

Happy is he that is happy in his children.

—Thomas Fuller

❧

Lo, children are an heritage of the Lord: and the fruit of the womb is his reward. As arrows are in the hand of a mighty man; so are children of the youth. Happy is the man that hath his quiver full of them.

—Psalm 127:3-5

What power there is in the smile of a child, in its play, in its crying—in short, in its mere existence. Are you able to resist its demand? Or do you hold out to it, as a mother, your breast, or, as a father, whatever it needs of your belongings?

—Max Stirner

Everyone...knows what the Pill is. It is a small object, not to be compared to the nuclear bomb in size, but its potential effect upon our society may be even more devastating.

—Pearl S. Buck

A boy is a magical creature—you can lock him out of your workshop, but you can't lock him out of your heart.

—Allan Beck

The joys of parents are secret, and so are their griefs and fears.

—*Francis Bacon*

The child is the father of the man.

—*William Wordsworth*

Children are our most valuable natural resource.

—*Herbert Hoover*

Better to be driven out from among men than to be disliked of children.

—*Richard Henry Dana*

ॐ

Children in a family are like flowers in a bouquet: there's always one determined to face in an opposite direction from the way the arranger desires.

—*Marcelene Cox*

Children are poor men's riches.

—*English Proverb*

And there was a certain man of Zorah, of the family of the Danites...and his wife was barren, and bare not. And the angel of the Lord appeared unto the woman, and said unto her, Behold now, thou art barren, and bearest not; but thou shalt conceive, and bear a son...and no razor shall come on his head: for the child shall be a Nazarite unto God from the womb: and he shall begin to deliver Israel out of the hand of the Philistines.

—*Judges 13:2,3,5*

Quiet is what home would be without children.

—*Anonymous*

Youth is that period when a young boy knows everything but how to make a living.

—*Carey Williams*

We never know the love of the parent till we become parents ourselves.

—*Henry Ward Beecher*

What gift has Providence bestowed on man that is so dear to him as his children?

—*Cicero*

The difficult thing about children is that they come with no instructions. You pretty well have to assemble them on your own.

—*James Dobson*

God sends children...to enlarge our hearts; and to make us unselfish and full of kindly sympathies and affections... My soul blesses the great Father, every day, that he has gladdened the earth with little children.

—*Mary Howitt*

[Book dedication:] To my own mother and father and to all parents like them, who have dedicated their lives to providing their children with the world's best inheritance—The Will to work and the Wisdom to Enjoy It.

—*Dr. Orlando A. Battista*

Today I have neglected my writing. The voice of a little girl calling to me, "Come out and play," drew me from my papers and my books. Was it not the final purpose of my toil that I should be free to frolic with her, and spend unharassed hours with the one who had given her to me? And so we walked and ran and laughed together, and fell in the tall grass, and hid among the trees; and I was young again.

Now it is evening; while I write, I hear the child's breathing as she sleeps in her cozy bed. And I know that I have found what I sought... Gladly I surrender myself to nature's imperative of love and parentage, trusting to her ancient wisdom.

—*Will Durant*

I have tried to put in simple words the friendliness, the beauty and even the holiness of childbirth, but its magnificence can only be felt by those who have learned to read in the original this masterpiece of the Creator.

—*Grantly Dick-Read*

We must preserve the value of bearing and raising children.

—James Dobson

Twenty years from now your sons and daughters probably will not remember just what you did in a strictly business or professional capacity, and they may not even be able to recall whether you were successful or just getting by. But they will never forget that you took time with them. The memories of the days you shared in the kitchen, on bicycles, or in the field and stream will be sharp enough to be related in detail to their own children.

—David & Virginia Edens

❦

You, mothers of America: you who have learned by the cradles of your own children to love and feel for all mankind—by the sacred love you bear your child; by your joy in his beautiful, spotless infancy; by the motherly pity and tenderness with which you guide his growing years; by the anxieties of his education; by the prayers you breathe for his soul's eternal good—I beseech you, pity the mother who has all your affections and not one legal right to protect, guide or educate the child of her bosom! By the sick hour of your child; by those dying eyes, which you never can forget; by those last cries that wrung your heart when you could neither help nor save; by the desolation of that empty cradle, that silent nursery, I beseech you pity those mothers that are constantly made childless by the American slave trade! And say, mothers of America—Is this a thing to be defended, sympathized with, passed over in silence?

—Harriet Beecher Stowe

Rocking is not only for soothing fussy children. It is for soothing cranky mothers, too. Frazzled nerves are easily rocked into a harmonious state... In short, rocking is a family affair. Holding a newborn close and rocking together creates a special kind of bond.

The birth of a new baby is a rebirth for mother... This passage into the delicate realm of nurturing may occur many times in the course of a woman's life... Each time, a good rocking chair can serve as your means of transition.

—Tricia Schleifer

It's an odd idea for someone like me to keep a diary; not only because I have never done so before, but because it seems to me that neither I—nor for that matter anyone else—will be interested in the unbosomings of a thirteen-year-old schoolgirl...

No one will believe that a girl of thirteen feels herself quite alone in the world, nor is it so. I have darling parents and a sister of sixteen. I know about thirty people whom one might call friends—I have strings of boy friends, anxious to catch a glimpse of me... I have relations, aunts and uncles, who are darlings too, a good home. No—I don't seem to lack anything. But it's the same with all my friends, just fun and joking, nothing more. I can never bring myself to talk of anything outside the common round...

I don't want to set down a series of bald facts in a diary like most people do, but I want this diary itself to be my friend, and I shall call my friend Kitty.

—Anne Frank

Infant damnation was in those days still part of the normal creed, but my father would have none of it, and my mother, having lost four beautiful little children, was raised to fury at the very mention of any child descending into hell. I had heard her comfort more than one young missionary mother beside the body of a dead child. "Your baby is in Heaven," she declared. "There are no babies in hell—no, not one. They are all gathered round the Throne of God the Father, and Jesus takes them in His bosom when they first come in, when they still feel strange to Heaven."

—Pearl S. Buck

Children's griefs are little, certainly; but so is the child, so is its endurance, so is its field of vision, while its nervous impressionability is keener than ours. Grief is a matter of relativity; the sorrow should be estimated by its proportion to the sorrower; a gash is as painful to one as an amputation to another.

—Francis Thompson

If gratitude is due from children to their earthly parent, how much more is the gratitude of the great family of men due to our Father in Heaven.

—Hosea Ballou

214

I congratulate poor young men upon being born to that ancient and honorable degree which renders it necessary that they should devote themselves to hard work.

—*Andrew Carnegie*

*W*henever I hear people discussing birth control, I always remember I was the fifth child.

—*Clarence Darrow*

*T*o a father waxing old, nothing is dearer than a daughter.

—*Euripides*

❧

*A*nd the daughter of Pharaoh came down to wash herself at the river; and her maidens walked along by the river's side; and when she saw the ark among the flags, she sent her maid to fetch it. And when she opened it, she saw the child: and behold, the babe wept. And she had compassion on him, and said, This is one of the Hebrews' children... And the child grew...and he became her son. And she called his name Moses: and she said, Because I drew him out of the water.

—*Exodus 2:5,6,10*

*T*he greatly maturing experience of helping others in time of need can rarely be had by a child whose chief associates are adults.

—*H.A. Overstreet*

I believe in one God, the creator of the universe. The most acceptable service we render to Him is doing good to His other children.

—*Benjamin Franklin*

*C*hildren are a great comfort in your old age—and they help you reach it faster, too.

—*Lionel M. Kauffman*

*N*ature kindly warps our judgment about our children, especially when they are young, when it would be a fatal thing for them if we did not love them.

—*George Santayana*

*B*eware of him who hates the laugh of a child.

—John Casper Lavater

*I*t is harder to marry a daughter well than to bring her up well.

—Thomas Fuller

*A*nd when he [Jesus] was twelve years old, they went up to Jerusalem after the custom of the feast...and it came to pass, that after three days they found him in the temple, sitting in the midst of the doctors, both hearing them, and asking them questions. And all that heard him were astonished at his understanding and answers... And Jesus increased in wisdom and stature, and in favour with God and man.

—Luke 2:42,46,47,52

*E*veryone tries to build his own monument. The nicest thing that can happen is for people to walk up to your children and say, "Your father was a fine man."

—Red Skelton

A babe in the house is a well-spring of pleasure, a messenger of peace and love, a resting place for innocence on earth, a link between angels and men.

—Martin F. Tupper

*I*t will be gone before you know it. The fingerprints on the wall appear higher and higher, then suddenly they disappear.

—Dorothy Evslin

I have been young, and now I am old; yet have I not seen the righteous forsaken, nor his seed begging bread.

—Psalm 37:25

*L*oving a child is a circular business...the more you give, the more you get, the more you get, the more you want to give.

—Penelope Leach

*T*here is nothing more thrilling in this world, I think, than having a child that is yours, and yet is mysteriously a stranger.

—Agatha Christie

216

I fold the drab maternity pants with the frayed elastic waistband and place them back in the box, then I put the box away—for now.

—*Carol Kort*

*A*ll the earth, though it were full of kind hearts, is but a desolation and desert place to a mother when her only child is absent.

—*Elizabeth Gaskell*

*B*eing a mother, as far as I can tell, is a constantly evolving process of adapting to the needs of your child while also changing and growing as a person in your own right.

—*Deborah Insel*

*S*eeing you sleeping peacefully on your back among your stuffed ducks, bears and basset hounds would remind me that no matter how good the next day might be, certain moments were gone forever.

—*Joan Baez*

*L*ittle children are still the symbol of the eternal marriage between love and duty.

—*George Eliot*

A child's sense of security and well-being is primarily rooted in the stability of his home and family.

—*James Dobson*

*T*eddy Bears shouldn't sit in closets when there's a child around who will love them.

—*Janet Dailey*

*D*oes it seem impossible that the child will grow up? That the bashful smile will become a bold expression...that a briefcase will replace the blue security blanket?

—*Anne Beattie*

*W*hile you can quarrel with a grownup, how can you quarrel with a newborn baby who has stretched out his little arms for you to pick him up?

—*Maria von Trapp*

217

The flowers of the field are the children of sun's affection and nature's love; and the children of men are the flowers of love and compassion.

—Kahlil Gibran

There never was child so lovely but his mother was glad to get him asleep.

—Ralph Waldo Emerson

A good man leaveth an inheritance to his children's children.

—Proverbs 13:22

A child is the root of the heart.

—Carolina Maria de Jesus

In the little world in which children have their existence, whosoever brings them up, there is nothing so finely perceived and so finely felt as injustice.

—Charles Dickens

Although today there are many trial marriages, there is no such thing as a trial child.

—Gary Wills

Welcome House, Incorporated...has grown through the years to gather many children... We are particular about our [adoptive] parents. They must want our babies for what they are, value the Asian heritage and be able to teach the child to value it. Once a prospective mother, looking at a lovely little part-Japanese girl, asked me, "Will her eyes slant more as she grows older?" My heart hardened. That woman would not be given one of our children. She had to think the tilted eyes were beautiful and if she did not then she was not the right one.

—Pearl S. Buck

I was visiting my aunt in the seaside resort of Punta del Este. One evening at a crafts market, I heard loud, rhythmic clapping break out. "It's a lost child," my aunt explained. "When a youngster is found wandering in a public place, passers-by crowd around and clap until a parent or guardian shows up."

—Elizabeth Schell

218

While my husband Frank and I were living in Pakistan many years ago, our six-month-baby died. An old Punjabi who heard of our grief came to comfort us.

"A tragedy like this is similar to being plunged into boiling water," he explained. "If you are an egg, your affliction will make you hard-boiled and unresponsive. If you are a potato, you will emerge soft and pliable, resilient and adaptable."

It may sound funny to God, but there have been many times when I have prayed, "O Lord, let me be a potato."

—*Billie Wilcox*

❦

The just man walketh in his integrity: his children are blessed after him.

—*Proverbs 20:7*

Adolescence is a kind of emotional seasickness. Both are funny, but only in retrospect.

—*Arthur Koestler*

The babe at first feeds upon the mother's bosom, but is always on her heart.

—*Henry Ward Beecher*

❦

Our children are our signature to the roster of history. I hope to leave them good health, an education, and possibly even a competence. But what are they going to do with these things if there are no more deer in the hills, and no more quail in the coverts? No more snipe whistling in the meadow, no more piping of pigeons and chattering of teal as darkness covers the marshes; no more whistling of swift wings when the morning star pales in the east! And when the dawn wind stirs through the ancient cottonwoods, and the gray light steals down from the hills over the old river sliding softly past its wide brown sandbars—what if there be no more goose music?

—*Aldo Leopold*

One of the precious payoffs to being a daughter is that, as we get older, our mothers seem to get better and better. The lessons they sometimes had to drive home to us with brickbats suddenly make perfect sense. The advice that once seemed colossally and hopelessly outdated becomes recognizable as the wisdom we refused to see. And the person who might once have been looked upon as life's chief roadblock—the adversary we were put on this earth to overcome—stands revealed as none other than the friend and ally that, in truth, she always was.

—Bette-Jane Raphael

Life begins as a quest of the child for the man and ends as a journey by the man to rediscover the child.

—Laurens van der Post

❦

My mother had a great deal of trouble with me, but I think she enjoyed it.

—Mark Twain

Like as a father pitieth his children, so the Lord pitieth them that fear him.

—Psalm 103:13

❦

Some couples have strange notions that children born out of wedlock are not likely to turn out as well as other children. That certainly has not been the case of adopted children within the range of my counseling experience. In fact, I have observed that parents who adopt children often want them more than natural parents want their children and consequently shower them with more love... What started out as a tragedy can, by the grace of God and the unselfish love of a Christian couple, save a life as well as a soul.

—Tim LaHaye

Each generation imagines itself to be more intelligent than the one that went before it and wiser than the one that comes after it.

—George Orwell

The glory of young men is their strength.

—*Proverbs 20:29*

The books of childhood are always with us. Lost in their pages, a child may swim in the bluest sea, rise on the highest swing, engage in the grandest adventure.

—*Gene Shalit*

❧

"For in its innermost depths youth is lonelier than old age." I read this saying in some book and I've always remembered it... Older people have formed their opinions about everything, and don't waver before they act. It's twice as hard for us young ones to hold our ground, and maintain our opinions in a time when all ideals are being shattered and destroyed, when people are showing their worst side, and do not know whether to believe in truth and right and God... It's really a wonder that I haven't dropped all my ideals... Yet I keep them.

—*Anne Frank*

❧

Few things are more satisfying than seeing your children have teenagers of their own.

—*Doug Larson*

Nature knows no sex limitations and does not bestow brains upon men alone. Daughters inherit gifts exactly as often and as much as sons.

—*Pearl S. Buck*

❧

Cherishing children is the mark of a civilized society.

—*Joan Ganz Cooney*

And your sons and your daughters shall prophesy...your young men shall see visions.

—*Joel 2:28*

Where is my wandering boy tonight,
   the boy of my tend'rest care,
The boy that was once my joy and light,
   the child of my love and prayer?

Once he was pure as morning dew, as
   he knelt at his mother's knee;
No face was so bright, no heart more
   true, and none was so sweet as he.

Oh, where is my boy tonight? Where
   is my boy tonight?
My heart o'erflows, for I love him, he knows,
Oh, where is my boy tonight?

—*Anonymous*

❦

I suppose there has never been a child who has not asked his mother at some time: "Mother, what will I be when I grow up?" One of the most romantic dreams of childhood is "When I grow up, I'm going to be..." It is this dream that lures us on and leads us to self-realization.
   —*Norman Vincent Peale & Smiley Blanton*

No tragedy is more wounding than the look of despair in the eyes of a starving child.
   —*Henry Kissinger*

Adolescence is a fascinating and crazy time of life.
   —*James Dobson*

When human life in its earliest form is no longer sacred, then human life in any form is no longer sacred.
   —*John T. Maempa*

He [newborn son Jason Emanuel Gould] is incredible, the only real contribution I will make to this world.
   —*Barbara Streisand*

$\mathscr{I}$ will pour my spirit upon thy seed, and my blessing upon thine offspring: And they shall spring up as among the grass, as willows by the water courses.

—Isaiah 44:3

❦

$\mathscr{O}$ur youth now love luxury. They have bad manners, contempt for authority; they show disrespect for their elders and love to chatter in places of exercise.

They no longer rise when others enter the room. They contradict their parents, chatter before company, gobble their food, and tyrannize their teachers.

—Socrates

❦

$\mathscr{T}$he best thing I can do for my children is to love their mother very well.
—Charlie Shedd

$\mathscr{Y}$outh is a wonderful thing. What a crime to waste it on children.
—George Bernard Shaw

$\mathscr{W}$hosoever therefore shall humble himself as this little child, the same is the greatest in the kingdom of heaven.

—Matthew 18:4

❦

$\mathscr{Y}$es, there is a Nirvana; it is in leading your sheep to a green pasture, and in putting your child to sleep, and in writing the last line of your poem.

—Kahlil Gibran

$\mathscr{W}$hat maintains one vice, would bring up two children.
—Benjamin Franklin

$\mathscr{I}$ do not know of a better shrine before which a father or mother may kneel or stand than that of a sleeping child. I do not know of a holier place, a temple where one is more likely to come into closer touch with all that is infinitely good, where one may come nearer to seeing and feeling God. From that shrine come matins of love and laughter, of trust and cheer to bless the new day; and before that shrine should fall our soft vespers, our grateful benedictions for the night. At the cot of a sleeping babe all man-made ranks and inequalities are ironed out, and all mankind kneels reverently before the image of the Creator.

—Value World

❦

$\mathscr{G}$eorge Washington visited the home of friends one evening, and when the hour came for him to leave, he said good-bye to the adults, then paused at the entrance where a little girl opened the door to let him out. Washington bowed to her and said, "I am sorry, my little dear, to give you so much trouble." She replied, "I wish, Sir, it was to let you in."

—W.B. Freeman Concepts

❦

$\mathscr{W}$hen I was a boy of 14, my father was so ignorant I could hardly stand to have the old man around. But when I got to be 21, I was astonished at how much the old man had learned in seven years.

—Mark Twain

❦

$\mathscr{B}$ut Samuel ministered before the Lord, being a child, girded with a linen ephod. Moreover his mother made him a little coat, and brought it to him from year to year, when she came up with her husband to offer the yearly sacrifice.

—I Samuel 2:18,19

$\mathscr{C}$hildren are like clocks: they must be allowed to run.

—James Dobson

224

$\mathcal{L}$ittle does the boy know... Little does he think, as he leans upon the lap of his mother, with his eye turned to her, in some earnest pleading for a fancied pleasure of the hour, or in some important story of his griefs, that such a sharing of his sorrows, and such sympathy with his wishes, he will find nowhere again.

—Donald Grant Mitchell

❦

$\mathcal{G}$od has mercifully given babies an uncanny ability to work into almost any parent's heart and carve out a special place of love. Rare indeed is that parent who can look his infant in the face and say, "I wish you had never been born." Instead, many who hesitated on the threshold of parenthood have responded to the paternal instinct once their child drew his first breath. In this day when planning or delaying a family is being over-emphasized, too many young couples are likely to cheat themselves out of one of life's most enriching experiences: being parents.

—Tim LaHaye

❦

$\mathcal{I}$ love little children, and it is not a slight thing when they, who are fresh from God, love us.

—Charles Dickens

❦

$\mathcal{B}$etween the dark and the daylight,
    When the night is beginning to lower,
Comes a pause in the day's occupations
    That is known as the Children's Hour.

—Henry Wadsworth Longfellow

❦

$\mathcal{I}$n Rama was there a voice heard, lamentation, and weeping, and great mourning, Rachel weeping for her children, and would not be comforted, because they are not.

—Matthew 2:18

225

*B*etween shows in Las Vegas, a man once asked Danny Kaye if he gambled. "Certainly," replied Kaye. "I love to gamble."

The man was puzzled. "Well, why don't we ever see you at the tables?" "Ah," said Kaye, "you equate gambling with winning or losing money. But that's not gambling for me... I will take a four-year-old child and put her on my knee in front of 30 million people, and not know what's going to come out of her mouth. Now that's gambling!"

—*Colin Dangaard*

ã

*I*t is a pitiful thing to hear a young girl say, when she is pregnant: "No, I am not married to him but I love him. I love him so much that I want to give him everything."

"But you had no right to give him a child," I tell her. "And he had no right to allow you to give him what he does not want—this helpless little child!"

—*Pearl S. Buck*

ã

A daughter is the companion, the friend, the confident of her mother...and the object of a pleasure, something like the love between the angels, of her father.

—*Richard Steele*

ã

I'd rather laugh a fair-haired boy, than reign a gray-haired king.

—*Oliver Wendell Holmes*

ã

*T*here's a feeling of eternity in youth.

—*William Hazlitt*

I don't know who my grandfather was. I am much more concerned about what his grandson will be.

—*Abraham Lincoln*

226

"*I* love you, Mother," said little John;
Then, forgetting his work, his cap went on,
And he was off to the garden swing,
And left her the water and wood to bring.
"I love you, Mother," said rosy Nell—
"I love you better than tongue can tell;"
Then she teased and pouted full half a day,
Till her mother rejoiced when she went to play.
"I love you, Mother," said little Fan;
"Today I'll help you all I can;
How glad I am that school doesn't keep!"
So she rocked the babe till it fell asleep.

Then, stepping softly, she fetched the broom,
And swept the floor and tidied the room;
Busy and happy all day was she,
Helpful and happy as child could be.
"I love you, Mother," again they said,
Three little children going to bed;
How do you think that mother guessed
Which of them really loved her best?

—*Joy Allison*

A man is still young as long as children smile at him.

—*Ralph Waldo Emerson*

*T*hat boy will do to depend on,
    I hold that this is true—
From lads in love with their mothers
    Our bravest heroes grew.
Earth's grandest hearts have been loving hearts,
    Since time and earth began.
And the boy who kissed his mother
    Is every inch a man.

—*Eben E. Rexford*

*C*hildren's children are the crown of old men: and the glory of children are their fathers.

—Proverbs 17:6

*W*e are born for a higher destiny than that of earth.

—Edward G. Bulwer-Lytton

*I*s this the little girl I carried,
  Is this the little boy at play?
I don't remember growing older—
  When did they?...

Sunrise, Sunset—
  Swiftly fly the years.
One season following another,
  Laden with happiness and tears.

—Sheldon Harnick

Nurturing and Training Children

Chapter Six
Nurturing and Training Children

*W*hat better thing of one's own can one do than share in the creation of a new life, thereafter integrating it into a loving and wholesome family and continuing to guide the formation of its personality and the molding of its character?

—Princess Grace of Monaco

I begin to love this little creature, and to anticipate his birth as a fresh twist to a knot, which I do not wish to untie.

—Mary Wollstoncroft

I remember leaving the hospital...thinking, "Wait, are they going to let me walk off with him? I don't know beans about babies! I don't have a license to do this."

—Anne Tyler

*I*n the sheltered simplicity of the first days after a baby is born, one sees again the magical closed circle, the miraculous sense of two people existing only for each other.

—Anne Morrow Lindbergh

I actually remember feeling delight, at two o'clock in the morning, when the baby woke for his feed, because I so longed to have another look at him.

—Margaret Drobble

*W*ho is getting more pleasure from their rocking, the baby or me?

—Nancy Thayer

A babe at the breast is as much pleasure as the bearing is pain.

—Marian Zimmer Bradley

*C*an a woman forget her suckling child, that she should not have compassion on the son of her womb...?

—Isaiah 49:15

*A*s a parent, you have to establish yourself as a leader early on and then work yourself out of a job thereafter.

—James Dobson

*M*y deep belief is that all human creatures deserve a happy childhood as a right and as a prerequisite to normal adulthood, and that the first essential to happiness is love. I have often observed that if a child does not have a wholehearted love from and for someone before he is five years old, he is emotionally stunted perhaps for the rest of his life. That is he is unable to love anyone wholeheartedly and is to that extent deprived of a full life. This loving and beloved person is hopefully father or mother or both, but lacking these, a kindhearted maid or nurse or grandmother will do, but it should be someone who has the physical care of him, so that through the daily washing and dressing and feeding and play he feels the pervading and continuing presence of love. It has to be real love. The professional coddling that a trained nurse or attendant gives a baby in a foundling home or hospital does not fool even the baby. It takes more than a clock-watching employee to make a child feel secure. It is amazing how discerning a baby can be. A child in the care of a good but unloving foster mother soon sinks into impassivity and begins to fade. Love is the sunshine of his growing soul, and when there is no sun, the soul stops and the body and mind begin to lag. That is why children in orphanages and boarding homes look dull and are either too silent or too noisy. Babies used to be kept in hordes in orphanages until it was discovered how quickly they died of nothing at all apparently. Of course they died for lack of true love.

—Pearl S. Buck

*H*e, whose infinite orderliness is everywhere in evidence, has not left His children without laws of life... There has been a tendency by some to say that this age-old counsel on conduct may have served a purpose in the past, but is no longer essential to human happiness... The Father of us all, in His love and wisdom pertaining to His children, hasn't said "Thou shalt" and "Thou shalt not" for no particular purpose.

—Richard L. Evans

234

If you are a mother, you should think of yourself as a sculptor. You can be a poor artist—and create sickly, underdeveloped children, or a great artist—and mold beautiful, happy lives. Keep this in mind; it reflects the importance of your daily tasks.

—Gayelord Hauser

The education of a child begins in infancy. At six months old it can answer smile by smile, and impatience with impatience. It can observe, enjoy, and suffer. Do you suppose it makes no difference to it that the order of the house is perfect and quiet, the faces of its father and mother full of peace, their soft voices familiar to its ear, and even those of strangers, loving.

—John Ruskin

❧

If a child lives with approval, he learns to live with himself.

—Dorothy Law Nolte

Children need models more than they need critics.

—Joseph Joubert

Children need love, especially when they do not deserve it.

—Harold S. Hubert

❧

Respect the child. Be not too much his parent. Trespass not on his solitude.

—Ralph Waldo Emerson

Talents for the education of youth are the gift of God; and...he on whom they are bestowed, whenever a way is opened for the use of them, is as strongly *called* as if he heard a voice from heaven.

—Benjamin Franklin

*N*othing is so contagious as example; and we never do any great good or evil which does not produce its like.

—Francous de la Rochefoucauld

*S*pare the rod and spoil the child—that is true. But, besides the rod, keep an apple to give him when he has done well.

—Martin Luther

*N*o job can compete with the responsibility of shaping and molding a new human being.

—James Dobson

*I*n the man whose childhood has known caresses and kindness, there is always a fibre of memory that can be touched to gentle issues.

—George Eliot

*C*hildren want some honest direction. They want a set of sensible rules to live by. The time has come to dust off the rule book.

—Jenkins Lloyd Jones

❧

*M*r. Ibuka's marvelous and gentle book [*Kindergarten Is Too Late!*] makes no earth-shaking pronouncements of any sort. He simply proposes that tiny children have within them the capacity to learn virtually anything while they are tiny. He proposes that what they learn without any conscious effort at two, three, or four years of age can be learned only with great effort, or may not be learned at all, in later life. He proposes that what adults learn painfully children learn joyfully. He proposes that what adults learn at a snail's pace, tiny children learn almost speedily. He proposes that adults sometimes avoid learning, while tiny children would rather learn than eat.

—Glenn Doman

*P*arents who neglect discipline are their children's worst enemies.

—F. Marion Dick

*C*hildren require guidance and sympathy far more than instruction.

—Ann Sullivan

236

If mothers would understand that much of their importance lies in building up the father image for the child, the children would turn out well.

—*Samuel S. Liebowitz*

I would develop in the child his hands, his brain and his soul. The hands have almost atrophied. The soul has been altogether ignored.

—*Mohandas Gandhi*

And all thy children shall be taught of the Lord; and great shall be the peace of thy children.

—*Isaiah 54:13*

✺

Little boys want to be men, but they need good men to show them how. The lucky boys have such men as fathers.

—*William J. Bennett*

A sense of belonging, the loving involvement of parents which creates a sense of worth, and a sense of purpose are what every child deserves to receive.

—*Cyril J. Barber*

✺

A mother is the medium through which the primitive infant transforms himself into a socialized human being.

—*Beata Rank*

I saw pure love when my son looked at me, and I knew that I had to make a good life for the two of us.

—*Suzanne Somers*

To make your children capable of honesty is the beginning of education.

—*John Ruskin*

*O*ur children...have been loaned to us temporarily for the purpose of loving them and instilling a foundation of values on which their future lives will be built. We will be accountable through eternity for the way we discharge that responsibility.

—James Dobson

*T*he arresting and somewhat terrifying fact about home is that in it new human beings are wholly at the disposal of the old. They come trailing clouds of glory; but what happens to these largely depends upon the adults who have the child in their control.

—H.A. Overstreet

*O*thou child of many prayers!
Life hath quicksands; life hath snares.

—Henry Wadsworth Longfellow

A child is fed with milk and praise.

—Charles Lamb

*L*et thy child's first lesson be obedience, and the second may be what thou wilt.

—Thomas Fuller

*H*onour thy father and thy mother; that thy days may be long upon the land which the Lord thy God giveth thee.

—Exodus 20:12

*T*he persons hardest to convince they're at the retirement age are children at bedtime.

—Shannon Fife

A good father will leave his imprint on his daughter for the rest of her life.

—James Dobson

*I*t is better to bind your children to you by a feeling of respect, and by gentleness, than by fear.

—Terence

238

$\mathcal{W}$e can list people's credentials, pinpoint the standards for a day-care center, but, as breast milk cannot be duplicated, neither can a mother. We cannot put mothering into a formula and come up with a person who has the special feeling for your child that you do.

—Sally E. Shaywitz

❦

$\mathcal{I}$f a child is to keep alive his inborn sense of wonder he needs the companionship of at least one adult who can share it, rediscovering with him the joy, excitement and mystery of the world we live in.

—Rachel Carson

❦

$\mathcal{T}$he rules for parents
are but three...
    Love,
    Limit,
And let them be!

—Elaine M. Ward

❦

$\mathcal{T}$he child you want to raise as an upright and honorable person requires a lot more of your time than your money.

—George Varky

❦

$\mathcal{O}$n average, American fathers spend a grand total of eight minutes talking—not nagging, yelling or reminding, but talking—to their kids on the typical weekday. Working mothers spend 11 minutes. Even stay-at-home moms average less than 30 minutes engaged in anything that can charitably be described as meaningful conversation.

—Dr. Ruth Westheimer

Children may be taught to read, without perceiving it to be anything but a sport, and play themselves into that which others are whipped for.

—*John Locke*

Train up a child in the way he should go: and when he is old he will not depart from it.

—*Proverbs 22:6*

Not the cry, but the flight of the wild duck, leads the flock to fly and follow.

—*Chinese Proverb*

Every child needs...a father and every father can make a difference... The mothers tended to be gentle and low-keyed with their babies. Fathers, on the other hand, were more playful, tickling and poking their babies more than the mothers did.

—*Dr. T. Berry Brazelton*

ॐ

Build me a son, O Lord, who will be strong enough to know when he is weak, and brave enough to face himself when he is afraid, one who will be proud and unbending in honest defeat, and humble and gentle in victory.

—*Douglas MacArthur*

In the effort to give good and comforting answers to the young questioners whom we love, we very often arrive at good and comforting answers for ourselves.

—*Ruth Goode*

The first step, my son, which one makes in the world is the one on which depends the rest of our days.

—*Voltaire*

Children have never been very good at listening to their elders, but they have never failed to imitate them.

—*James Baldwin*

$\mathcal{L}$ove—real love—demands that you do what is best for your child, not necessarily what your child wants you to do, or what is easiest for you.

—Zig Ziglar

$\mathcal{O}$ne hundred years from now, it will not matter what kind of car I drove, what kind of house I lived in, how much money I had, or what my clothes looked like. But the world may be a little better, the universe a little brighter, because I was important to a child.

—Anonymous

$\mathcal{I}$f you have no prayer life yourself, it is rather a useless gesture to make your child say his prayers every night.

If you never enter a church, it is rather futile to send your child to Sunday School.

If you make a practice of telling social lies, it will be difficult to teach your child to be truthful.

If you say cutting things about your neighbors and about fellow members in the church, it will be hard for your child to learn the meaning of kindness.

—Peter Marshall

❧

$\mathcal{H}$ear, ye children, the instruction of a father, and attend to know understanding.

—Proverbs 4:1

$\mathcal{O}$ur children are living messages we send to a time and place we will never see.

—Anonymous

$\mathcal{T}$he vast majority of Americans share a respect for certain fundamental traits of character: honesty, compassion, courage, and perseverance. These are virtues. But because children are not born with this knowledge, they need to learn what these virtues are. We can help them gain a grasp and appreciation of these traits by giving children material to read about them... There are many wonderful stories of virtue and vice with which our children should be familiar.

—William J. Bennett

Christmas is for children. But it is for grown-ups too. Even if it is a headache, a chore, a nightmare, it is a period of necessary defrosting of chill and hide-bound hearts.

—Lenora Mattingly Weber

Can't you see the Creator of the universe, who understands every secret, every mystery...sitting patiently and listening to a four-year-old talk to Him?

—James Dobson

As I stood there gazing at the old house, it was as though I could see the door open and my mother come out. My mother had fair skin and blue eyes and blonde hair. Although it was an ancient style, I always seem to picture her in a dress with one of those chokers at the neck that came way up under the chin and held a women's head up straight. And she would have her hair piled up some way—and perched on top of it was a big hat. And those big balloon sleeves—I could see my mother coming out of the house like that and down the steps. I remembered sitting on that porch with her years ago, when she had been telling me that we had to economize... She said, "I won't go in debt... No one should ever go in debt. Don't get it until you can pay for it..."

"Well, now, Norman," she remonstrated... "I don't care about your having money. I want you to have enough money to pay your bills, but I don't want you to make money the aim of your life..."

"Ambition, Norman...is good, if God controls it... What I want you to be is a clean, decent, honorable, upright Christian man with love in your heart, serving God and His children. And I want you so to live that when you finish your course of life, long after I have preceded you, I'll meet you somewhere in the eternities of our Lord."

—Norman Vincent Peale

We should never permit ourselves to do anything that we are not willing to see our children do.

—Brigham Young

Correct thy son, and he shall give thee rest; yea, he shall give delight unto thy soul.

—Proverbs 29:17

My father...among his instructions to me when a boy, frequently repeated a proverb of Solomon, "Seest thou a man diligent in his calling, he shall stand before kings, he shall not stand before mean men." I thence considered industry as a means of obtaining wealth and distinction, which encouraged me, though I did not think that I should ever literally *stand before kings,* which, however, has since happened; for I have stood before *five,* and even had the honor of sitting down with one, the King of Denmark, to dinner.

—Benjamin Franklin

It is a tower of strength for a boy to have a hero.

—Andrew Carnegie

It is not book-learning young men need, nor instruction about this and that, but a stiffening of the vertebrae which will cause them to be loyal to a trust, to act promptly, concentrate their energies: do the thing.

—Elbert Hubbard

It is no help to your children to leave them money, but if you leave them education, if you leave them Christian and noble character, if you leave them a wide circle of friends, if you leave them an honorable name, it is far better than that they should have money.

—Russell H. Conwell

I was born in Augusta, Georgia, and we children were taught early on what the world is really like. We were told that we must work very hard and that we could become anything we wanted to be.

—Jessye Norman

A parent's love is more important to a child than wealth or education or any form of material possession... The home can fall far short of perfection in many areas; this lack will serve to prepare the child for life in an imperfect world. But the one thing he must have for a positive mental attitude is love.

—Tim LaHaye

Loving a child doesn't mean giving in to all of his whims; to love him is to bring out the best in him, to teach him to love what is difficult.

—Nadia Boulanger

243

*S*trange is our situation here upon this earth. Each of us comes for a short visit, not knowing why, yet sometimes seeming to a divine purpose. From the standpoint of daily life, however, there is one thing we do know: That we are here for the sake of others...for the countless unknown souls with whose fate we are connected by a bond of sympathy. Many times a day, I realize how much my own outer and inner life is built upon the labors of people, both living and dead, and how earnestly I must exert myself in order to give in return as much as I have received.

—Albert Einstein

*I*t's very important for us to use our best china, silver and linens... I've had many children's teas and nothing gets broken. In fact, it's the parents that are watching, worrying that my good china will get broken. I don't worry at all. It never happens.

—Barbara Rosenthal

*I*t is almost impossible to raise an honest child who remains immature in most other respects, since honesty is linked to other maturities, especially to the maturity of consideration and understanding of others.

—Dr. John A. Schindler

[*S*he loved and honored her grandfather, Thomas Jefferson:] above all earthly beings... And well I might. From him seemed to flow all the pleasures of my life... His nature was so eminently sympathetic that, with those he loved, he could enter into their feelings, anticipate their wishes, gratify their tastes, and surround them with an atmosphere of affection...

He talked with us freely, affectionately, never lost an opportunity of giving a pleasure or a good lesson. He reproved without wounding us, and commended without making us vain... Our smaller follies he treated with good-humored raillery, our graver ones with kind and serious admonition. He was watchful over our manners, and called our attention to every violation of propriety.

—Ellen W. Coolidge

*B*efore becoming a mother I had a hundred theories on how to bring up children. Now I have seven children and only one theory: love them, especially when they least deserve to be loved.

—Kate Samperi

244

The very idea of removing by social surgery a woman's or man's connected love for a child is part of a coming ice age of relationships— the dehumanizing of mankind. We may find that intellectual activity is not enough, that achievement in the industrial, technological world, while important, is not sufficient, and that we also, man and woman alike, need the roots into biology, the touch of one another that childrearing brings.

—*Anne Roiphe*

When a child suffers something precious is being compromised.

—*Sophia Loren*

Anyone who writes down to children is simply wasting his time. You have to write up, not down. Children are demanding. They are the most attentive, curious, eager, sensitive, quick and generally congenial readers on earth. They accept, almost without question, anything you present them with, as long as it is presented honestly, fearlessly and clearly... Children are game for anything. I throw them hard words, and they backhand them over the net. They love words that give them a hard time, provided they are in a context that absorbs their attention.

—*E.B. White*

Children need adults who can go for casual walks and talk about fishing and stuff like that...and slow down to look at pretty leaves and caterpillars...and answer questions about God and the nature of the world as it is.

—*James Dobson*

My parents were among [those few missionary families who chose to live among the Chinese]. Happy for me that I had such parents, for instead of the narrow and conventional life of the white man in Asia, I lived with the Chinese people and spoke their tongue as I spoke my own.

Did I see sights which children should not see and hear talk not fit for children's ears? If I did, I cannot remember. I saw poor and starving people in a famine year, but my parents bade me help them, and I learned early that suffering can always be relieved, if there is a will to do it, and in that knowledge I have found escape from despair throughout my life... It is better to learn early of the inevitable depths, for then sorrow and death take their proper place in life, and one is not afraid.

—*Pearl S. Buck*

*C*hildren are travellers newly arrived in a strange country of which they know nothing.

—*John Locke*

*T*he proper attitude toward a child's disobedience is this: "I love you too much to let you behave like that."

—*James Dobson*

*I*f you want a baby, have a new one. Don't baby the old one.

—*Jessamyn West*

*L*ittle drops of water,
    Little grains of sand,
Make the mighty ocean
    And the pleasant land.

Thus the little minutes,
    Humble though they be
Make the mighty ages
    Of eternity.

—*Julia A. Carney*

*J*ohn Parke (Jacky) Custis was four years old, and little Martha (Patsy) only two, when their mother married Washington. He welcomed them into his household as though they were his own. They took to him right away, calling him "Poppa" and responding to his kindness and gifts with genuine affection. "Poppa" Washington proved to be thoughtful and conscientious in his treatment of the children. "I conceive there is much greater circumspection by a guardian than a natural parent, who is only accountable to his own conscience for his conduct." He considered it his duty to be "generous and attentive" to the children, and these convictions guided his actions as long as they lived with him.

—*Andrew M. Allison & Jay A. Parry*

A six-year-old boy came home from school one day with a note from his teacher suggesting that he be taken from school as he was "too stupid to learn." "My boy is not stupid," said the mother. "I will teach him myself." She did, and Thomas A. Edison was the result.

—*Edward W. Bok*

Obedience is the gateway through which knowledge—yes, and love, too—enter the mind of a child.

—*Anne Sullivan*

Every parent knows how crucial the choice of friends is for every child. Childhood friendships tell parents which ways their children are tending. They are important because good friends bring you up, and bad friends bring you down. So it matters who our children's friends are. And it matters, as examples to our children, who our friends are. Friends should be allies of our better natures.

—*William J. Bennett*

☙

Work while you work,
    Play while you play;
One thing each time,
    That is the way.
All that you do,
    Do with your might;
Things done by halves
    Are not done right.

—*McGuffey's Primer*

Are all the children in? The night is falling,
    And storm clouds gather in the threatening west;
The lowing cattle seek a friendly shelter,
    The bird hies to her nest;
The thunder crashes; wilder grows the tempest,
    And darkness settles o'er the fearful din.
Come, shut the door, and gather round the hearthstone.
    Are all the children in?

—*Elizabeth Rossen*

My mother was always looking to home influences as the best means of keeping her two boys in the right path. She used to say that the first step in this direction was to make home pleasant.

—*Andrew Carnegie*

247

*T*is education forms the common mind:
As the twig is bent the tree's inclined.

—Alexander Pope

*N*ature fits all her children with something to do.
He who would write and can't write, can surely review.

—James Russell Lowell

*C*hildren are what the mothers are.
No fondest father's fondest care
Can fashion so the infant heart.

—Walter Savage Landor

*J*ohn and Charles Wesley were two of eighteen children. Yet their
mother made time to spend an hour every week individually with each
child, as though that child were the only one she had.

John Wesley became a remarkable Christian leader, traveling eight
thousand miles a year on horseback and eventually renewing the whole
church. His brother Charles wrote over five thousand hymns, many of
which we still sing. The self-esteem Susanna Wesley built into her
children produced two spiritual geniuses.

—Norman Vincent Peale

*D*ost thou love life? Then do not squander time, for that is the stuff life
is made of.

—Benjamin Franklin

*B*itter are the tears of a child:
    Sweeten them.
Deep are the thoughts of a child:
    Quiet them.
Sharp is the grief of a child:
    Take it from him.
Soft is the heart of a child:
    Do not harden it.

—Lady Pamela Wyndham Glenconner

One father is more than a hundred school-masters.

—*George Herbert*

Ride with an idle whip, ride with an unused heel,
But, once in a way, there will come a day
When the colt must be taught to feel
The lash that falls, and the curb that galls,
And the sting of the rowelled steel.

—*Rudyard Kipling*

꙾

What will a child learn sooner than a song?

—*Alexander Pope*

Give a little love to a child, and you get a great deal back.

—*John Ruskin*

There is nothynge that more dyspleaseth God,
Than from theyr children to spare the rod.

—*John Skelton*

꙾

How pleasant is Saturday night,
When I've tried all the week to be good,
And not spoke a word that was bad,
    And obliged every one that I could.

—*Nancy Dennis Sproat*

A child should always say what's true
And speak when he is spoken to,
And behave mannerly at table;
At least as far as he is able.

—*Robert Louis Stevenson*

249

Children, obey your parents in all things; for this is well pleasing unto the Lord. Fathers, provoke nor your children to anger, lest they be discouraged.

—*Colossians 3:20-21*

Birds in their little nests agree;
    And 'tis a shameful sight
When children of one family
    Fall out, and chide, and fight.

—*Isaac Watts*

❦

Blessed be the hand that prepares a pleasure for a child, for there is no saying when and where it may bloom forth.

—*Douglas Jerrold*

Children have more need of models than of critics.

—*Joseph Joubert*

❦

Values are not taught to children: they are caught by children.

—*James Dobson*

Whilst that the child is young, let him be instructed in virtue and literature.

—*John Lyly*

❦

The best way to make children good is to make them happy.

—*Oscar Wilde*

Instruction increases inborn worth, and right discipline strengthens the heart.

—*Horace*

When you can't do anything else to a boy, you can make him wash his face.

—Ed Howe

And thou shalt teach them [the commandments] diligently unto thy children, and shalt talk of them when thou sittest in thy house, and when thou walkest by the way, and when thou liest down, and when thou risest up.

—Deuteronomy 6:7

Hearts, like doors, will open with ease
To very, very little keys,
And don't forget that two of these
Are "I thank you" and "If you please."

—Anonymous

"Do I have to say I am sorry when I am not?" One of my own sons, when small, made this demand after injustice to his younger sister.

"Indeed you must say you are sorry, and whether you are or not," I replied. "You must *do* right, however you *feel*. You cannot make yourself feel something you do not feel, but you can make yourself do right in spite of your feelings. And you'll be surprised, because when you have learned the habit of saying you are sorry when you should be, you will actually begin to feel sorry."

—Pearl S. Buck

You send your child to the schoolmaster, but 'tis the schoolboys who educate him.

—Ralph Waldo Emerson

Be ever gentle with the children God has given you. Watch over them constantly; reprove them earnestly, but not in anger.

—Elihu Burritt

All around us, living in the very shadow of our large churches and beautiful cathedrals, children are growing up without a particle of religious training or influence.

—Peter Marshall

251

*P*oliteness, etiquette, good manners, civility—the habits these words represent are underrated and underused in our time.

—*William J. Bennett*

*W*ith children we must mix gentleness with firmness. They must not always have their own way, but they must not always be thwarted. If we never have headaches through rebuking them, we shall have plenty of heartaches when they grow up.

—*Charles Haddon Spurgeon*

*T*he idea that we can leave entirely to the children the choices of the vital essentials is unsafe... Children are entitled to counsel, and to knowing the principles that have been proved by the experience of the past. It is part of the heritage they have. They are entitled to example, to prayerful guidance, and righteous persuasion in the living of their lives. And even though they may react contrarily at times, they will be everlastingly grateful for early teachings taught, for early lessons learned, for the love and living example of a good parent's life.

—*Richard L. Evans*

*G*ood Christian people, here [in your children] lies for you an inestimable loan;—take all heed thereof, in all carefulness employ it. With high recompense, or else with heavy penalty, will it one day be required back.

—*Thomas Carlyle*

*C*hildren want their parents more than they want the junk we buy them.

—*James Dobson*

*N*othing we ever do is in strict scientific literalness wiped out... Could the young but realize how soon they will become mere walking bundles of habits, they would give more heed to their conduct while in the plastic state. We are spinning our own fates, good or evil... Every smallest stroke of virtue or of vice leaves its never so little scar... We are...imitators and copiers of our past selves.

—*William James*

*O*nly a life lived for others is a life worthwhile.

—*Albert Einstein*

*U*nless a tree has borne blossoms in spring, you will vainly look for fruit on it in autumn.

—*August W. Hare*

*I*f you bungle raising your kids, I don't think whatever else you do well matters very much.

—*Jacqueline Kennedy Onassis*

*E*ven a child is known by his doings, whether his work be pure, and whether it be right.

—*Proverbs 20:11*

*B*estow thy youth so that thou mayest have comfort to remember it when it hath forsaken thee.

—*Sir Walter Raleigh*

*N*ever cut a tree down in the wintertime. Never make a negative decision in the low time. Never make your most important decisions when you are in your worst mood. Wait. Be patient. The storm will pass. The spring will come.

—*Robert H. Schuller's Father*

*M*oral virtues come from habit... The habits we form from childhood make no small difference, but rather they make all the difference.

—*Aristotle*

*K*eep a watch on your words, my darling,
    For words are wonderful things;
They are sweet like the bees' fresh honey,
    Like the bees they have terrible stings;
They can bless like the warm, glad sunshine,
    And brighten a lonely life;
They can cut, in the strife of anger,
    Like an open, two-edged knife.

—*Mrs. E.R. Miller*

*M*y children, the three acts of faith, hope, and charity contain all the happiness of man upon the earth.

—*John Vianney*

$\mathcal{W}$e have to teach our young that they will never find contentment until they put themselves into the mainstream of human life. And then, in the wonderful, rewarding way that life has, peace and happiness—when not sought for their own sakes—come stealing in through the doors of duty fulfilled. Duty is not hateful or tedious or destructive. Duty fulfilled is gratifying and enjoyable and restoring to the soul, and serenity is its fruit.

—Pearl S. Buck

$\mathcal{A}$ teacher of days gone by...made it a practice to bow low before his class when he entered the classroom. When asked why he did so, his reply was, "Every time I look at my class of boys, I wonder for what important position in life each one is being prepared." One member of that class was none other than Martin Luther.

—Evelyn LeTourneau

ॐ

$\mathcal{I}$f at first you don't succeed,
Try, try again;
Then your courage should appear,
For, if you will persevere,
You will conquer, never fear;
Try, try again.

—McGuffey's Second Reader

$\mathcal{L}$ives of great men all remind
us we can make our lives sublime,
And, departing, leave behind us
footprints on the sands of time.

—Henry Wadsworth Longfellow

$\mathcal{L}$ittle strokes fell great oaks.

—Benjamin Franklin

$\mathcal{M}$y grandfather once told me that there are two kinds of people: those who do the work and those who take the credit. He told me to try to be in the first group; there was less competition there.

—Indira Gandhi

254

$\mathcal{I}$ do not believe we can love our children too much. I think we ought to take all the comfort we can in them while they are spared to us and if we must give them up we ought to be thankful that we were blessed by their angelic presence even for a little while... I am more and more impressed with the responsibility of training children properly... It requires great caution and firmness to do the right thing always. It seems to me there can be no stronger motive for improvement than the thought of the influence on our children. It is what *we are*, not what we do in reference to them, which will make its impress on their lives. They will be sure to find out our weak points whatever professions we make.

—*Louisa Torrey Taft*

$\mathcal{Y}$ou've got to do your own growing, no matter how tall your grandfather was.

—*Irish Proverb*

$\mathcal{C}$onsider your origin; you were not formed to live like brutes, but to follow virtue and knowledge.

—*Dante*

$\mathcal{D}$o not wait for some extreme emergency to show...tenderness for your children. When your little boy passes by, pat him on the head and say, "You little dear," or take your little girl in your arms and say, "You are the kind of little girl I always wanted." Or rest your hands on your older son's shoulder and say, "What a fine boy you are. I am so proud of you." These things should not be said occasionally, but daily!... This will help keep your children from going astray.

—*Helen B. Andelin*

$\mathcal{I}$t is with youth as with plants, from the first fruits they bear we learn what may be expected in the future.

—*Demophilus*

$\mathcal{L}$et us teach our children to study man as well as mathematics, and to build cathedrals as well as power stations.

—*Sir David Eccles*

$\mathcal{T}$o teach is to learn.

—*Japanese Proverb*

255

My father taught me that a bill is like a crying baby and has to be attended to at once.

—Anne Morrow Lindbergh

Oh, that it were my chief delight
  To do the things I ought!
Then let me try with all my might
  To mind what I am taught.

—Ann Taylor

A torn jacket is soon mended, but hard words bruise the heart of a child.

—Henry Wadsworth Longfellow

It would be more honorable to our distinguished ancestors to praise them less in words, but in deeds to imitate them more.

—Horace Mann

Too many parents seem actually afraid of their children. They make little or no effort to enforce discipline. They seem to act on the helpless assumption that children can't really be controlled, so why bother to try? The result is that children never learn discipline or how to control themselves.

—Norman Vincent Peale

We should teach our children to be not what we are, but what they should be.

—William Penn

The right of parents to select their child's religious orientation must be protected. No teacher or administrator should be allowed to contradict what the child has been taught at home.

—James Dobson

They who provide much wealth for their children but neglect to improve them in virtue do like those who feed their horses high, but never train them to be useful.

—Socrates

$\mathscr{I}$ have no greater joy than to hear that my children walk in truth.

—III John, Verse 4

$\mathscr{A}$ wise parent allows the children to make mistakes. It is good for them once in a while to burn their fingers.

—Mohandas Gandhi

❦

$\mathscr{I}$t is time that we had uncommon schools, that we did not leave off our education when we begin to be men and women.

—Henry David Thoreau

$\mathscr{N}$ever give a child an unnecessary order, but when you do give one, make it stick!

—Smiley Blanton

$\mathscr{L}$et me enjoin it upon you [son John] to attend constantly and steadfastly to the precepts and instructions of your father.

—Abigail Adams

$\mathscr{I}$ would like them [children] to be the happy end of my story.

—Margaret Atwood

❦

$\mathscr{O}$ur children are not going to be "our children" they are going to be other people's husbands and wives and the parents of our grandchildren.

—Mary S. Calderone

$\mathscr{L}$ife teaches if the student is willing.

—Peter R. Stone

$\mathscr{C}$hildren are likely to live up to what you believe of them.

—Lady Bird Johnson

One of the wisest principles I ever learned was given to me years ago by Mother. One night in our farm home up in Pennsylvania my mother, my brothers and I were playing cards... We were not using regular playing cards, for my mother was very straight-laced...[but] an old-fashioned game called "Flinch," or something.

Anyway, Mother was the dealer and she dealt me the worst possible hand. I knew I hadn't the slightest chance of winning with a hand like that and since I always did like to win, I began complaining and griping. Mother said, "All right, boys, put your cards face down on the table, especially you, Ike."

She said, "This is only a game, but it's like life itself. You're going to have many a bad hand dealt to you. What you've got to do is to take up each hand, good or bad, and don't whine or complain, but take that hand and play it out. If you're men enough to do that—to play out the hand—God will help you and you'll come out all right in the end."

—*Dwight D. Eisenhower*

Hearing the truth from friends or strangers may sometimes shame us. Like many medicines, shame may not feel good, but its bitter taste can help set us straight.

—*William J. Bennett*

[To her daughters:] I long to put the experience of fifty years at once into your young lives, to give you at once the key to that treasure chamber every gem of which has cost me tears and struggles and prayers, but you must work for these inward treasures yourselves.

—*Harriet Beecher Stowe*

The good education of youth has been esteemed by wise men in all ages as the surest foundation of the happiness both of private families and of commonwealths.

—*Benjamin Franklin*

It is probably no accident that as the number of working mothers has increased, so has the incidence of juvenile delinquency of all kinds and the decline of sex morals among young people.

—*Norman Vincent Peale*

There is so much to teach, and the time goes so fast.
—*Erma Bombeck*

He that spareth his rod hateth his son: but he that loveth him chasteneth him betimes.
—*Proverbs 13:24*

A successful career means nothing without a personal life. So the children were always with me.
—*Janet Leigh*

The duty upon parents is much more than merely to provide. It is also to teach and train, to counsel, and, as necessary, correct—to live the part of parents, with gentleness and firmness so intermixed as never to avoid wise discipline or the doing of duty; to show forth leadership, and remember never to leave out love.
—*Richard L. Evans*

What do girls do who haven't any mothers to help them through their troubles?
—*Louisa May Alcott*

[*Ob*jections to sending a young man to Europe for schooling:] He is led by the strongest of all human passions into a spirit for female intrigue, destructive of his own and others' happiness, or a passion for whores, destructive of his health, and in both cases learns to consider fidelity to the marriage bed as an ungentlemanly practice, and inconsistent with happiness; he recollects the voluptuary dress and arts of the European women, and pities and despises the chaste affections and simplicity of those of his own country.
—*Thomas Jefferson*

Whenever one learns to do anything he has never to wait long for an opportunity of putting his knowledge to use.
—*Andrew Carnegie*

[*Boys*] know truth from counterfeit as quick as a chemist does. They detect weakness in your eye and behavior...before you open your mouth.
—*Ralph Waldo Emerson*

259

The greatest satisfaction comes not from without, but from within. The greatest rewards come not from the discipline applied by others, your teachers and your parents, but from the most beautiful and severe of all disciplines, that which you exert on yourself.

—Pearl S. Buck

I grew up believing...in love for one's family and kindness toward others. I grew up believing that malicious gossip led to the downfall of one's own character, that reading was the best occupation for an only child, that doing well in school was the only reward a parent wanted, and that friends, good friends, must be made and kept for life. I still believe those things.

—Lois Wyse

The best thing we can do for our children is to consciously work at being role models for them. Teach them by your example, and they'll remember and even try to imitate... Other than guiding them by example, there isn't much we can do for them except to be around to pick them up whenever they fall. That's not asking too much, is it?

—Og Mandino

Don't let these parenting years get away from you. Your contributions to your children and grandchildren could rank as your greatest accomplishments in life.

—James Dobson

Hearken unto the father that begat thee, and despise not thy mother when she is old.

—Proverbs 23:22

There are three great questions which in life we have over and over again to answer: Is it right or wrong? Is it true or false? Is it beautiful or ugly? Our education ought to help us to answer these questions.

—John Lubbock

Never fear spoiling children by making them too happy. Happiness is the atmosphere in which all good affections grow.

—Thomas Bray

260

*M*any schoolteachers are afraid to bring up moral and spiritual questions for fear that they violate the Constitution. It's a tragedy, intellectually as well as morally and spiritually. This might relate to the educational problems among some children. A large number of the schools' assumptions are materialist and agnostic; there's a culture conflict between families and schools. That conflict may have some bearing on what children learn and what they don't learn, and how children behave in school.

—Robert Coles

I was not just the child of my parents—I was in fact a child of the entire neighborhood. When I was out of sight of the folks and thought I could get away with something, Mr. Jones or Mrs. Smith down the block was sure to step in and administer appropriate, corrective caring—whether I liked it or not... But through it I learned certain values that were reinforced at every turn by my church and school: self-esteem, self-discipline, the desire to learn, responsibility and service. In short, my neighborhood built around me a culture of character—an ethic of personal responsibility.

—Louis W. Sullivan

*W*hoso loveth wisdom rejoiceth his father.

—Proverbs 29:3

*I*f you want your children to improve, let them overhear the nice things you say about them to others.

—Dr. Haim Ginott

*O*ur fathers teach us what we should become; our mothers teach us what we are.

—Peter Davison

*I*f you want your children to keep their feet on the ground, put some responsibility on their shoulders.

—Abigail Van Buren

*A*dherence to a standard is an important element of discipline.

—James Dobson

*E*ach of us must come to care about everyone else's children. We must recognize that the welfare of our children and grandchildren is intimately linked to the welfare of all others people's children. After all, when one of our children needs lifesaving surgery, someone else's child will perform it. If one of our children is threatened or harmed by violence, someone else's child will be responsible for the violent act. The good life for our own children can be secured only if a good life is also secured for all other people's children.

—Lillian Katz

*C*orrection does much, but encouragement does more.

—Johann Wolfgang von Goethe

*F*ears are educated into us and can, if we wish, be educated out.

—Dr. Karl A. Menninger

*S*ometimes the poorest man leaves his children the richest inheritance.

—Ruth E. Renkel

*P*arents are the bones on which children cut their teeth.

—Peter Ustinov

I now plainly perceive what great obligations I am under to love and honour my parents. I have great reason to believe that their counsel and education have been my making; though, in the time of it, it seemed to do me so little good.

—Jonathan Edwards

*W*e must teach our children to dream with their eyes open.

—Harry Edwards

[*T*o her son, John Wesley]: Would you judge the lawfulness or unlawfulness of pleasure, then use this rule: Whatever weakens your reason, impairs the tenderness of your conscience, obscures your sight of God; takes from you your thirst for spiritual things; increases the authority of your body over your mind, that thing to you is evil no matter how plausibly or insidiously it may be presented to you.

—Susanna Wesley

262

$\mathcal{P}$atricia Neal recalls that her father had a motto above his desk that read: When you call upon a Thoroughbred, he gives you all the speed, strength of heart and sinew in him. When you call on a jackass, he kicks.

—As I Am

$\mathcal{P}$arents of teens would make great tightrope artists—we've had so much practice. We are always walking that fine line between too far away and too close. We must never be snoopy but always be interested... We should blend in with the scenery but stand firm as a rock when needed, which is more often than we may think.

—Helen Bottel

❧

$\mathcal{F}$or you must take this for a certain truth, that let them have what instructions you will, and ever so learned lectures...daily inculcated into them, that which will most influence their carriage will be the company they converse with, and the fashion of those about them.

—John Locke

$\mathcal{M}$y father taught me that only through self-discipline can you achieve freedom. Pour water in a cup and you can drink. Without the cup, the water would splash all over. The cup is discipline.

—Ricardo Montalban

❧

$\mathcal{K}$ids in school are exposed to many subjects and many different fields, all of which require many different skills. That's good. The trouble comes when the school expects a kid to be good at all of them. And individual teachers have a way of thinking that all the students in their class ought to be good at their subject. That's ridiculous; it would even be humorous if it didn't make so many students feel so inadequate. Since nobody is good at everything, but since the adult world often expects this of kids, kids often feel they are failures. It is important to recognize that no adult expects another adult to be good at everything. After all, that would be asking too much. Ask any adult.

—Jonah Kalb & David Viscott

I want my daughters to be beautiful, accomplished, and good; to be admired, loved and respected; to have a happy youth, to be well and wisely married, and to lead useful, pleasant lives, with as little care and sorrow to try them as God sees fit to send. To be loved and be chosen by a good man is the best and sweetest thing which can happen to a woman; and I sincerely hope my girls may know this beautiful experience.

—*Louisa May Alcott*

*Y*oung people need pleasure as truly as they need food and air. When I see the throngs of factory-girls on our streets in the evening, it seems to me that the pitiless city sees in them just two possibilities: first, the chance to use their tender labor-power by day, and then the chance to take from them their little earnings at night by appealing to their need for pleasure.

—*Jane Addams*

*C*hildren, obey your parents in the Lord; for this is right. Honour thy father and mother; which is the first commandment with promise.

—*Ephesians 6:1,2*

❦

I think I can tell you in six words what you are waiting for. You are waiting to be free. Free from the nagging voice of conscience and the gray shadow of guilt. Free to give all of yourself, not a panicky fraction... The fastidious and perfectionist part of you has always wanted the best, not the second best. That's why you are such a wonderful person. And that's why you are holding out. Something in you, some deep extinct, knows what a tremendous experience your first complete union with another person can be—and that same instinct keeps telling you not to blur it, not to waste it, not to make it small.

—*A Father's Letter, told to Norman Vincent Peale*

*F*ollowing an unimportant mistake to pass without a comment is a wonderful social grace... Children who have the habit of constantly correcting should be stopped before they grow up to drive spouses and everyone else crazy by interrupting stories to say, "No, dear—it was Tuesday, not Wednesday."

—*Judith Martin*

264

The best things you can give children, next to good habits, are good memories.
—*Sydney J. Harris*

The child who has not been disciplined with love by his little world will be disciplined, generally without love, by the big world.
—*Zig Ziglar*

The great aim of every boy should be to do something beyond the sphere of his duties—something which attracts the attention of those over him.
—*Andrew Carnegie*

Too many parents leave too much to the schools... The schoolteacher is not a substitute parent. We parents have to do the job ourselves—and it's not always easy.
—*Princess Grace of Monaco*

The much-derided apron string can come in handy, especially when its fibers are the virtues we've learned at home. Those bonds stay with us.
—*William J. Bennett*

Power is of two kinds. One is obtained by the fear of punishment and the other by the art of love. Power based on love is a thousand times more effective and permanent than the one derived by the fear of punishment.
—*Mohandas Gandhi*

It is not that I disapprove of Allegra for her own sake. She is like many other girls, pretty, sweet and shallow. She will make some man quite happy, a man who does not need much. He will be happy with Allegra and she with him for the heart of each has the measure of a cup and no more, and so they fulfill one another. But you, Rennie, need a fountain of love, living and eternal. You must find a deep woman, my son, a woman with an overflowing heart. When you find her, believe me, I shall never lie awake again, however late you come home.
—*Pearl S. Buck*

I hope, therefore, that some of my descendants may follow the example and reap the benefit [of attempting moral perfection].

—*Benjamin Franklin*

We will walk on our own feet; we will work with our own hands; we will speak our own minds.

—*Ralph Waldo Emerson*

❧

Seventy percent of the kids with affectionate parents did well for themselves socially, compared with only 30 percent of the kids with cold-fish parents; and dad's hugs were found to be as important as Mom's.

—*Journal of Personality and Social Psychology*

A wise son maketh a glad father: But a foolish son is the heaviness of his mother.

—*Proverbs 10:1*

❧

What are parents for? Not simply for food and shelter and physical necessities, although this is a great service in itself. But parents are also counselors, builders of character, teachers of truth, and must not abdicate their particular position as parents. They are those to whom God has given children, with the prime responsibility as the molders and shapers of manners and morals.

—*Richard L. Evans*

❧

If we could have but one generation of properly born, trained, educated and healthy children, a thousand other problems of government would vanish.

—*Herbert Hoover*

Singing and dancing and having fun are fine, but...preparation for life must include readiness for sterner stuff as well.

—*William J. Bennett*

266

*M*other would have taken her two boys, one under each arm, and perished with them rather than they should mingle with low company in their extreme youth... Anything low, mean, deceitful, shifty, coarse, underhand, or gossipy was foreign to that heroic soul. Tom and I could not help growing up respectable characters, having such a mother and such a father, for the father, too, was one of nature's nobleman, beloved by all, a saint.

—*Andrew Carnegie*

ॐ

1. *N*ever put off until tomorrow what you can do today.
2. Never trouble another for what you can do yourself.
3. Never spend your money before you have earned it.
4. When angry, count to ten before you speak; if very angry, count to one hundred.

—*Thomas Jefferson*

ॐ

*T*o youth, I have but three words of counsel—work, work, work.

—*Bismarck*

ॐ

I do not know what your destiny will be, but one thing I know: the only ones among you who will really be happy are those who have sought and found how to serve.

—*Albert Schweitzer*

ॐ

I have reason to hope that my parents' prayers for me have been, in many things, very powerful and prevalent; that God has, in many things, taken me under His care and guidance, provision and direction, in answer to their prayers for me.

—*Jonathan Edwards*

267

$\mathscr{A}$ parent should pray for his children and let them know that he does. Prayer of this kind, I'm convinced, forms a kind of invisible envelope of love that surrounds them wherever they go.

—*Norman Vincent Peale*

❧

$\mathscr{M}$y son, if sinners entice thee, consent thou not.

—*Proverbs 1:10*

$\mathscr{I}$f you can talk with crowds and keep your virtue,
Or walk with Kings—nor lose the common touch.
Yours is the Earth and everything that's in it,
And—which is more—you'll be a Man, my son!

—*Rudyard Kipling*

❧

$\mathscr{Y}$our children are always your "babies" even if they have gray hair.

—*Janet Leigh*

❧

$\mathscr{S}$ex education programs in public schools are dangerous because of their moral neutrality. Right and wrong must be approached directly, rather than through the back doors of anatomy and physiology.

—*James Dobson*

$\mathscr{W}$hoso curseth his father or his mother, his lamp shall be put out in obscure darkness.

—*Proverbs 20:20*

❧

$\mathscr{T}$he essential thing about mothers—one needs to know that they are there, particularly at that age when, paradoxically, one is trying so hard to break away from parental influence.

—*Margot Fonteyn*

*Y*ou cannot take the total responsibility for the outcome of your children; for they do have a free will, and some are determined to exercise it.

—James Dobson

*R*ules for Raising Children

Don'ts
1. Don't give your children too many things.
2. Don't saddle them with your own fears, prejudices, or frustrations.
3. Don't be overprotective.
4. Where discipline is concerned, don't vacillate.
5. Don't stifle their talent for religion.

Do's
1. Show affection.
2. Trust them.
3. Encourage them to think for themselves.
4. Cultivate the ability to communicate with them.
5. Show them what self-discipline is.

—Norman Vincent Peale

A good man dies when a boy goes wrong.

—Anonymous

I would, if I were the teacher, educate the young male and female first of all in what it means to be born, to struggle for life, and then to find oneself deprived of family and home. Perhaps when this lonely individual becomes a reality for them, they will consider their own bodies, their sexual capacities and functions, and perceive the necessity to understand and to control and to use wisely the strong and significant power of sex.

Am I implying the word *sacred*? It is not a fashionable word or one often used in our modern time... Nevertheless, I will use it, for I believe that the physical creation is sacred, as art is sacred, and for the same reason. It is creation.

—Pearl S. Buck

*O*ur kids are shaped forever by the love and training received at home. They will always be influenced by the experiences that characterized the family in which they were reared. Not one experience is ever completely lost. Even at fifty years of age, they will "remember" and be guided by that which was taught in childhood. It's an awesome thought.

—*James Dobson*

*O*my young friends, the world is beautiful and...life is full of promise.

—*Phillips Brooks*

❦

Mothers and Grandmothers

Chapter Seven
Mothers and Grandmothers

And Adam called his wife's name Eve; because she was the mother of all living.

—Genesis 3:20

The woman who creates and sustains a home, and under whose hands children grow up to be strong and pure men and women, is a creator second only to God.

—Helen Hunt Jackson

❧

Ahimsa means infinite love... Who but woman, the mother of man, shows this capacity in the largest measure? She shows it as she carries the infant and feeds it during nine months and derives joy in the suffering involved. What can beat the suffering caused by the pangs of labour? But she forgets them in the joy of creation. Who again suffers daily so that her babe may wax from day to day?

—Mohandas Gandhi

When God thought of mother, He must have laughed with satisfaction, and framed it quickly—so rich, so deep, so divine, so full of soul, power, and beauty was the conception.

—Henry Ward Beecher

The mother in her office holds the key of the soul; and she it is who stamps the coin of character.

—Old Play

The tie which links mother and child is of such pure and immaculate strength as to be never violated, except by those whose feelings are withered by vitiated society.

—Washington Irving

*W*ork toward a positive birth experience, whether or not it is a cesarean. Work from the mother instinct, from the inner voice. Work from the inner knowledge that tells us women were made to give birth to their babies. Replace the fears and misinformation with good information, support, and self-love... If we continue to let medical technology take over the birthing process—beginning with our reproductive options—we give up a task that rightfully belongs to women. Our task is to bring the next generation into the world. That is the way it has always been and the way it has got to be. Medical technology is not meant to be the primary force for bringing new life into the world.

—Mothering

*M*other is the name for God in the lips and hearts of little children.

—William Makepeace Thackeray

*T*he moment a child is born,
The mother is also born.
She never existed before.
The woman existed, but the mother, never.
A mother is something absolutely new.

—Rajneesh

*S*he named the infant "Pearl," as being of great price—purchased with all she had.

—Nathaniel Hawthorne

A mother's arms are made of tenderness, and children sleep soundly in them.

—Victor Hugo

*I*f there is one scene in heaven or on earth, capable of calling forth the most refined sensibilities of our nature, it is the expressions of love which kindle into rapture, and which flow out in the soul of a woman towards her infant.

So pure, chaste, so tender and benevolent, so simple, so ardent and sincere, and so disinterested is this principle, that it could only have been kindled by the inspiration of a spirit direct from the fountain of eternal, everlasting love.

—Parley P. Pratt

*L*ord who ordainst for mankind
Benignant toils and tender cares,
We thank Thee for the ties that bind
The mother to the child she bears.

—William Cullen Bryant

*O*f all the rights of women, the greatest is to be a mother.

—Lin Yutang

*W*hen you are a mother, you are never really alone in your thoughts. You are connected to your child and to all those who touch your lives; a mother always has to think twice, once for herself and once for her child.

—Sophia Loren

*T*hey say that man is mighty,
He governs land and sea;
He wields a mighty scepter
O'er lesser powers that be;
But a mightier power and stronger,
Man from his throne has hurled;
And the hand that rocks the cradle
Is the hand that rules the world.

—Alfred, Lord Tennyson

*A*nd when Rachel saw that she bare Jacob no children, Rachel envied her sister; and said unto Jacob, Give me children, or else I die.

—Genesis 30:1

*N*othing that has been said
nothing that could be said
    or that ever will be said,
would be eloquent enough, expressive enough, or adequate to
make articulate that peculiar emotion we feel for our mothers.

—Peter Marshall

*M*y first job is to be a good mother.

—Faye Dunaway

The fully feminine woman—the woman who is glad she's a woman—normally raises alert, well-balanced youngsters, and gets a great deal of fun from the process. Pregnancy for her is a period of pleasure. As the months advance she becomes a picture of contentment and serenity. She feels she has achieved a perfect trinity because she has in a sense her husband, her child and herself, all within her own person.

—*Dr. Marynia F. Farnham*

The mother is the precious possession of the nation, so precious that society advances its highest well being when it protects the functions of the mother.

—*Ellen Key*

It [motherhood] is still the biggest gamble in the world. It is the glorious life force. It's huge and scary—it's an act of infinite optimism.

—*Gilda Radner*

❦

If you would civilize a man, begin with his grandmother.

—*Victor Hugo*

There is a legend that an angel came to earth to take something beautiful back to heaven, and he took a bouquet of roses, a baby's smile, and a mother's love. When he reached the heavenly realms the roses had withered, the baby's smile had vanished, but the mother's love endured forever.

—*Anonymous*

There is no influence so powerful as that of the mother.

—*Sarah Josepha Hale*

Is there any happiness that can be compared with that of a woman with her small babies? Is there any love so unselfish and so inspiring as the love of a mother for her child? To healthy-minded women it is the realization of their highest ambition, the fulfillment of their instinctive urge, and the ultimate perfection of their bodily functions.

—*Grantly Dick-Read*

278

*O*bserve how soon, and to what a degree, a mother's influence begins to operate!

—Lydia H. Sigourney

*M*ighty is the force of motherhood! It transforms all things by its vital heat; it turns timidity into fierce courage, and dreadless defiance into tremulous submission; it turns thoughtlessness into foresight, and yet stills all anxiety into calm content; it makes selfishness become self-denial, and gives even to hard vanity the glance of admiring love.

—George Eliot

I have learned to place a high estimate upon the love of mother... The love of a true mother comes nearer being like the love of God than any other kind of love.

—Joseph F. Smith

*I*s not a young mother one of the sweetest sights which life shows us?

—William Makekpeace Thackeray

*A*nd Rachel travailed, and she had hard labour... The midwife said unto her, Fear not: thou shalt have this son also. And it came to pass, as her soul was in departing, (for she died) that she called his name Benoni; but his father called him Benjamin.

—Genesis 35:16,18

A grandmother is a person with too much wisdom to let that stop her from making a fool of herself over her grandchildren.

—Phil Moss

*W*hat I inherited from my mother is inside me. I love people too easily, as she did. But then my first memory is of love. To be able to think back, as I can...and to remember, as I do, nothing but love, overwhelming love, provides the atmosphere to one's whole life. So loved for one's self, one loves in return, easily and richly—and sometimes too often and too faithfully. For this gift of loving, I thank my beloved mother.

—Pearl S. Buck

279

Who ran to help me when I fell,
And would some pretty story tell,
Or kiss the place to make it well?
   My mother.

—Jane Taylor

I learned at that best academy—a mother's knee.

—Lowell

I had been apt enough to learn, and willing enough, when my mother and I lived alone together. I can faintly remember learning the alphabet at her knee. To this day, when I look upon the fat black letters in the primer, the puzzling novelty of their shapes, and the easy good-nature of O and Q and S, seem to present themselves again before me as they used to... I seemed to have walked along a patch of flowers...and to have been cheered by the gentleness of my mother's voice and manner all the way.

—Charles Dickens

Stories first heard at a Mother's knee are never wholly forgotten, a little spring that never dries up in our journey through scorching years.

—Ruffini

Into the woman's keeping is committed the destiny of the generations to come after us. In bringing up your children you mothers must remember that while it is essential to be loving and tender it is no less essential to be wise and firm. Foolishness and affection must not be treated as interchangeable terms; and besides training your sons and daughters in the softer and milder virtues, you must seek to give them those stern and hardy qualities when in after life they will surely need.

—Theodore Roosevelt

Mothers bear children...grandmothers enjoy them.

—Spanish Proverb

There is no such thing as a nonworking mother.

—Hester Mundis

280

*B*lessed is the mother who treats her child as she would be treated, for her home shall be filled with happiness.

—Lenora Zearfoss

*C*hildren, look in those eyes, listen to that dear voice, notice the feeling of even a single touch that is bestowed upon you by that gentle hand! Make much of it while you yet have that most precious of all good gifts, a loving mother.

—Thomas Macaulay

❦

*T*he early years of my life, which were spent in the little cabin, were not very different from those of thousands of other slaves. My mother, of course, had little time in which to give attention to the training of her children during the day. She snatched a few moments for our care in the early morning before her work began and at night after the day's work was done. One of my earliest recollections is that of my mother cooking a chicken late at night, and awakening her children for the purpose of feeding them. How or where she got it I do not know. I presume, however it was procured from our owner's farm. Some people may call this theft...but taking place at the time it did, and for the reason that it did, no one could ever make me believe my mother was guilty of thieving. She was simply a victim of the system of slavery.

—Booker T. Washington

*M*y mother was a busy woman, but all her work did not prevent her neighbors from soon recognizing her as a wise and kindly woman whom they could call upon for counsel or help in times of trouble... Wherever we resided, rich and poor came to her with their trials and found good counsel. She towered among her neighbors wherever she went.

—Andrew Carnegie

I have only the best of memories of my mother, who was a woman of great faith and determination... She was a strong woman, a tremendous inspiration to me, a person who always tried to do what was right. My mother told me I could go as far as I wanted in life if I would just work hard.

—Paula Hawkins

"*The* pain never goes away," [says a 15-year-old whose mother died when he was eleven.] He is only starting to realize it, but at each crucial passage of life—graduation, marriage, the birth of children—there will be a face missing from the picture, a kiss never received, a message of joy bottled up inside, where it turns into sorrow. His sleep will be shadowed by ghosts, and the bittersweet shock of awakening back into a world from which his mother is gone forever. If he lives to be 100, with a score of descendants, some part of him will still be the boy whose mother left for the hospital one day and never came back.

—Jerry Adler

The change from hand loom to steam loom weaving was disastrous to our family. My father did not recognize the impending revolution, and was struggling under the old system. His looms sank greatly in value, and it became necessary for that power which never failed in any emergency—my mother—to step forward and endeavor to repair the family fortune. She opened a small shop in Moodie Street and contributed to the revenues which, though slender, nevertheless at that time sufficed to keep us in comfort and "respectable,"

—Andrew Carnegie

When I was a small boy, my brother Bob and I sometimes visited our grandparents in Lynchburg, Ohio, for a few days. One night, just as Grandma had put us to bed, a terrible storm came up. A great wind shook the house. Lightning flashed and thunder rolled while the rain hurled itself in great sheets against the windowpanes. From the bed I could see the huge maple tree outside our windows lashing back and forth in the fury of the storm. I was terrified. I said to Bob, "That tree will never last this out. It's going down."

Both of us jumped out of bed and scurried downstairs to where Grandma was reading by a kerosene lamp. When we told her our fears, she bundled us up and took us out on the porch. "There's nothing to be afraid of," she said. "God is in the rain and the storm. That tree is having a good time with the wind. See how it bends? The tree doesn't fight the wind, it cooperates with it by bending back and forth. I think it will be there for a long time. Now you boys go back to bed. Remember that God is in this storm and all storms ultimately pass."

—Norman Vincent Peale

My mother taught me a small, casual thing that may seem meaningless but to me was most important: My mother taught me to walk proud and tall, "as if the world was mine." I remember that line, and I think it brought me some luck. My first important film was *The Gold of Naples*, in which I walked through the streets of Naples exactly as she had taught me. This was my first big success, according to the critics.

—Sophia Loren

It is a tragedy that generally speaking our girls are not taught the duties of motherhood... To be an ideal mother is no easy task. The procreation of children has to be undertaken with a full sense of responsibility...and she who gives intelligent, healthy and well brought up children to the country is surely rendering a service.

—Mohandas Gandhi

Where there is a mother in the house, matters speed well.

—Amos Bronson Alcott

My mom assured me that nothing except a lack of will would prevent me from reaching goals I set for myself. I took her seriously.

—Geraldine Ferraro

There is in all this cold and hollow world no fount of deep, strong, deathless love, save that within a mother's heart.

—Felicia Dorothea Hemans

My mother wanted me to be her wings, to fly as she never quite had the courage to do. I love her for that. I love that she wanted to give birth to her own wings.

—Erica Jong

An hour before my 13th birthday party, she took my favorite lemon cake out of the oven. When she came back half an hour later to put icing on, she noticed it had fallen, and not just a little.

Not to worry. She filled the crater with extra icing, found a small plastic man in the toy box, rigged up a toothpick and string, and had a theme cake, the ol' fishing hole. It was one of my most popular parties. Everyone wanted a piece of the pond.

—Sharon Scruton

[*My* mother] could hold an audience spellbound with her extraordinary ability to tell a story. Although she had only a high school education, she continued to teach herself by reading, by listening, and by participating in everything from religion to public affairs. While supervising missionary work for the National Foreign Missionary Society of the Methodist Church, she made an extended trip to the Far East and in that connection spoke to many audiences. Later when we lived in Findlay, Ohio, she was the first woman to be elected to the city school board.

—*Norman Vincent Peale*

[*Grandmother Louisa Adams was*] singularly peaceful, a vision of silver gray, an exotic, like her Sevres china; an object of deference to everyone.

—*Henry Adams*

Granny, oh, darling Granny, how little we understood of what she suffered, or how sweet she was. And besides all this, she knew a terrible secret which she carefully kept to herself the whole time [a severe internal disease]. How faithful and good Granny always was; she would never have let one of us down. Whatever it was, however naughty I had been, Granny always stuck up for me.

—*Anne Frank*

My mother was the most beautiful woman I ever saw... All I am I owe to my mother... I attribute all my success in life to the moral, intellectual, and physical education I received from her.

—*George Washington*

All that I am, my mother made me.

—*John Quincy Adams*

All that I am or hope ever to be I get from my mother. God bless her.

—*Abraham Lincoln*

Blessed is the mother who teaches respect, for she shall be respected.

—*Lenora Zearfoss*

*S*he [Mother] never lifted her voice to us in anger... She guided us by example... We were aware that she had strength beyond the energies of her small body. We believed as she did because we wanted the same kind of haven in time of storm.

—Marian Anderson

*T*here came a night when I was ill and crying both with headache and toothache and distressed because my mother did not come to me. That was because she was ill too; and what was odd was that there were several doctors in her room, and voices and comings and goings all over the house and doors shutting and opening. It seemed to last for hours. And then my father, in tears, came into my room and began to try to convey to my terrified mind things it had never conceived before...

With my mother's death all settled happiness, all that was tranquil and reliable, disappeared from my life...no more of the old security. It was sea and islands now; the great continent had sunk like Atlantis.

—C.S. Lewis

*A*nd the best bread was of my mother's own making—the best in all the land!

—Sir Henry James

*A*n ounce of Mother is worth a pound of clergy.

—Spanish Proverb

A happy birthday to you, dearest Mother, and many, many returns of the day! How good it is to think of you visiting us again. It means that you will be there to see something of my new and larger work. Whatever success comes to me seems incomplete because you are so often not at my side to be glad with me. But now you will have a chance to realize more fully into what new worlds of thought, feeling and aspiration I am entering... Your affectionate child, Helen.

—Helen Keller

*M*y mother has been to me: a gracious presence, beautiful, courageous, and compact of love, ready at any time to put herself between me and danger, and with the light that she herself possessed to drive back into the night any treacherous thing that might draw near to harm me.

—Father Andrew [Henry Ernest Hardy]

285

*M*ost mothers are instinctive philosophers.

—Harriet Beecher Stowe

*M*y mother always seemed to me a fairy princess: a radiant being, possessed of limitless riches and power. She shone for me like the evening star. I loved her dearly.

—Winston Churchill

*S*he [Mother] was quiet and shy. But she was the strongest person I ever knew.

—Lyndon B. Johnson

*M*other is the heartbeat in the home; and without her, there seems to be no heart throb. She is the pulse in the home; and when she is gone, the life current is weak. She is the light in the home; and when that light goes out, shadow falls over it. She is life in the home; and when she dies, the home seems dead.

—LeRoy Brownlow

*M*y mother used to say that a hearing of Bach's *Chaconne* always reminded her of the Sermon on the Mount, and that the introduction of the major variations represented the Beatitudes.

—Albert Spalding

*M*y mother was an angel upon earth... Her heart was the abode of heavenly purity. She had no feelings but of kindness and beneficence... She had known sorrow, but her sorrow was silent... If there is existence and retribution beyond the grave, my mother is happy.

—John Quincy Adams

I induced my mother to get hold of a book for me. How or where she got it I do not know, but in some way she procured a copy of Webster's "blue-back" spelling-book... Though she was totally ignorant, so far as mere book knowledge was concerned, she had high ambitions for her children, and a large fund of good, hard, common sense which seemed to enable her to meet and master every situation. If I have done anything in life worth attention, I feel sure that I inherited the disposition from my mother.

—Booker T. Washington

*S*he [Mother] was a discreet and virtuous woman.

—Benjamin Franklin

*T*he noblest thought my soul can claim,
The holiest words my tongue can frame,
Unworthy are to praise the name
    More sacred than all other.
An infant, when her love first came—
A man, I find it just the same;
Reverently I breathe her name.
    The blessed name of mother.

—George Griffith Fetter

*I*t is always safe to follow the religious belief that our mother taught us; there never was a mother yet who taught her child to be an infidel.

—Henry Wheeler Shaw

*D*ana Gentry of Las Vegas recently discovered the added power that music can have when we share it with others... [One of] Gentry's earliest memories is of her grandmother holding her in her arms, singing their favorite song, "True Love." Now Gentry's grandmother is in a nursing home, her mind lost to Alzheimer's disease.

One day Gentry knelt beside the woman's wheelchair and sang "their" song. "At first," Gentry says, "I noticed a glimmer of recognition on her face. Then she joined in and sang the entire song in harmony. As tears rolled down my cheeks she cried, too, as if realizing what she had accomplished. We sing our song every visit now. It turns a sad time into a happy time."

—David M. Mazie

I have never met anybody in my life, I think, who loved his mother as much as I love you. I don't believe there ever was anybody who did, quite so much, and quite in so many wonderful ways... The reason I am a poet is entirely because you wanted me to be and intended I should be, even from the very first. You brought me up in the tradition of poetry, and everything I did you encouraged. I cannot remember once in my life when you were not interested in what I was working on, or even suggested that I should put it aside for something else.

—Edna St. Vincent Millay

My mother had a slender, small body, but a large heart—a heart so large that everybody's grief and everybody's joys found welcome in it, and hospitable accommodation.

—Mark Twain

I learned in my childhood...that no love in all the world can equal the love of a true mother... I am at a loss to know how it would be possible for anyone to love her children more truly than did my mother... How could the Father love his children more than my mother loved her children?... She loved her children with all her soul. She would toil and labor and sacrifice herself day and night for the temporal comforts and blessings that she could meagerly give... There was no sacrifice of self...that was considered for a moment, when it was compared with her duty and her love to her children.

—Joseph F. Smith

The late Ida Stover Eisenhower, mother of the former President... lived to be eighty-four, [and said] that her favorite diversion was fancywork, such as crocheting and knitting. But she had been taught as a child that she must earn the right to do fancywork. Only after the cooking, laundering, cleaning, mending and gardening had been completed could she reach for her sewing basket and indulge in the pleasures of her pastime.

She raised her remarkable children according to this philosophy, too. Her boys were assigned specific chores, and only when these were satisfactorily completed did they earn the right to play baseball or football.

—Robert Peterson

As one whom his mother comforteth, so will I comfort you.

—Isaiah 66:13

Money was scarce, but Cora Millay, who had been a singer and loved literature, saw to it that her girls had wonderful books, piano and singing lessons, and pretty ribbons for their hair. "Although we sometimes did without a few of life's necessities," Edna Millay later recalled, "we rarely lacked for its luxuries."

—Elizabeth Barnett

My mother liked to sing... At night with the lights out, after she had heard our prayers, my mother would sing to James and me... She'd sing "Down by the Old Mill Stream" or some Cole Porter hit she knew from college... She would whisper with a low, wonderful laugh, smiling and bending over us to wetly kiss our cheeks, her hair down, long and black, and sweeping against my chest and chin, smelling soapy and dry. And if the moon was out it lit up the lake, and the lake light shone into the room... When she left she always kept the door slightly unlatched, the lamp from the hall framing the door in cracks of light... She always called in a whisper, "Good night, my sweet sparrows."

—Lorrie Moore

In her youth she [Mother] had learned to bind shoes in her father's business for pin-money, [and after her marriage] for the benefit of the family... This wonderful woman...earned four dollars a week by binding shoes. Midnight would often find her at work... When household cares would permit...my young brother sat on her knee threading needles and waxing thread for her, [while] she recited to him, as she had to me, the gems of Scottish minstrelsy which she seemed to have by heart, or told him tales which failed not to contain a moral.

—Andrew Carnegie

Most of all the other beautiful things in life come by twos or threes, by dozens and hundreds; plenty of roses, stars, sunsets, rainbows, brothers and sisters, aunts and cousins, but only one mother in all the wide world.

—Kate Douglas Wiggin

The shadow of my mother danced around the room to a tune that my shadow sang.

—Jamaica Kincaid

When my mother insisted that we always wear a shirt to the table, refrain from putting our elbows on the table, say please to one another, and use good manners in our treatment of each other, she remarked, "You will never be in better company than in the company you are in right now." I am most grateful for her insistence upon these things, because I married a wife who enjoys courtesy and politeness—and I am inclined to believe that most women do.

—Tim LaHaye

*M*ake it possible for healthy married women to have all the children they want; make it profitable, and one of the main causes of domestic unhappiness and social unrest will fade into thin air. Give us back the Victorian mothers of seven and ten children, and we shall again be swayed by the quiet but irresistible goodness of true motherhood.

—Grantly Dick-Read

*E*ver since I can remember, my grandmother has been a most wonderful example of fun, laughter, and warmth and above all, exquisite taste in so many things. For me she has always been one of those extra-ordinary, rare people whose touch can turn everything into gold... She belongs to that priceless brand of human beings whose greatest gift is to enhance life for others through her own effervescent enthusiasm for life.

—Prince Charles

A mother, has, perhaps, the hardest earthly lot; and yet no mother worthy of the name ever gave herself thoroughly for her child who did not feel that, after all, she reaped what she had sown.

—Henry Ward Beecher

ॐ

*T*here is a center to each home
From which all joys must start—
the center of the home? It is
A Mother's heart.

—Anonymous

*M*other's love grows by giving.

—Charles Lamb

*B*lessed is the mother who answers simply the startling questions, for she shall always be trusted.

—Lenora Zearfoss

*M*ohammed...charged his followers to "reverence the womb" that bore them.

—Edith Deen

290

[Abraham Lincoln] was born in the Kentucky wilderness, reared among the poor, drinking avidly of knowledge from a few books that he borrowed, without benefit of formal schooling... Just a lanky boy stretched out at night with a book in front of the open fire. How in the world did he ever get anywhere?... He had the ability to think and to pray and to dream. Moreover, he had a mother, one of the sweetest characters in history, Nancy Hanks.

As she did her housework, Nancy Hanks sang hymns, hymns about heaven. "There's a land that is fairer than day, And by faith we can see it afar..." But with scrubbing and toiling, she worked her youth and strength away. And in her 30s, she was seized with the milk sickness, a terrible scourge that swept across those frontier communities, and she succumbed.

Later, a wonderful stepmother came into the family. She often called her tall, ungainly, lanky son to her side and, with all her aversion to sin and crudity and poverty and lack of culture, she said to him: "Abe, be somebody." Years later, when at the Capitol in Washington he took the oath of office as President, I wonder if he did not hear out of the yesterdays the soft, sweet, yet strong voice of a pioneer mother saying, "Abe, be somebody."

—Norman Vincent Peale & Smiley Blanton

Never was a woman more richly mother than this woman. Bubbling over with a hundred little songs and scraps of gay nonsense to beguile a child from tears...yet her hands were swift to tenderness and care and quiet brooding, tending when need arose. Never was she more perfect mother than during the summers on the mountain top when she could give herself freely to her children.

She led them here and there in search of beauty and she taught them to love cliffs and rugged rocks outlined against the sky, and to love also little dells where moss grew about a pool. Beauty she brought into her house too and filled the rooms with ferns and flowers.

—Pearl S. Buck

For when you looked into my mother's eyes you knew, as if He had told you, why God had sent her into the world—it was to open the minds of all who looked, to beautiful thoughts.

—Sir James M. Barrie

*F*or several years my mother had not been in good health, but I had no idea, when I parted from her the previous day, that I should never see her alive again... In a very short time...our little home was in confusion. My sister Amanda...was too young to know anything about keeping house... Sometimes we had food cooked for us, and sometimes we did not... Our clothing went uncared for, and everything about our home was soon in a tumble-down condition. It seems to me that this was the most dismal period of my life.

—Booker T. Washington

*M*y mother has the prettiest tricks
    Of words and words and words.
Her talk comes out as smooth and sleek
    As breasts of singing birds.

God wove a web of loveliness,
    Of clouds and stars and birds,
But made not anything at all
    So beautiful as words.

They are as fair as bloom of air;
    They shine like any star,
And I am rich who learned from her
    How beautiful they are.

—Anna Hemstead Branch

*H*e had a face only a mother could love.

—Traditional

*R*icher than I
you can never be—
    I had a Mother
who read to me!

—Anonymous

*M*other—that was the bank where we deposited all our hurts and worries.

—Thomas DeWitt Talmage

The greatest man I ever met was not a man, but a woman, my mother. She was not well educated from the standpoint of formal schooling, but she had insight, understanding and wisdom, deep wisdom.

—*Dwight W. Eisenhower*

My Mother, God bless her, taught me when I was little never to carry yesterday on my back. It didn't matter what had happened—yesterday was dead. I remember her saying: "There's nothing you can do about it now. If you get in the habit of carrying yesterday around on your back, you'll be bent double by the time you're 21."

—*Danny Thomas*

Mother had one of those strong, restful, yet widely sympathetic natures, in whom all around seemed to find comfort and repose.

—*Harriet Beecher Stowe*

Now, as always, the most automated appliance in the household is a mother.

—*Beverly Jones*

No language can express the power and beauty and heroism and majesty of a mother's love. It shrinks not where man cowers, and grows stronger where man faints.

—*Edwin Hubbell Chapin*

❧

There is no love like the good old love—the love that Mother gave us.

—*Eugene Field*

When I try to recall my mother as she was at that time, nothing appears to me but her brown eyes, which always expressed love and goodness.

—*Leo Tolstoy*

All mothers are rich when they love their children. There are no poor mothers, no ugly ones, no old ones. Their love is always the most beautiful of the joys.

—*Maurice Maeterlinck*

293

*B*lessed is the mother who guides by the path of righteousness, for she shall be proud of her offspring.

—*Lenora Zearfoss*

*Y*ou wrote no lofty poems
That critics counted art,
But with a nobler vision
You lived them in your heart.

—*Thomas Fessenden*

*S*he [Mother] had the sort of ability which is rare in man and almost never found in woman—the ability to say a humorous thing with a perfect air of not knowing it to be humorous.

—*Mark Twain*

*A*ll women become like their mothers. That is their tragedy. No man does. That is his.

—*Oscar Wilde*

*W*hat are Raphael's Madonnas but the shadow of a mother's love, fixed in permanent outline forever?

—*Thomas Wentworth Higginson*

❧

*P*ride is one of the seven deadly sins; but it cannot be the pride of a mother for her children, for that is a compound of two cardinal virtues— faith and hope.

—*Charles Dickens*

*H*is sweetest dreams were still of that dear voice that soothed his infancy.

—*Robert Southey*

A mother is the truest friend we have. When friends...desert us, when troubles thicken around us, she still clings to us, and endeavors...to dissipate the clouds of darkness and cause peace to return to our hearts.

—*Washington Irving*

294

I feel that, in the Heavens above,
   The angels, whispering to one another,
Can find, among their burning terms of love,
   None so devotional as that of "Mother."

—Edgar Allan Poe

*M*y dear mother, with the truthfulness of a mother's heart, ministered to all my woes, outward and inward, and even against hope, kept prophesying good.

—Thomas Carlyle

*M*y mother had no feelings but of kindness and beneficence, yet her mind was as firm as her temper was mild and gentle.

—John Quincy Adams

*T*here is a religion in all deep love, but the love of a mother is the veil of a softer light between the heart and the heavenly Father.

—Samuel Taylor Coleridge

*N*o man is poor who has had a godly mother.

—Abraham Lincoln

*U*nhappy is the man for whom his own mother has not made all other mothers venerable.

—Jean Paul Richter

*F*or the mother is and must be, whether she knows it or not, the greatest, strongest, and most lasting teacher her children have.

—Hannah Whitall Smith

*A*ll-gracious! grant to those who bear
A mother's charge, the strength and light
   To guide the feet that own their care
In ways of Love and Truth and Right.

—William Cullen Bryant

*I*f the whole world were put into one scale, and my mother into the other, the world would kick the beam.

—Lord Langdale

295

A kiss from my mother made me a painter.

—Benjamin West

*N*ow my sister was no ordinary woman—no woman ever is, but to me, my sister less than any. When my mother died, she, my sister, had become my mother, and more mother to me than any mother could ever have been. I was immensely proud of her. I shone in the reflection of her green-eyed, black-haired, gypsy beauty. She sang at her work in a voice so pure that the local men said she had a bell in every tooth and was gifted by God.

She had eyes so hazel-green and open that, to preserve them from too much knowledge of evil, should have been hooded and, not as they were, terrible in their vulnerability. She was innocent and guileless and infinitely predictable. She was naive to the point of saintliness and wept a lot at the misery of others. She felt all tragedies except her own. I had read of the Knights of Chivalry, and I knew that I had a bounden duty to protect her above all other creatures.

—Richard Burton, Actor

*M*others are the only goddesses in whom the whole world believes.

—Anonymous

I had...[when] I entered the telegraph service, but one linen suit of summer clothing; and every Saturday night, no matter if it was my night on duty and I did not return till near midnight, my mother washed those clothes and ironed them, and I put them on fresh on Sabbath morning. There was nothing that heroine did not do in the struggle we were making for elbow room in the western world.

—Andrew Carnegie

*W*hat is home without a mother?
What are all the joys we meet,
When her loving smile no longer
Greets the coming, coming of our feet?

—Alice Hawthorne

*W*here there is a grandmother in the house, the children always have a friend.

—Swedish Saying

It was a memory that met us everywhere, for every person in town, from the highest to the lowest, seemed to have been so impressed by my mother's character and life that they constantly reflected some portion of it back on us.

—*Harriet Beecher Stowe*

I do not extol the art of motherhood without a sincere belief that it is a force of incomprehensible magnitude and worthy of the highest place among the major considerations of our time.

—*Grantly Dick-Read*

Mother and child—think of it, my friends, on Christmas day. What more beautiful sight is there in the world? That man must be very far from the kingdom of God whose heart has not been touched by the sight of his first child in its mother's bosom.

—*Walter Kingsley*

[*Mother*] was a great talker, but a significant thing about her was that she said something when she talked... She had a fascinating personality. I used to go home to Ohio occasionally and usually managed to get there for breakfast, for that was one meal my mother believed in... These reunions were a glorious time.

—*Norman Vincent Peale*

Any mother could perform the jobs of several air-traffic controllers with ease.

—*Lisa Alther*

The bravest battle that ever was fought;
Shall I tell you where and when?
On the maps of the world you'll find it not.
It was fought by the mothers of men.

—*Joaquin Miller*

My mother was the source from which I derived the guiding principles of my life.

—*John Wesley*

297

$\mathcal{F}$or me, a line from mother is more efficacious than all the homilies preached in Lent.

—*Henry Wadsworth Longfellow*

$\mathcal{W}$hen Neil A. Armstrong first set foot on the moon, and the heavens became a part of man's world, his mother, Mrs. Viola Armstrong, rose forth...as she spoke to the waiting world, "Praise God from whom all blessings flow."

—*Edith Deen*

$\mathcal{I}$ did not have my mother very long, but in that length of time she cast over me an influence which has lasted all my life... If it had not been for her appreciation and faith in me at a critical time in my experience, I should very likely never have became an inventor.

—*Thomas Edison*

$\mathcal{T}$he greatest difference which I find between my mother and the rest of the people whom I have known is this...while others felt a strong interest in a few things, she felt a strong interest in the whole world and everything and everybody in it.

—*Mark Twain*

$\mathcal{M}$aternity! ecstatic sound! so twined round our heart, that it must cease to throb ere we forget it. It is our first love, it is part of our religion.

—*The Ladies Museum*

ॐ

$\mathcal{T}$here is an enduring tenderness in the love of a mother to a son that transcends all other affections of the heart. It is neither to be chilled by selfishness, nor daunted by danger, nor weakened by worthlessness, nor stifled by ingratitude. She will sacrifice every comfort for his convenience; she will surrender every pleasure to his enjoyment; she will glory in his fame, and exalt in his prosperity; and if adversity overtake him, he will be the dearer to her by misfortune; and if disgrace settle upon his name, she will still love and cherish him; and if all the world beside cast him off, she will be all the world to him.

—*Washington Irving*

298

*W*e search the world for truth; we cull
The good, the pure, the beautiful,
From graven stone and written scroll,
From all old flower-fields of the soul;
And, weary seekers of the best,
We come back laden from our quest,
To find that all the sages said
Is in the Book our mothers read.

—John Greenleaf Whittier

*I*f it had not been for my mother's conviction and determination that music was my destiny, it is quite conceivable that I would have become a carpenter.

—Pablo Casals

*M*y mother was as mild as any saint, and nearly canonized by all she knew, so gracious was her tact and tenderness.

—Alfred, Lord Tennyson

[*G*randmother was] a person possessed of more literature than was common in persons of her sex and station, a diligent reader and a most exemplary woman in all the relations of life.

—John Quincy Adams

*S*he worried whenever he rode "that dumb motorcycle." A ten minute ride to the supermarket and she was a bundle of nerves. So, when John Drimmer announced his plans for a cross-country trip to Seattle and back, he expected some resistance from his mother. Surprisingly, though, she just smiled and gave her blessings, calling the journey a valuable life experience. After nine days on the road John stopped at a gift shop for a Mother's Day present, something special that would express his appreciation for her love, understanding, and abilities as an actress.

—An Advertisement

*D*o you know that if Mother were alive I should feel so much safer. I have always thought her prayers had much to do with my success.

—Grover Cleveland

As I approached the door about nine o'clock in the evening, I heard my mother engaged in prayer. During the prayer she referred to me, her son away, God only knew where, and asked that he might be preserved in health to return to her and comfort her in her old age. At the conclusion of the prayer I quietly raised the latch and entered. I will not attempt to describe the scene which followed.

—*James A. Garfield*

The faith of my mother is beautiful. I suppose some might say it is old-fashioned, Well, if it is, we should have more of it. For her faith sustains her and gives her spiritual courage and goodness of heart... It has seen her through many stormy seas, sickness in the family, death, trials and troubles of all kinds. Through them all she has always emerged with all flags flying... And the beautiful thing is she thinks she is so ordinary.

—*Rawley Meyers*

ॐ

All progress, both moral and physical, ultimately depends upon the perfection of motherhood.

—*Grantly Dick-Read*

Dr. Raj Chopra [was] born in India [and] at the age of ten he lost his father to cancer. A few months later he witnessed the fighting between Moslems and Hindus that resulted in the murder of his Mother's parents and the slaughter of thousands of natives.

In the turmoil Raj hid with his mother and siblings until they were taken to a refugee camp. There he started raising goats to provide food for his family. He would probably be one of India's hapless millions today if he had not had a devout grandmother.

After searching for months, Raj's paternal grandmother found the family. She told the boy: "You have a greater purpose in life, Raj, than tending goats. You are somebody. You are going to get an education. God has a special plan for you."

—*Norman Vincent Peale*

There seems to be an age-old, life-long link between the virtues of men and their love for their mothers.

—*William J. Bennett*

I suppose she would have considered her life a failure if she had judged it by the measure of what she had meant it to be... But if she judged her life fallen short, to us, among whom she lived, what a life it was! I do not think one of us would have called her a saintly woman. She was far too practical, far too vivid and passionate, too full of humor and change of temper for that. She was the most human person we have ever known, the most complex in her swift compassion, in her gusts of merriment and in her utter impatiences; she was the best friend and companion to us.

—Pearl S. Buck

It may be a time-worn cottage,
Standing back among the trees;
And its window panes may rattle
In the searching autumn breeze;
Or it may be more a mansion,
Built of marble, firm and grand;
And its beauties may be many,
Stretching out on every hand.
But what e'er be its construction,
In our heart deep feeling swells,
When we single out the "home nest"—
The place where Mother dwells.

—Sarah E. Milton

They came and told her [Sarah Bush Lincoln, that her step-son was dead]. The newspapers wrote the longest pieces about his real mother, and that was like it should be, but some folks came and asked her what sort of boy Abe had been... "Abe was a good boy," she said. "He never gave me a cross word or look. His mind and mine...seemed to run together." And then she added, "He loved me truly, I think."

Often, during the four years that remained to her, she would sit of an evening and think of Abe. Being a mother, she did not think about him as President, as the man about whom they sang... She remembered him as a little boy. She was baking johnny-cake for him; she was weaving him a shirt; she was covering him with a blanket when he had fallen asleep over his books, trying to keep him safe from the cold.

—Bernadine Bailey & Dorothy Walworth

301

I thank God for my mother as for no other gift of His bestowing.

—Williard

*M*en are what their mothers made them.

—Ralph Waldo Emerson

A mother is not a person to lean on, but a person to make leaning unnecessary.

—Dorothy Canfield Fisher

*H*ad she [Mother, Abigail Adams] lived in the age of the Patriarchs, every day of her life would have been filled with clouds of goodness and love. There is not a virtue that could abide in the female heart but it was the ornament of hers. She had been fifty-four years the delight of my father's heart, the sweetener of all his toils, the comforter of all his sorrows, the sharer and brightener of all his joys.

—John Quincy Adams

*M*y dear Mother... Last Sunday was Mother's Day in America... The custom is a beautiful one, but is in danger from the American evil of commercializing even the sacred festivals... I felt during the day how much I owed MY mother, and although I was 5,000 miles away from you, your influence, your faith in me, and your hopes in me were and are always near and real to me. You have planted well, and the seed which you have planted is bearing fruit.

I esteem your pride in me more precious than all the honours I have received since coming here. When I come home, and you hear me preach, your "well done" will be sweeter music than the platitudes I hear continuously...

So I send you not gifts, but appreciations that must be taken for granted, until I can show you by my presence and my life that I mean what I say. You have given me memories that are precious. You have furnished me with the background upon which I am trying to paint the picture you have dreamed of. Anything accomplished by me is not the result of my own efforts, but the result of your prayers and your dreams for my success—not in material things, but in the things that count, that are eternal... Your affectionate son, Peter.

—Peter Marshall

302

I should have been a French atheist if it had not been for one recollection, and that was that my departed mother used to take my little hand in hers, and cause me, on my knees, to say, "Our Father which art in heaven."

—*John Randolph*

*T*he person I really admire is my grandma—I call her Mamo. She raised seven children of her own, 26 foster boys, helped raise many of her 26 grandchildren, and now has nine great-grandchildren. Mamo was never famous, eloquent, graceful, or artistic, yet she has touched many lives with her fortitude, perseverance, patience, and unselfish love. That is why I admire Mamo more than anyone else in the world.

—*Reader, Goodhousekeeping Poll*

*Y*outh fades; love droops; the leaves of friendship fall;
A mother's secret hope outlives them all!

—*Oliver Wendell Holmes*

*B*eing a successful mother-in-law is one of the most difficult tasks in the world... Mothers-in-law have been unhonored almost since the start of time. "Whistler's Mother" is a famous painting...but what artist has ever painted a portrait of his mother-in-law? Hundreds of songs about "Mother" have been written...but what composer has written a song about his mother-in-law? Name one sonnet written by a poet about a mother-in-law...

It must have started centuries ago... Mothers-in-law became stereotyped as nagging, meddlesome, bossy, possessive old women. It's simply not true... For every mother-in-law who nags and meddles, there are 100 kindly women who refuse to take sides, who have nothing but the greatest respect and admiration for the men their daughters marry, and for the women who marry their sons.

—*Dan Valentine*

*T*he outstanding impression my mother has left on my memory is that of saintliness. She was deeply religious. She would not think of taking her meals without her daily prayers... She would take the hardest vows and keep them without flinching. Illness was no excuse for relaxing them.

—*Mohandas Gandhi*

303

*Backward, turn backward,
O time, in your flight!
Make me a child again, just for tonight!
Mother, come back from the echoless shore,
Take me again to your heart as of yore—
Kiss from my forehead the furrows of care,
Smooth the few silver threads out of my hair—
Over my slumbers your loving watch keep—
Rock me to sleep, Mother—rock me to sleep!*

—Elizabeth Akers Allen

*S*he inherited from her mother the dignity, refinement, and air of the cultivated lady. Perhaps some day I may be able to tell the world something of this heroine, but I doubt it. None could ever really know her—I alone did that. After my father's early death she was all my own. The dedication of my first book tells the story. It was: "To my favorite Heroine, My Mother."

—Andrew Carnegie

*O*ne day in our village I saw a vicious devil of a Corsican...chasing his grown daughter past cautious male citizens with a heavy rope in his hand and declaring he would wear it out on her. My mother spread her door wide to the refugee and then, instead of closing and locking it after her, stood in it and stretched her arms across it, barring the way. The man swore, cursed, threatened her with his rope, but she did not flinch or show any sign of fear; she only stood straight and fine and lashed him, shamed him, derided him, defied him in tones not audible to the middle of the street but audible to the man's conscience and dormant manhood; and he asked her pardon and gave her his rope and said with a most great and blasphemous oath that she was the bravest woman he ever saw; and so he went his way without another word and troubled her no more. He and she were always good friends after that, for in her he had found a long-felt want—somebody who was not afraid of him.

—Mark Twain

*T*he great painters of the past have searched for the reality of beauty, and have chosen to represent it in motherhood.

—Grantly Dick-Read

[*President* James A. Garfield] became the victim of the assassin's bullet. During the long, weary weeks of suffering, he wrote but one letter and that was to his mother... "I must write Mother," he said; and calling for pen and ink he wrote to her the only letter he penned after the assassin struck him down.

—LeRoy Brownlow

I actually think they ought to pin medals on people like my mother. They don't get their names in headlines for heroic deeds—all they do is just hold our whole society together, that's all. It is the large number of people of her character and upright code of conduct who have made our nation great.

—Rawley Meyers

M is for the million things she gave me,
O means only that she's growing old,
T is for the tears she shed to save me,
H is for her heart of purest gold;
E is for her eyes, with love-light shining,
R means right, and right she'll always be.
Put them all together; they spell MOTHER,
A word that means the world to me.

—Howard Johnson

When a mother tree is logged, blown over, or destroyed by fire—when, in other words, she dies—the trauma stimulates the burl's growth hormones. The seeds release, and trees sprout around her, creating the circle of daughters. The daughter trees grow by absorbing the sunlight their mother cedes to them when she dies. And they get the moisture and nutrients they need from their mother's root system, which remains intact underground even after her leaves die. Although the daughters exist independently of their mother above ground, they continue to draw sustenance from her underneath... [My mother] lives on beneath everything I do. Her presence influenced who I was, and her absence influences who I am.

—Hope Edelman

305

A mother's love!
If there be one thing pure,
Where all beside is sullied,
That can endure,
When all else passes away;
If there be aught
Surpassing human deed or word, or thought,
It is a mother's love.

—*Marchioness d' Spadara*

č

*M*otherhood is, after all, woman's great and incomparable work.

—*Edward Carpenter*

*W*ho is it that loves me and will love me forever with an affection which no chance, no misery, no crime of mine can do away? My dear mother.

—*Thomas Carlyle*

*I*n all times and places, the dearest thing is the tear of mother love.

—*William J. Bennett*

č

*S*he [Grandmother Ida Palmer Nielson] stood erect in the middle of the room, ninety years old and straight as an arrow. I stepped back to look at her... There, in all her unassumed glory, stood my gracious grandma. She wore comfortable looking sneakers, a loose blouse, navy blue trousers and a cloudy blue knitted sweater. Her glittering eyes studied me at the same time. I wondered why it had taken so long to get back here...

It was after midnight. Grandma's stories had held me captive for hours. She had shared them in tones that lacked regret, lacked complaint or remorse. I wondered, in that tired hour, if I had ever heard Grandma complain, or speak spitefully, or say any unkind thing. I could think of no such instance.

—*Lyman Hafen*

$\mathcal{I}$d often find her crying at home or at work... My mother told me that one of my brothers died of intoxication [forced to work where coffee plants were being sprayed]. I saw another of them die of hunger, of starvation... I saw her sweat and work but she never complained.

—*Rigoberta Menchú*

$\mathcal{I}$t is time that we recognize motherhood as our most vital—and one of our most highly skilled professions, and exalt it as such.

—*Dr. Marynia F. Farnham*

❦

$\mathcal{S}$itting alone in an old rockin' chair,
I saw an old mother with silvery hair.
She seemed so neglected by those who should care,
Rockin' alone in an old rockin'chair.

Her hands were calloused and wrinkled and old,
A life of hard work was the story they told,
And I thought of angels as I saw her there,
Rockin' alone in an old rockin' chair...

I look at her and I think what a shame,
The ones who forgot her she loves just the same,
And I think of angels as I see her there,
Rockin' alone in an old rockin' chair.

—*Bob Miller*

$\mathcal{I}$f I were damned of body and soul,
I know whose prayers would make me whole,
    Mother o' mine.

—*Rudyard Kipling*

$\mathcal{I}$love to think her like a blessed candle
    Burning through life's long night,
Quietly useful, simple, gentle, tender,
    And always giving light.

—*Lee Shippey*

*There's a spot in my heart which no Colleen may own,
There's a depth in my heart never sounded or known:
There's a place in my mem'ry, my life, that you fill,
No other can take it, no one ever will...

Sure, I love the dear silver that shines in your hair,
And the brow that's all furrowed and wrinkled with care.
I kiss the dear fingers, so toil-worn for me,
Oh, God bless you and keep you, Mother Machree!*

—*Ernest R. Ball*

&

We buried her physical body in a little country cemetery in southern Ohio. My heart was very heavy that day. It was in the summertime, and when autumn came, I wanted to be with my mother again. I was on the train all night and kept telling myself that it would never be as it used to be. I arrived at that little town on a cold, overcast autumn day and walked to the cemetery. The fallen leaves rustled as I walked. I sat by her grave, very lonely, feeling very small and sad.

Then, quite suddenly, the clouds parted and the sun came through... Sitting there, I seemed to "hear" her voice. It was as if she said, "Why seek ye the living among the dead? I am not here." ...Suddenly I was happy inside, and I knew the truth—she was alive... I got up, put my hand on the tombstone, and saw it for what it was—only a place where lie the mortal remains of a body that was dear, like a coat that had been laid aside when the wearer no longer needed it. I walked out of that place and have been back in it only once since.

—*Norman Vincent Peale*

&

*A mother is a mother still,
The holiest thing alive.*

—*Samuel Taylor Coleridge*

A good grandmother can cure most of a family's ills.

—*Chinese Proverb*

[*K*night's toast to his mother:]
"I drink to one," he said,
"Whose image never may depart,
Deep graven on this grateful heart,
Till memory be dead.
To one whose love for me shall last
When lighter passions long have passed,
So holy 'tis, and true."

—Anonymous

&

*I*n my library there are thirty-seven volumes, each leather bound and stamped in gold, "Mother's Letters. From 1915 to 1941." These manuscripts of indescribable beauty are not to an only son, for I was number six of seven children born in nine years. Schooldays and Cambridge, the London Hospital, the Great War, are recalled and reviewed in terms of sympathy and understanding, admonition and advice. Betrothal, marriage and parenthood are discussed... Year after year this fount of mother love has poured its influence into my life and still, at eighty-six, this grand old lady fills me with pride when I read her views on things of today, written in the light of long years of quiet observation and deduction.

—Grantly Dick-Read

*W*hereas the service rendered the United States by the American mother is the greatest source of the country's strength and admiration...we declare that the second Sunday of May will henceforth be celebrated as Mother's Day.

—Congressional Resolution, 1914

*W*hen the wayward child is overcome by temptation, strays from the pathway of right, sinfully wanders into the gutter and is left there to die unnoticed and unaided by a cruel and heartless world, you may be sure that if his mother is living he still has a friend. That dear old mother will come and gather him up into her feeble arms and carry him home and tell him of all his virtues until he almost forgets that his soul was ever disfigured by vice.

—LeRoy Brownlow

309

*O*men, respect women who have borne you.

—*The Koran*

*O*nly once she mentioned her death... "Child, if I should seem afraid at the end, it will be only because this old body takes advantage of me for the moment..."

There were no last words or any sign. She died in her sleep, and at the moment of passing her face lit up with a great smile, and then fell into great gravity. But none of us knew the meaning of that smile. It was as though she simply withdrew from us all and went on alone, leaving us only her life to remember, a vivid, full, bitter-sweet life. We dressed her in the lavender silk gown she loved and put about her the silver grey and pale gold chrysanthemums of autumn. It was on an autumn day we buried her, a windy, misty day under a grey sky. The brave words of the song she had told us to sing over her went out like the challenge of all human life in its desperate cry against inevitable death everywhere around. Thus ended all of her life that we can know.

—*Pearl S. Buck*

*E*ven He that died for us upon the cross, in the last hour, in the unutterable agony of death, was mindful of His mother, as if to teach us that this holy love would be our last worldly thought—the last point of earth from which the soul should take its flight for heaven.

—*Henry Wadsworth Longfellow*

Words of Women

Chapter Eight
Words of Women

*A*nd Mary said, My soul doth magnify the Lord, and my spirit hath rejoiced in God my Saviour. For he hath regarded the low estate of his handmaiden: for, behold, from henceforth all generations shall call me blessed.

—Luke 1:46-48

*T*he world is sown with good; but unless I turn my glad thoughts into practical living and till my own field, I cannot reap a kernel of the good.

—Helen Keller

*B*e true in all words and actions; and unnecessarily deliver not your opinion, but when you do, let it be just, and considered, and plain.

—Ann Fanshawe

I am never resigned to any condition that is wrong anywhere. I will not be resigned so long as I live to anything unjust and unequal between human beings. But I dare not go about righting that wrong unless I feel my own spirit is simple and kind and free from bitterness and hatred even against the unjust. I will remember that often, perhaps always, the unjust man is the ignorant man, and I will not blame him for ignorance—I will try to inform him. Or he may be the man who has suffered some wrong himself and suffering has turned bitter in him. I will try to look beyond the individual in any case, and myself hold no bitterness.

—Pearl S. Buck

*T*hese are the times in which a genius would wish to live. It is not in the still calm of life or the repose of a pacific station, that great characters are formed... The habits of a vigorous mind are formed in contending with difficulties... Great necessities call out great virtues.

—Abigail Adams

*T*ell her that the lesson taught her far outweighs the pain.

—Adelaide Proctor

315

*A*ction that is clearly right needs no justification.

—Elisabeth Elliot

*I*f I can stop one heart from breaking,
I shall not live in vain;
If I can ease one life the aching,
Or cool one pain,
Or help one fainting robin
Unto his nest again,
I shall not live in vain.

—Emily Dickinson

I see heaven's glories shine, and faith shines equal, arming me from fear.

—Emily Bronte

*B*e faithful in little things, for in them our strength lies. To the good God nothing is little, because He is so great and we so small.

—Mother Teresa

*M*an has no nobler function than to defend the truth.

—Ruth McKenney

O God, give me the grace to be ever the lover and herald of truth, and for this truth I shall gladly give my life.

—Catherine of Siena

*A*ny coward can fight a battle when he's sure of winning; but give me the man, who has pluck to fight when he's sure of losing. That's my way, sir; and there are many victories worse than a defeat.

—George Eliot

*N*othing strengthens the judgment and quickens the conscience like individual responsibility.

—Elizabeth Cady Stanton

316

*F*aith in small things has repercussions that ripple all the way out. In a huge, dark room a little match can light up the place.

—*Joni Eareckson Tada*

*F*aith is for that which lies on the other side of reason. Faith is what makes life bearable, with all its tragedies and sudden, startling joys.

—*Madeleine L'Engle*

*Y*ou may have to fight a battle more than once to win it.

—*Margaret Thatcher*

*L*ife is the first gift, love is the second, and understanding the third.

—*Marge Pier*

*W*e are weaving the future on the loom of today.

—*Grace Dawson*

*G*oals are dreams with deadlines.

—*Diana Scharif*

*W*ere there no God, we would be in this glorious world with grateful hearts and no one to thank.

—*Christina Rossetti*

I used to pray that God would do this or that; now I pray that God will make His will known to me.

—*Madame Chiang Kai-Shek*

*D*on't confuse fame with success. Madonna is one; Helen Keller is the other.

—*Erma Bombeck*

*E*very fallen woman represents a man as guilty as herself, who escapes human detection, but whose soul lies open before God.

—*Julia Ward Howe*

Happiness is not a state to arrive at, but a manner of traveling.

—*Margaret Lee Runbeck*

Hold fast your dreams!
Within your heart
Keep one, still, secret spot
Where dreams may go,
And sheltered so,
May thrive and grow.

—*Louise Driscoll*

Some things...arrive in their own mysterious hour, on their own terms and not yours, to be seized or relinquished forever.

—*Gail Godwin*

Treat your friends as you do your pictures, and place them in their best light.

—*Jennie Jerome Churchill*

I would rather walk in the dark with God than go alone in the light.

—*Mary Gardiner Brainard*

The trouble with being in the rat race is that even if you win, you're still a rat.

—*Lily Tomlin*

You have to count on living every single day in a way you believe will make you feel good about your life—so that if it were over tomorrow, you'd be content with yourself.

—*Jane Seymour*

Pain nourishes courage. You can't be brave if you've only had wonderful things happen to you.

—*Mary Tyler Moore*

The man who treasures his friends is usually solid gold himself.

—*Marjorie Holmes*

318

Opinion is a flitting thing,
But Truth, outlasts the Sun—
If then we cannot own them both—
Possess the oldest one.

—Emily Dickinson

All serious daring starts from within.

—Eudora Welty

Laziness may appear attractive, but work gives satisfaction.

—Anne Frank

Red Cross founder Clara Barton made it a policy to never hold a grudge. When asked if she remembered a particular wrong that had been done her, Clara said, "No, I distinctly remember forgetting that."

—Timepeace Daily Calendar

I had early to accept the fact that there are persons, both men and women, who are incurably and willfully cruel and wicked. But, forced to this recognition, I retaliated spiritually by making the fierce resolution that wherever I saw evil and cruelty at work I would devote all I had to delivering its victims. This resolution has stayed with me throughout my life and it has not always been easy to follow, for I am not an aggressive person by nature.

—Pearl S. Buck

My heart was bursting with the anguish excited by the cruelty and injustice our nation was showing to the slave, and praying God to let me do a little, and to cause my cry for them to be heard. Weeping many a time as I thought of the slave mothers whose babes were torn from them, I put my lifeblood, my prayers, my tears into the book [*Uncle Tom's Cabin*].

—Harriet Beecher Stowe

Hope is the feeling you have that the feeling you have isn't permanent.

—Jean Kerr

Reach high, for stars lie hidden in your soul.
Dream deep, for every dream precedes the goal.

—Pamela Vaull Starr

Trust in God and *do* something.

—Mary Lyon

Optimist—one who makes the most of all that comes and the least of all that goes.

—Sara Teasdale

The best remedy for a short temper is a long walk.

—Jacqueline Schiff

I expect some new phases of life this summer and shall try to get some honey from each moment.

—Lucy Stone

Few wishes come true by themselves.

—June Smith

A bad habit never disappears miraculously; it's an undo-it-yourself project.

—Abigail Van Buren

If I didn't start painting, I would have raised chickens.

—Anna Mary Robertson [Grandma] Moses

Concern should drive us into action and not into depression.

—Karen Horney

Love beauty; it is the shadow of God on the universe.

—Gabriela Mistral

Yesterday I dared to struggle.
Today I dare to win.

—Bernadette Devlin

I need thee every hour,
Most gracious Lord.
No tender voice like thine
Can peace afford.

I need thee every hour;
Stay thou near-by.
Temptations lose their pow'r
When thou art nigh.

I need thee every hour,
In joy or pain.
Come quickly and abide,
Or life is vain.

I need thee every hour,
Most holy One.
Oh, make me thine indeed,
Thou blessed Son!

I need thee, oh, I need thee;
Every hour I need thee!
Oh, bless me now, my Savior;
I come to thee!

—Annie S. Hawkes

When in doubt listen.

—Lucretia Mott

Identity is not found... Identity is built.

—Margaret Halsey

Freedom breeds freedom; nothing else does.

—Anne Roe

Love your enemy, it will drive him nuts.

—Eleanor Doan

[*On* her eightieth birthday:] Keep breathing.

—*Sophie Tucker*

We never know how high we are
Till we are asked to rise
And then if we are true to plan
Our statures touch the skies—

—*Emily Dickinson*

Nothing contributes so much to tranquilize the mind as a steady purpose.

—*Mary Wallstonecroft*

Blessed is the influence of one true, loving soul on another.

—*George Eliot*

I believe that science has great beauty. A scientist in his laboratory is not a mere technician; he is also a child confronting natural phenomena that impress him as though they were fairy tales.

—*Marie Curie*

The little cares that fretted me,
    I lost them yesterday
Among the fields above the sea,
    Among the winds at play;
Among the lowing of the herds,
    The rustling of the trees,
The singing of the birds,
    The humming of the bees.

—*Elizabeth Barrett Browning*

Done is better than perfect.

—*Anne Mollegen Smith*

Remember, age is not important unless you are a cheese.

—*Helen Hayes*

There is a fountain of youth: it is your mind, your talents, the creativity you bring to your life and the lives of people you love.

—*Sophia Loren*

Always be smarter than the people who hire you.

—*Lena Horne*

❦

Ever since light and intelligence began to dawn within my being, I had a love of knowledge... There was a hunger in my soul that never seemed appeased... It seems to me a strange class of circumstances that finally determined my going to attend Woman's Medical College of Pennsylvania, and I feel that it was only though the divine interposition of Providence that I was enabled ever to bring myself to pass through the ordeal [leaving her own little ones behind, sleeping as a guard in the anteroom of a hall of cadavers, teaching sewing to pay her way, and giving birth to a baby only the day after passing her examinations with honors].

—*Dr. Ellis R. Shipp*

If I had my life to live over...I would start barefoot earlier in the spring and stay that way later in the fall. I would go to more dances. I would ride more merry-go-rounds. I would pick more daisies.

—*Nadine Stair*

There is something to be said for losing one's possessions after nothing can be done about it. I had loved my Nanking home and the little treasures it had contained. Well, that was over. Nothing was ever as valuable to me again, nothing, that is, in the way of place or beloved objects, for I knew now that anything material can be destroyed. On the other hand, people were more than ever important and human relationships more valuable.

—*Pearl S. Buck*

We live in the present, we dream in the future, and we learn eternal truths from the past.

—*Madame Chiang Kai-shek*

*N*ever mistake knowledge for wisdom. One helps you make a living; the other helps you make a life.

—*Sandra Carey*

*O*n every level of life from housework to heights of prayer, in all judgment and all efforts to get things done, hurry and impatience are sure marks of the amateur.

—*Evelyn Underhill*

*R*ose-colored glasses are never made in bifocals. Nobody wants to read the small print in dreams.

—*Ann Landers*

*N*o witchcraft, no enemy action had silenced the rebirth of life in this stricken world. The people had done it themselves.

—*Rachel Carson*

❦

*T*he only people with whom you should try to get even are the ones who have helped you.

—*Mae Maloo*

*S*ee into life—don't just look at it.

—*Anne Baxter*

*N*o one can make you feel inferior without your consent.

—*Eleanor Roosevelt*

*I*n making dinner for a friend, don't forget the love.

—*Jeanne Moreau*

*K*ind words can be short and easy to speak, but their echoes are truly endless.

—*Mother Teresa*

*N*ever be afraid to trust an unknown future to a known God.

—*Corrie ten Boom*

*W*ork! Thank God for the swing of it, for the clamoring, hammering ring of it.

—Angela Morgan

*I*f a door slams shut it means that God is pointing to an open door further on down.

—Anna Delaney Peale

❧

*T*he world stands out on either side
No wider than the heart is wide;
Above the world is stretched the sky—
No higher than the soul is high.
The heart can push the sea and land
Farther away on either hand;
The soul can split the sky in two,
And let the face of God shine through.

—Edna St. Vincent Millay

❧

*P*rayer begins where human capacity ends.

—Marian Anderson

*T*here are three answers to prayer: yes, no, and wait awhile. It must be recognized that no is an answer.

—Ruth Stafford Peale

[*W*hen paralyzed] I told the doctors that God was my partner and I believed he would help me walk again.

—Jane Withers

*E*very day give yourself a good mental shampoo.

—Sara Jordan

*A*ll in the end is harvest.

—Edith Sitwell

325

Since it has pleased Providence to place me in this station, I shall do my utmost to fulfill my duty towards my country. I am young, and perhaps in many, though not all things, inexperienced, but I am sure that very few have more real good will and more real desire to do what is fit and right than I have.

—*Queen Victoria*

❧

Tis God gives skill, but not without men's hands. He could not make Antonio Stradivari's violins without Antonio.

—*George Eliot*

If suffering alone taught, all the world would be wise.

—*Anne Morrow Lindbergh*

❧

I'm Nobody! Who are you?
Are you—Nobody—Too?
Then there's a pair of us?
Don't tell! they'd advertise—you know!

—*Emily Dickinson*

❧

Why do grownups quarrel so easily, so much, and over the most idiotic things? Up till now I thought that only children squabbled and that that wore off as you grew up. Of course, there is sometimes a real reason for a quarrel, but this is just plain bickering.

—*Anne Frank*

❧

We pull ourselves together when we need to. We do the things that have to be done. But we need to give ourselves times and places in which to mourn. This is strength, not weakness.

—*Madeleine L'Engle*

Who has seen the wind?
    Neither I nor you:
But when the leaves hang trembling,
    The wind is passing through.

Who has seen the wind?
    Neither you nor I:
But when the trees bow down their heads,
    The wind is passing by.

—*Christina Rossetti*

When God invites a soul to follow him in the heights of love, and that soul acquiesces, it does not become transformed in an instant from a human being, with all its frailties and passions of the flesh, into an angel of perfection. On the contrary, it sometimes begins to encounter staggering difficulties and temptations. To reach the glory of a resurrection which brings a delightful foretaste, even in this world, of the eternal heaven, the soul must know hunger and want, neglect and misunderstanding, the sorrow and loneliness of a Gethsemane even God seems to have forsaken, and a more or less protracted crucifixion of fleshly desires, ambitions and vanities.

—*St. Teresa of Avila*

If the radio's slim fingers
Can pluck a melody from night
And toss it over continent and sea;
If the petaled white notes of a violin
Are blown across the mountains of
        the city's din;
If songs, like crimson roses, are
        culled from thin blue air—
Why should mortals wonder if God
        hears prayer?

—*Ethel Romig Fuller*

No life is so hard but you can't make it easier by the way you take it.
—*Ellen Glasgow*

$\mathcal{G}$od spoke to me and called me to His service.

—Florence Nightingale

$\mathcal{I}$f you have knowledge, let others light their candles at it.

—Margaret Fuller

$\mathcal{T}$he best and most beautiful things in the world cannot be seen or even touched. They must be felt with the heart.

—Helen Keller

$\mathcal{T}$here is happiness in living, learning, studying, working and loving—doing the best I can in my own small orbit.

—Kate Smith

$\mathcal{M}$ine eyes have seen the glory of the coming of the
    Lord:
He is trampling out the vintage where the grapes of
    wrath are stored;
He hath loosed the faithful lightning of his terrible
    swift sword:
His truth is marching on...

He has sounded forth the trumpet that shall never call
    retreat;
He is sifting out the hearts of men before his
    judgment-seat:
O, be swift, my soul, to answer him! be jubilant, my
    feet!
Our God is marching on.

In the beauty of the lilies Christ was born across the
    sea,
With a glory in his bosom that transfigures you and
    me;
As he died to make men holy, let us die to make men free,
  While God is marching on.

—Julia Ward Howe

*D*on't be scared to fight for your rights; George Washington wasn't, and even the British like him now.

—Ethel Merman

*H*onor must hope always; for no real evil can befall the virtuous, either in this life or in the next.

—Jane Porter

*H*e who loves best his fellow man
Is loving God the holiest way he can.

—Alice Cary

*H*e who never ate his bread in tears and who never sat weeping on his bed during nights of sorrow, does not know the powers of heaven.

—Queen Louise

I only need to see my path for this one day.

—Mary Frances Butts

*A*ll those who journey soon or late
Must pass within the garden's gate;
Must kneel alone in darkness there
And battle; with some fierce despair.
God pity those who cannot say:
"Not mine, but Thine;" who only pray
"Let this cup pass," and cannot see
The purpose in Gethsemane.

—Ella Wheeler Wilcox

*H*ope is the thing with feathers
That perches in the soul,
And sings the tune without words,
And never stops at all.

—Emily Dickinson

*P*raise loudly; blame softly.

—Catherine II

$\mathcal{W}$hen you get into a tight place, and everything goes against you and it seems as if you couldn't hold on a minute longer, never give up then, for that is just the place and time the tide will turn.

—*Harriet Beecher Stowe*

$\mathcal{E}$ndurance of inescapable sorrow one must learn alone. And only to endure is not enough. Endurance can be harsh and bitter. There must be acceptance, the knowledge that sorrow fully accepted brings its own gifts. For there is an alchemy in sorrow. It can be transmuted into wisdom, which can bring happiness.

—*Pearl S. Buck*

$\mathcal{W}$e hand folks over to God's mercy and show none ourselves.

—*George Eliot*

$\mathcal{A}$ poor man served by thee shall make thee rich.

—*Elizabeth Barrett Browning*

$\mathcal{L}$ook at a day when you are supremely satisfied at the end. It's not a day when you lounge around doing nothing. It's when you've had everything to do, and you've done it.

—*Margaret Thatcher*

$\mathcal{L}$ife is sad
Because we never know
That what we have
Is what we'll be loving so
When it's gone.

—*Freda Carrigean*

$\mathcal{N}$othing is hopeless that is right.

—*Susan B. Anthony*

$\mathcal{T}$he future belongs to those who believe in the beauty of their dreams.

—*Eleanor Roosevelt*

$\mathcal{T}$he less you talk, the more you're listened to.

—*Abigail Van Buren*

If a man amounts to much in this world, he must encounter many and varied annoyances whose number mounts as his effectiveness increases.

—Grace Coolidge

It would be impossible [to accept money for the discovery of radium]. It would be contrary to the scientific spirit. Besides radium is going to be used in treating disease, and it would be impossible to take advantage of that.

—Marie Curie

You only really get to know people when you've had a jolly good row with them. Then and then only can you judge their true characters!

—Anne Frank

Here a star, and there a star,
Some lose their way.
Here a mist, and there a mist:
Afterwards—day!

—Emily Dickinson

I wonder sometimes whether we are progressing. In my childhood days life was different in many ways. We were slower, still we had a good and happy life, I think. People enjoyed life more in their way... They don't take time to be happy nowadays... I look back on my life like a good day's work, it was done and I feel satisfied with it. I was happy and contented. I knew nothing better and made the best out of what life offered. And life is what we make it, it always has been, always will be.

—Anna Mary Robertson [Grandma] Moses

I learned early that next to Heaven, our highest duty was to love and serve our country and support its laws.

—Clara Barton

After all, sight and hearing are but two of the most beautiful blessings which God has not given me. The most precious, the most wonderful of his gifts was still mine. My mind remained clear and active "though fled for'er the light."

—Helen Keller

331

$\mathcal{I}$thought, maybe the difference between white folks and colored is just this matter of reading and writing. I made up my mind I would know my letters.

—*Mary McCleod Bethune*

❦

$\mathcal{L}$et me rescue some of American's miserable children from vice and guilt.

—*Dorothea Dix*

❦

$\mathcal{D}$id ever any kingdom or state regain its liberty, when once it was invaded, without bloodshed?

—*Abigail Adams*

❦

$\mathcal{R}$ocks have been shaken from their solid base,
But what shall move a firm and dauntless mind?

—*Joanna Baillie*

❦

$\mathcal{I}$had a pleasant time with my mind, for it was happy.

—*Louisa May Alcott*

❦

$\mathcal{G}$od wrote His loveliest poem on the day
He made the first tall silver poplar tree,
And set it high upon a pale-gold hill
For all the new enchanted earth to see.

—*Grace Noll Crowell*

Ere you left your room this morning,
  Did you think to pray?
In the name of Christ, our Savior,
  Did you sue for loving favor
As a shield today?...

When sore trials came upon you,
  Did you think to pray?
When your soul was full of sorrow,
  Balm of Gilead did you borrow
At the gates of day?

Oh, how praying rests the weary!
  Prayer will change the night to day.
So, when life gets dark and dreary,
  Don't forget to pray.

—Mary A. Pepper Kidder

Blessed is the memory of those who have kept themselves unspotted *from* the world! Yet more blessed and more dear the memory of those who have kept themselves unspotted in the world.

—Mrs. Jameson

Then give to the world the best you have,
And the best will come back to you.

—Mary Ainge De Vere

The most reckless spendthrift in the world is the one who squanders time. Money lost may be regained, friendships broken may be renewed, houses and lands may be sold or buried or burnt, but may be bought or gained or built again. But what power can restore the moment that has passed, the day whose sun has set, the year that has been numbered with the ages gone?

—Anna R. Brown Lindsay

Grief may be joy misunderstood.

—Elizabeth Barrett Browning

$\mathcal{I}$t is surely better to pardon too much than to condemn too much.

—*George Eliot*

$\mathcal{T}$he library looked beautiful this morning in the sunlight—quiet and full of the sort of promise that books give when they are waiting on the shelves.

—*Pearl S. Buck*

$\mathcal{T}$he kiss of the sun for pardon,
   The song of the birds for mirth,—
One is nearer to God's heart in a garden
   Than anywhere else on earth.

—*Dorothy Frances Blomfield Gurney*

ॐ

$\mathcal{I}$ slept and dreamed that life was beauty.
I woke—and found that life was duty.

—*Ellen Sturgis Hooper*

$\mathcal{I}$f the world seems cold to you,
Kindle fires to warm it!

—*Lucy Larcom*

$\mathcal{G}$ive me your tired, your poor,
Your huddled masses yearning to breathe free,
The wretched refuse of your teeming shore.
Send these, the homeless, tempest-tossed, to me.
I lift my lamp beside the golden door.

—*Emma Lazarus*

$\mathcal{O}$ World, I cannot hold thee close enough!
Thy winds, thy wide gray skies!
Thy mists, that roll and rise!
Thy woods, this autumn day, that ache and sag
And all but cry with color.

—*Edna St. Vincent Millay*

334

Courage is the price that life exacts for granting peace.
The soul that knows it not, knows no release
From little things;
Knows not the livid loneliness of fear,
Nor mountain heights where bitter joy can hear
The sound of wings.

—*Amelia Earhart*

I never saw a moor,
I never saw the sea;
Yet know I how the heather looks,
And what a wave must be.

I never spoke with God,
Nor visited in heaven;
Yet certain am I of the spot
As if the chart were given.

—*Emily Dickinson*

ॐ

I have often in my mind compared society to a vast orchestra which, properly led, gives forth a heavenly music, and which, ill conducted, utters harsh discordant sounds.

—*Julia Ward Howe*

Congenial work, no matter how much there is of it, has never yet killed anyone.

—*Anna Howard Shaw*

I worked for a menial's hire,
   Only to learn, dismayed,
That any wage I had asked of Life,
   Life would have paid.

—*Jessie Belle Rittenhouse*

O Liberty! Liberty! how many crimes are committed in thy name!

—*Madame Roland*

335

*W*hen I can look Life in the eyes,
Grown calm and very coldly wise,
Life will have given me the Truth,
And taken in exchange—my youth.

—*Sara Teasdale*

*S*ad soul, take comfort, nor forget
That sunrise never failed us yet.

—*Celia Laighton Thaxter*

*G*od does not send strange flowers every year.
When the spring winds blow o'er the pleasant places,
The same dear things lift up the same fair faces,
The violet is here.

—*Adeline Dutton Train Whitney*

*O*ne must not start killing people, not even by wishing them dead. One simply must not—or where will it end? Hitler did just that. He first killed the mentally ill, declaring them useless. Then of what use were the cripples or retarded children, or the aged: He killed them, and after them it was Jews, and then anyone who did not agree with him. Where does one draw the line? At the beginning! One must not take a human life, for any reason.

—*Pearl S. Buck*

*L*ife is either a daring adventure or nothing.

—*Helen Keller*

*L*et us say again that the lessons of great men are lost unless they reinforce upon our minds the highest demands which we make upon ourselves; that they are lost unless they drive our sluggish wills forward in the direction of their highest ideals.

—*Jane Addams*

*I*ntreat me not to leave thee, or to return from following after thee; for whither thou goest, I will go; and where thou lodgest, I will lodge; thy people shall be my people, and thy God my God.

—*Ruth 1:16*

For books are more than books, they are the life,
The very heart and core of ages past,
The reason why men lived and worked and died,
The essence and quintessence of their lives.

—*Amy Lowell*

Who has made us Jews different from all other people? Who has allowed us to suffer so terribly up till now? It is God that has made us as we are, but it will be God, too, who will raise us up again. If we bear all this suffering and if there are still Jews left, when it is over, then Jews, instead of being doomed, will be held up as an example. Who knows, it might even be our religion from which the world and all peoples learn good, and for that reason and that reason only do we have to suffer now.

—*Anne Frank*

The sunrise wakes the lark to sing,
The moonrise wakes the nightingale.
Come, darkness, moonrise, everything
That is so silent, sweet, and pale:
Come, so ye wake the nightingale.

—*Christina Rossetti*

They speak of hope to the fainting heart,
With a voice of promise they come and part,
They sleep in dust through the wintry hours,
They break forth in glory—bring flowers, bright flowers!

—*Felicia Dorothea Hemans*

The red upon the hill
Taketh away my will;
If anybody sneer,
Take care, for God is here,
That's all.

—*Emily Dickinson*

No civilization is complete which does not include the dumb and defenseless of God's creatures within the sphere of charity and mercy.

—*Queen Victoria*

337

One must be poor to know the luxury of giving.

—George Eliot

How easy to be amiable in the midst of happiness and success.

—Anne Sophie Swetchine

Freedom—it is today more than ever the most precious human possession.

—Pearl S. Buck

All change is not growth; all movement is not forward.

—Ellen Glasgow

No man ever repented of being a Christian on his death bed.

—Hannah More

If we could sell our experiences for what they cost us, we'd all be millionaires.

—Abigail Van Buren

We have no more right to put our discordant states of mind into the lives of those around us and rob them of their sunshine and brightness than we have to enter their houses and steal their silverware.

—Julia Moss Seton

Diplomacy is the art of letting someone have your way.

—Daniele Vare

No man is responsible for his father. That is entirely his mother's affair.

—Margaret Turnbull

People throw away what they could have by insisting on perfection, which they cannot have, and looking for it where they will never find it.

—Edith Schaeffer

We can do no great things—only small things with great love.

—Mother Teresa

You can make the pathway bright,
Fill the soul with heaven's light,
If there's sunshine in your heart;
Turning darkness into day,
As the shadows fly away,
If there's sunshine in your heart today...

You can live a happy life
In this world of toil and strife,
If there's sunshine in your heart;
And your soul will glow with love
From the perfect Light above,
If there's sunshine in your heart today.

If there's sunshine in your heart,
You can send a shining ray
That will turn the night to day;
And your cares will all depart,
If there's sunshine in your heart today.

—Helen Silcott Dungan

I saw dawn creep across the sky,
And all the gulls go flying by.
I saw the sea put on its dress
Of blue mid-summer loveliness,
And heard the trees begin to stir
Green arms of pine and juniper.
I heard the wind call out and say:
"Get up, my dear, it is today!"

—Rachel Field

Books are men of Higher Stature,
And the only men that speak aloud for future times to hear!
—Elizabeth Barrett Browning

The clearsighted do not rule the world, but they sustain and console it.
—Agnes Repplier

$\mathcal{N}$o entertainment is so cheap as reading, nor any pleasure so lasting.

—*Mary Wortley Montagu*

$\mathcal{N}$o coward soul is mine,
　No trembler in the world's storm-troubled sphere;
I see heaven's glories shine,
　And faith shines equal, arming me from fear.

—*Emily Bronte*

$\mathcal{L}$et nothing disturb thee,
Let nothing afright thee.
All things are passing.
God never changes.
Patience gains all things.
Who has God wants nothing.
God alone suffices.

—*St. Theresa of Avila*

$\mathcal{N}$othing in life is to be feared. It is only to be understood.

—*Marie Curie*

$\mathcal{U}$nless we form the habit of going to the Bible in bright moments as well as in trouble, we cannot fully respond to its consolations, because we lack equilibrium between light and darkness.

—*Helen Keller*

$\mathcal{O}$ne cannot collect all the beautiful shells on the beach. One can collect only a few, and they are more beautiful if they are few.

—*Anne Morrow Lindbergh*

$\mathcal{T}$oday is a new day. You will get out of it just what you put into it... If you have made mistakes, even serious mistakes, there is always another chance for you. And supposing you have tried and failed again and again, you may have a fresh start any moment you choose, for this thing that we call "failure" is not the falling down, but the staying down.

—*Mary Pickford*

$\mathcal{B}$eauty is not caused. It is.

—*Emily Dickinson*

$\mathcal{T}$he uncommitted life is not worth living... We either believe in something or we don't... Commitment is willingness to stand up and be counted. It is a human must for young and old, for black and white, for Christian, Moslem and Buddhist. It is skill plus goodwill. It is a thoughtful decision on the part of an individual to participate passionately in the events of his time... Commitment will bring sadness as well as joy, loneliness as well as friendship, but whichever it is, it brings excitement and demands the use of all a person's resources. Even beyond this, it increases our capacity for the generous enjoyment of life and colors all we do with a concern for others... With commitment, we can move mountains. Without it we cannot move a molehill.

—*Pearl S. Buck*

$\mathcal{T}$here can be no happy life without strenuous, unremitting work in it—work which occupies mind, body, heart, and soul.

—*Anna R. Brown Lindsay*

$\mathcal{B}$uild a little fence of trust
    Around today;
Fill the space with loving works,
    And therein stay;

Look not through the sheltering bars
    Upon tomorrow;
God will help thee bear what comes
    Of joy or sorrow.

—*Mary Frances Butts*

$\mathcal{T}$he more we know, the better we forgive;
Whoe'er feels deeply, feels for all who live.

—*Madame de Stael*

$\mathcal{W}$hat is done cannot be undone, but one can prevent it happening again.

—*Anne Frank*

$\mathcal{W}$ear a smile and have friends; wear a scowl and have wrinkles. What do we live for if not to make the world less difficult for each other?

—*George Eliot*

What a resource is a cultivated mind! What can people do when old and sick without intellectual resources?

—*Louisa Torry Taft*

It is good to have an end to journey towards; but it is the journey that matters in the end.

—*Ursula LeGuin*

Life appears to me to be too short to be spent in nursing animosity or in registering wrongs... With this creed, revenge never worries my heart, degradation never too deeply disgusts me, injustice never crushes me too low. I live in calm, looking to the end.

—*Charlotte Bronte*

A little Madness in the Spring
Is wholesome even for the King.

—*Emily Dickinson*

I have written my life in small sketches, a little today, a little yesterday, as I have thought of it, as I remember all the things from childhood on through the years, good ones, and unpleasant ones. That is how they come out and that is how we have to take them.

—*Anna Mary Robertson [Grandma] Moses*

Spring rides no horses down the hill,
But comes on foot, a goose-girl still.
And all the loveliest things there be
Come simply so, it seems to me.

—*Edna St. Vincent Millay*

What is nobody's business is my business.

—*Clara Barton*

The responsibility of tolerance lies with those who have the wider vision.

—*George Eliot*

A straight line is the shortest in morals as in mathematics.

—*Maria Edgeworth*

From your parents you learn love and laughter and how to put one foot before the other. But when books are opened you discover that you have wings.

—*Helen Hayes*

Strength is born in the deep silence of long-suffering hearts, not amidst joy.

—*Felicia Dorothea Hemans*

Have not many of us in the weary way of life felt, in some hours, how far easier it were to die than to live?

The martyr, when faced even by a death of bodily anguish and horror, finds in the very terror of his doom a strong stimulant and tonic. There is a vivid excitement, a thrill and fervor, which may carry through any crisis of suffering that is the birth-hour of eternal glory and rest.

But to live, to wear on, day after day of mean, bitter, low harrassing servitude, every nerve dampened and depressed, every power of feeling gradually smothered—this long and wasting-heart-martyrdom, this slow, daily bleeding away of the inward life, drop by drop, hour after hour—this is the true searching test of what there may be in man or woman.

—*Harriet Beecher Stowe*

Our opinion of people depends less upon what we see in them than upon what they make us see in ourselves.

—*Sarah Grand*

❦

He ate and drank the precious word.
His spirit grew robust;
He knew no more that he was poor,
Nor that his frame was dust.
He danced along the dingy days,
And this bequest of wings
Was but a book. What liberty
A loosened spirit brings!

—*Emily Dickinson*

343

The real art of conversation is not only to say the right thing in the right place, but to leave unsaid the wrong thing at the tempting moment.

—*Dorothy Nevill*

I don't see why I am always asking for private, individual, selfish miracles when every year there are miracles like white dogwood.

—*Anne Morrow Lindbergh*

If the world's a vale of tears,
Smile, till rainbows span it!

—*Lucy Larcom*

Sandwich every bit of criticism between two layers of praise.

—*Mary Kay Ash*

If I had my life to live over...instead of wishing away nine months of pregnancy, I'd have cherished every moment and realized that the wonderment growing inside me was my only chance in life to assist God in a miracle... There would have been more I love you's...more I'm sorry's...but mostly, given another shot at life, I would seize every minute...look at it and really see it...live it...and never give it back.

—*Erma Bombeck*

The best remedy for those who are afraid, lonely or unhappy is to go outside, somewhere where they can be quite alone with the heavens, nature and God. Because only then does one feel that all is as it should be and that God wishes to see people happy, amidst the simple beauty of nature. As long as this exists, and it certainly always will, I know that then there will always be comfort for every sorrow, whatever the circumstances may be.

—*Anne Frank*

The use of the sea and air is common to all; neither can a title to the ocean belong to any people or private persons, forasmuch as neither nature nor public use and custom permit any possession thereof.

—*Queen Elizabeth I*

While forbidden fruit is said to taste sweeter, it usually spoils faster.

—*Abigail Van Buren*

344

It may not be on the mountain height
  Or over the stormy sea;
It may not be at the battle's front
  My Lord will have need of me.
But if, by a still, small voice he calls
  To paths that I do not know,
I'll answer, dear Lord, with my hand in thine:
  I'll go where you want me to go...

There's surely somewhere a lowly place
  In earth's harvest fields so wide
Where I may labor through life's short day
  For Jesus, the Crucified.
So trusting my all to thy tender care,
  And knowing thou lovest me,
I'll do thy will with a heart sincere:
  I'll be what you want me to be.

I'll go where you want me to go, dear Lord,
  Over mountain or plain or sea;
I'll say what you want me to say, dear Lord;
  I'll be what you want me to be.

—Mary Brown

❧

Just pray for a tough hide and a tender heart.

—Ruth Graham

Some keep the Sabbath going to church;
  I keep it staying home,
With bobolink for a chorister,
  And the orchard for a dome.

—Emily Dickinson

No soul is desolate as long as there is a human being for whom it can feel trust and reverence.

—George Eliot

And Hannah prayed, and said, My heart rejoiceth in the Lord, mine horn is exalted in the Lord... There is none holy as the Lord: for there is none beside thee: neither is there any rock like our God... The bows of the mighty men are broken, but they that stumbled are girded with strength. They that were full have hired out themselves for bread; and they that were hungry ceased: so that the barren hath born seven; and she that hath many children is waxed feeble. The Lord killeth, and maketh alive: he bringeth down to the grave, and bringeth up. The Lord maketh poor, and maketh rich: he bringeth low and lifteth up. He raiseth up the poor out of the dust and lifteth up the beggar from the dunghill, to set them among princes, and to make them inherit the throne of glory: for the pillars of the earth are the Lord's, and he hath set the world upon them.

—I Samuel 2:1-8

The only difference between a rut and a grave is their dimensions.

—Ellen Glasgow

If you want to understand a nation, look at its dances and listen to its folk songs—don't pay any attention to its politicians.

—Agnes de Mille

We are not dispirited here, if our men are all drawn off and we should be attacked, you would find a race of Amazons in America.

—Abigail Adams

Know yourself. Don't accept your dog's admiration as conclusive evidence that you are wonderful.

—Ann Landers

Carve not upon a stone when I am dead
    The praises which remorseful mourners give
To women's graves—a tardy recompense—
    But speak them while I live.

—Elizabeth Akers Allen

Some folks never exaggerate—they just remember big.

—Audrey Snead

My words are little jars
For you to take and put upon a shelf.
Their shapes are quaint and beautiful,
And they have many pleasant colours and lustres
To recommend them.
Also the scent from them fills the room
With sweetness of flowers and crushed grasses.

—*Amy Lowell*

I solemnly pledge myself before God, and in the presence of this
assembly, to pass my life in purity, and to practice my profession
faithfully. I will do all in my power to maintain and elevate the standard
of my profession, and will hold in confidence all personal matters
committed to my keeping and all family affairs coming to my knowledge
in the practice of my calling. With loyalty will I endeavor to aid the
physician in his work, and devote myself to the welfare of those
committed to my care.

—*The Florence Nightingale Pledge*

[*On* her battle with breast cancer:] We human beings are remarkable. We
plant trees, knowing that by the time they're big enough to climb, we'll be
too old to climb them. We write constitutions for people who won't be
born for 100 years and may not deserve them. And we try to take care of
our sick, although we all have a disease we're going to die from, which, I
think, makes us very brave. And in the course of that we sometimes stand
tall and take the time to look at the sun and laugh.

I have always felt that laughter in the face of reality is probably the
finest sound there is and will last until the day when the game is called on
account of darkness. In this world, a good time to laugh is any time
you can.

—*Linda Ellerbee*

*H*appiness is not a goal, it is a by-product.

—*Eleanor Roosevelt*

*D*on't wait around for other people to be happy for you. Any happiness
you get you've got to make yourself.

—*Alice Walker*

347

*E*very private citizen has a public responsibility.

—*Myra Janco Daniels*

*Y*ou know you're old when you've lost all your marvels.

—*Merry Browne*

*T*here is an Indian belief that everyone is a house of four rooms: a physical, a mental, an emotional and a spiritual room. Most of us tend to live in one room most of the time, but unless we go into every room every day, even if only to keep it aired, we are not complete.

—*Rumer Godden*

*E*very fragment of song holds a mirror to a past moment for someone.

—*Fanny Cradock*

❦

*M*orality is its own advocate; it is never necessary to apologize for it.

—*Edith L. Harrell*

*S*tanding in the middle of the road is very dangerous; you get knocked down by the traffic from both sides.

—*Margaret Thatcher*

*Y*ou can't act like a skunk without someone's getting wind of it.

—*Lorene Workman*

*U*ntil you make peace with who you are, you'll never be content with what you have.

—*Doris Mortman*

A word is dead
When it is said,
    Some say.
I say it just
    Begins to live
That day.

—*Emily Dickinson*

In spite of the cost of living, it's still popular.

—*Kathleen Norris*

Miracles are instantaneous. They cannot be summoned, but come of themselves, usually at unlikely moments and to those who least expect them.

—*Katherine Anne Porter*

That book [the Bible] accounts for the supremacy of England.

—*Queen Victoria*

A letter pulls people together like nothing else. It can make you cry or shout for joy. There's no finer caress than a love letter, because it makes the world very small, and the writer and reader, the only rulers... A letter is life!

—*Cecilia Capuzzi*

Why is it when you're seven, today is forever and tomorrow never; but when you're 70, tomorrow's yesterday before you knew it was today?

—*Sue Jane Purcell*

By what strange law of mind is it that an idea long overlooked, and trodden under foot as a useless stone, suddenly sparkles out in new light as a discovered diamond!

—*Harriet Beecher Stowe*

Faith is like radar that sees through the fog—the reality of things at a distance that the human eye cannot see.

—*Corrie ten Boom*

How noble and good everyone could be if, every evening before falling asleep, they were to recall to their minds the events of the whole day and consider exactly what has been good and bad. Then, without realizing it, you try to improve yourself at the start of each new day; of course, you achieve quite a lot in the course of time.

—*Anne Frank*

Courage is not the towering oak that sees storms come and go. It is the fragile blossom that opens in the snow.

—*Alice Mackenzie Swaine*

The pedigree of honey
Does not concern the bee;
A clover, any time to him
Is aristocracy.

—*Emily Dickinson*

O my Father, thou that dwellest
   In the high and glorious place,
When shall I regain thy presence
   And again behold thy face?
In thy Holy habitation,
   Did my spirit once reside?
In my first primeval childhood,
   Was I nurtured near thy side?...

I had learned to call thee Father,
   Thru thy Spirit from on high,
But, until the key of knowledge
   Was restored, I knew not why.
In the heav'ns are parents single?
   No, the thought makes reason stare!
Truth is reason; truth eternal
   Tells me I've a mother there.

When I leave this frail existence,
   When I lay this mortal by,
Father, Mother, may I meet you
   In your royal courts on high?
Then, at length, when I've completed
   All you sent me forth to do,
With your mutual approbation
   Let me come and dwell with you.

—*Eliza R. Snow*

When life knocks you to your knees, and it will, why, get up! If it knocks you to your knees again, as it will, well, isn't that the best position from which to pray?

—Ethel Barrymore

❧

Genesis reads: "And the Lord God planted a garden eastward in Eden." It may well be that every making of a garden is an attempt to return to Eden. It even may be that every garden is an Eden in itself; that for the while we are immersed in it we can retain a vision of what we were meant to be.

—Betsy Holland Gehman

❧

Blessed is the man who, having nothing to say, abstains from giving us wordy evidence of the fact.

—George Eliot

❧

You can get through life with bad manners, but it's easier with good manners.

—Lillian Gish

❧

All that is necessary to break the spell of inertia and frustration is this: Act as if it were impossible to fail. That is the talisman, the formula, the command of right-about-face which turns us from failure towards success.

—Dorothea Brande

❧

The Lord judges not as men judge.

—Anne Hutchinson

351

*A*ny concern too small to be turned into a prayer is too small to be made into a burden.

—*Corrie ten Boom*

*M*ake no judgments where you have no compassion.

—*Anne McCaffrey*

*A*lways laugh at yourself first—before others do.

—*Elsa Maxwell*

I will be the gladdest thing
    Under the sun!
I will touch a hundred flowers
And not pick one.

I will look at cliffs and clouds
    With quiet eyes,
Watch the wind bow down the grass,
    And the grass rise.

When the lights begin to show
    Up from the town,
I will mark which must be mine,
    And then start down!

—*Edna St. Vincent Millay*

I am very much against killing and that includes...abortion. I have learned to respect life more at the beginning.

—*Elizabeth Kubler-Ross*

*T*hey say: "Indians are poor because they don't work, because they're always asleep..." But I know from experience that we're outside ready for work at three in the morning... This is what motivated me, and also motivated many others. Above all the mothers and fathers. They remember their children. They remember the ones...who died of malnutrition...or had to be given away because they had no way of looking after them.

—*Rigoberta Menchú*

*P*raise is warming and desirable. But it is an earned thing. It has to be deserved, like a hug from a child.

—Phyllis McGinley

*I*t is a wholesome and necessary thing for us to turn again to the earth and in the contemplation of her beauties to know the sense of wonder and humility.

—Rachel Carson

*T*oday there is so much talk about freedom and finding oneself. I'm for the dignity of the individual, but I don't think anyone has a successful marriage or career or anything without sacrifice. Discipline seems to be a word that has almost disappeared from today's vocabulary. I learned discipline in Catholic schools, by being brought up in a strict family and in the theater.

—Princess Grace of Monaco

*W*hat frightens me is that men are content with what is not life at all.

—Elizabeth Barrett Browning

*I*t is one of my sources of happiness never to desire knowledge of other people's business.

—Dolly Madison

*E*ducate the women and the men will be educated... Let the ladies understand the great doctrine of seeking the greatest good, of loving their neighbors as themselves; let them indoctrinate their children in the fundamental truth, and we shall have wise legislators.

—Mary Lyon

*I*f you want a place in the sun, you've got to put up with a few blisters.

—Abigail Van Buren

*F*ame is a bee.
It has a song—
It has a sting—
Oh, too, it has a wing.

—Emily Dickinson

*L*ight and Power come only with Growth.

—*Ida M. Tarbell*

*H*alf the misery in the world comes of want of courage to speak and hear the truth plainly, and in a spirit of love.

—*Harriet Beecher Stowe*

[*At* the approach of the Spanish Armada:] I know I have a body of a weak and feeble woman, but I have the heart and stomach of a king, and of a king of England too; and think foul scorn that Parma or Spain, or any prince of Europe should dare to invade the borders of my realm.

—*Queen Elizabeth I*

*S*eated one day at the organ,
I was weary and ill at ease,
And my fingers wandered idly
Over the noisy keys.

I do not know what I was playing,
Or what I was dreaming then;
But I struck one chord of music,
Like the sound of a great Amen...

I have sought, but I seek it vainly,
That one lost chord divine,
That came from the soul of the organ
And entered into mine.

—*Adelaide Procter*

*I*f it is natural to feed the hungry and care for the sick, it is certainly natural to give pleasure to the young, comfort to the aged, and to minister to the deep-seated craving for social intercourse that all men feel.

—*Jane Addams*

I feel a pleasure in being able to sacrifice my selfish passions to the general good, and in imitating the example which has taught me to consider myself and my family but as the small dust of the balance, when compared with the great community.

—*Abigail Adams*

*F*aith means having courage
To know as days go by
That just as long as
Faith lives on
Hope can never die.

—Minerva Shultz

*A*s we grow older, God sees to it our eyesight grows dimmer, so that when we look at ourselves in the mirror, we can say, "I still look as good as ever."

—Helen Hayes

*T*his is the bitterest of all, to wear the yoke of our wrongdoing.

—George Eliot

*T*he finest kind of friendship is between people who expect a great deal of each other but never ask it.

—Sylvia Bremer

*H*urt no living thing:
Ladybird, nor butterfly,
Nor moth with dusty wing,
Nor cricket chirping cheerily,
Nor grasshopper so light of leap,
Nor dancing gnat, nor beetle fat,
Nor harmless worms that creep.

—Christina Rossetti

A ship is safe when it is in harbor, but that isn't what ships are for.

—Grace Lowe

*B*eing a Christian means thinking of our brothers around us, and that everyone of our Indian race has a right to eat...that it is not God's will that we should live in suffering...but that men on earth have imposed this suffering, poverty, misery and discrimination on us...

It is the duty of Christians to create the kingdom of God on earth among our brothers. This kingdom will exist only when we have enough to eat, when our children...don't have to die from hunger and malnutrition.

—Rigoberta Menchú

$\mathscr{I}$do not ask for any crown
    But that which all may win:
Nor try to conquer any world
    Except the one within.
Be thou my guide until I find,
    Led by a tender hand,
The happy kingdom in myself
    And dare to take command.

—Louisa May Alcott

$\mathscr{I}$beg you take courage; the brave soul can mend even disaster.

—Catherine II

$\mathscr{O}$ut of the earth, the rose,
    Out of the night, the dawn;
Out of my heart, with all its woes,
    High courage to press on.

—Laura Lee Randall

$\mathscr{O}$nly when a tree has fallen can you take the measure of it. It is the same
with a man.

—Anne Morrow Lindbergh

$\mathscr{H}$e knows so little and knows it so fluently.

—Ellen Glasgow

$\mathscr{O}$h, the comfort—the inexpressible comfort of feeling safe
with a person,
Having neither to weigh thoughts,
Nor measure words—but pouring them
All right out—just as they are—
Chaff and grain together—
Certain that a faithful hand will
Take and sift them—
Keep what is worth keeping—
And with the breath of kindness
Blow the rest away.

—Dinah Maria Mulock Craik

Today as I look back, I am convinced that the whole ordeal of my paralysis was inspired by God's love. I wasn't the brunt of some cruel divine joke. God had reasons behind my suffering, and learning some of them has made all the difference in the world.

—*Joni Eareckson Tada*

God can't give His best till we have given ours!

—*Mary Slessor*

[She attributed her success:] to my excellent training: first, under my father, who taught me to wonder and to test; second, under my husband, who understood and encouraged me; and third, under my children, who question me!

—*Marie Curie*

Don't be sad.
I'm not leaving.
I'm arriving.

—*Last Words of Gaby Morlay*

I came at morn; 'twas spring, I smiled.
The fields with green were clad;
I walked abroad at noon, and lo!
'Twas summer—I was glad;
I sat me down; 'twas autumn eve,
And I with sadness wept;
I laid me down at night, and then
'Twas winter, and I slept.

—*Mary Pyper*

The voice of conscience is so delicate that it is easy to stifle it, but it is also so clear that it is impossible to mistake it.

—*Madame de Stael*

We are not interested in the possibility of defeat.

—*Queen Victoria*

It's better to be a lion for a day than a sheep all your life.

—*Elizabeth Kenny*

*D*iamonds are only chunks of coal,
That stuck to their jobs, you see.

—*Minnie Richard Smith*

*L*ife, believe, is not a dream
So dark as sages say;
Oft a little morning rain
Foretells a pleasant day.

—*Charlotte Bronte*

*A*nd when he [Pilate] was set down on the judgment seat, his wife sent unto him, saying, Have thou nothing to do with this just man: for I have suffered many things this day in a dream because of him.

—*Matthew 27:19*

*I*t's easy to find reasons why other folks should be patient.

—*George Eliot*

*T*he most beautiful discovery true friends make is that they can grow separately without growing apart.

—*Elisabeth Foley*

*A*s for inhibitions, I've spent a lifetime developing them, and I don't intend to lose them.

—*Pearl S. Buck*

I always seek the good that is in people and leave the bad to Him who made mankind and knows how to round off the corners.

—*Katharina Textor von Goethe*

I believe in the immortality of the soul because I have within me immortal longings... I believe in the life to come I shall have the senses I have not had here and that my home there will be beautiful with color, music, and the speech of flowers and faces I love... I believe that life is given us so that we may grow in love and I believe that God is in me as the sun is in the color and fragrance of a flower—the Light in my darkness, the Voice in my silence.

—*Helen Keller*

*N*earer, my God, to Thee,
    Nearer to Thee!
E'en though it be a cross
    That raiseth me;
Still all my song shall be,
    Nearer, my God, to Thee,
Nearer, my God, to Thee,
    Nearer to Thee!

Though like the wanderer,
    The sun gone down,
Darkness be over me,
    My rest a stone;
Yet in my dreams I'd be
    Nearer, my God, to Thee,
Nearer to Thee!...

Then, with my waking thoughts
    Bright with Thy praise,
Out of my stony griefs
    Bethel I'll raise;
So by my woes to be
    Nearer, my God, to Thee,
Nearer to Thee!

Or if on joyful wing
    Cleaving the sky,
Sun, moon, and stars forgot,
    Upward I fly,
Still all my song shall be,
    Nearer, my God, to Thee,
Nearer to Thee!

—Sarah F. Adams

$\mathcal{L}$ord, Thou knowest better than I know myself that I am growing older and will someday be old. Keep me from the fatal habit of thinking I must say something on every subject and on every occasion. Release me from craving to straighten out everybody's affairs. Make me thoughtful but not moody; helpful but not bossy. With my vast store of wisdom, it seems a pity not to use it all, but Thou knowest Lord that I want a few friends at the end.

Keep my mind free from the recital of endless details; give me wings to get to the point. Seal my lips on my aches and pains. They are increasing, and love of rehearsing them is becoming sweeter as the years go by. I dare not ask for grace enough to enjoy the tales of other's pains, but help me to endure them with patience.

I dare not ask for improved memory, but for a growing humility and a lessing cocksureness when my memory seems to clash with the memories of others. Teach me the glorious lesson that occasionally I may be mistaken.

Keep me reasonably sweet; I do not want to be a Saint—some of them are so hard to live with—but a sour old person is one of the crowning works of the devil. Give me the ability to see good things in unexpected places, and talents in unexpected people. And, give me, O Lord, the grace to tell them so. Amen.

—17th Century Nun's Prayer

$\mathcal{I}$n spite of everything I still believe that people are really good at heart. I simply can't build up my hopes on a foundation consisting of confusion, misery, and death. I see the world gradually being turned into a wilderness, I hear the ever-approaching thunder, which will destroy us too. I can feel the sufferings of millions and yet, if I look up into the heavens, I think that it will all come right, that this cruelty too will end, and that peace and tranquillity will return again.

—Anne Frank

Women
to
Remember

Chapter Nine
Women to Remember

The first woman distinctly portrayed in the dramatic history of man's spiritual development is Sarah, beloved wife of Abraham, founder of the House of Israel. The story of the beautiful and distinguished Sarah and her husband, "Father of Faithful," covers more space in the Genesis account than does that of the entire human race from the Creation down to their time... She was to be the Mother of Nations.

—Edith Deen

*A*nne Sullivan...was one of those rare geniuses who flower out of the muck of poverty and disease. Her father was a ne'er-do-well drunkard, her brother had died of tuberculosis, and she herself had been threatened with total blindness up to the age of eighteen, when a successful operation had partially cured her. At twenty, when she became Helen [Keller]'s teacher, she had recovered enough of her vision to read for the child and to lead her into a new world.

—Henry & Dana Lee Thomas

*I*n the Queensland port of Townsville she [Elizabeth Kenny] set up a clinic in the backyard of a private home. It had an earthen floor, an awning for a roof, and a zinc bathtub. Water was heated in a kerosene tin hung by a chain over the galley fire. Her assistants were the parents of her patients. The Sylvia Stretcher [which she had invented] paid expenses. There were seventeen patients, all of whom had been given up as hopeless by their doctors.

Each case provided its own drama. A baby girl had both feet deformed. The attendant physician had said that only an operation would permit the baby to walk and advised the parents to take her to a bone specialist a thousand miles distant. Because they had no money for the journey or the operation, they let Sister Kenny take over. In her care the baby was able to walk in four months. She was ten when Sister Kenny next saw her, a happy schoolgirl with no memory of having been crippled.

—Robin McKown

If the planet earth could sing, it would sound something like Marian Anderson.

—*Jessye Norman*

If I am remembered, I want it to be not because I am a woman, but also because of what I have accomplished, and for the help I've given my people [as chief of Cherokee Nation].

—*Wilma Mankiller*

Her motto was "Keep going." Born into slavery on a Maryland farm, Harriet Tubman made her escape in 1849, guided only by the North Star. She returned South 19 times despite a $12,000 bounty on her head and shepherded more than 300 slaves to freedom.

—*Life*

Gandhi went out among India's downtrodden poor. He found people dumb with despair, living in filth and ignorance...and Kasturbai [Gandhi's wife] must help too. Kasturbai was uneducated but she could teach women how to keep their mud huts clean. Pushing aside her prejudices she went into the Untouchables' hovels and, seeing the misery there, her heart was moved... Gradually Kasturbai became absorbed in her husband's mission of service. She taught hygiene, she campaigned against the use of drugs and liquor, and she taught peasants how to spin their own cloth.

—*Betty Schechter*

Things got simpler where she [Eleanor Roosevelt] was. Good became good again, the nonsense nonsense, and evil evil, and a man could live again and even pity.

—*Archibald MacLeish*

How came you [Florence Sabine] to possess these many skills and virtues? [in exploration and discoveries of the lymph system]... It has been, I think, because of your great humanity. You have cared deeply for your kind. And men have come to recognize in you that rare total person—of wisdom and of sentiment—heart and mind in a balanced union.

—*Dr. Alfred Cohn*

$\mathcal{O}$ne of the most beautiful buildings in the world is the Taj Majal. It was built by the Mongul emperor Shah Jehan at Delhi, India, as a tomb for his favorite wife... Artists and craftsmen were brought from all over Asia to assist the thousands of Hindus employed in the construction. About 20 years were needed to complete the building. The emperor used it as a pleasure palace during his lifetime. When he died he was buried beside his beloved empress. The building takes its name from one of her titles, Taj Mahal, "crown of the palace."

—Compton's Encyclopedia

$\mathcal{W}$inston's old nurse, Mrs. Everest, fell ill. Churchill, hearing the news, obtained leave from his regiment, went to London, and engaged a specialist and two doctors to attend her. He called on her in her house in North London. It had been raining and his old nurse, ignoring her own fatal illness, felt his jacket which was wet and would not rest until he had taken it off and it was dried.

Winston had to leave her bedside at midnight... [but] returned and was with Mrs. Everest in her final moments. Winston Churchill never forgot Mrs. Everest and her great care and love for him. In his later years in Parliament, [he initiated programs for pensions and medical care for the elderly].

—Leonard Wibberly

$\mathcal{B}$y coincidence I came across a diary [by a mere child, Anne Frank] that was written during the war. The Netherlands State Institute for War Documentation already has about 200 of such diaries, but it would surprise me if there was one other which was as pure, as intelligent and yet as human as this one.

—Professor Jan Romein

$\mathcal{H}$er [Sarah Bernhardt's] strength as an artist always cheated death... This sickly actress with the immortal soul went on living for seventy-nine years... In her middle age she fell while playing Hamlet and phlebitis developed in one of her legs... The poison in her leg crept upward and...when she was seventy-one, the doctors warned her that an amputation would be necessary. She submitted cheerfully to the ordeal. From then on she sat in a wheelchair to play her roles. But the glory of her voice and the magic of her art were not diminished.

—Henry & Dana Lee Thomas

*M*ark Twain fell in love with the woman he was to marry before he ever saw her. It happened one afternoon during a cruise...when Charles Langdon, a young fellow passenger, showed him a miniature painting of his sister, Olivia. She was a strikingly beautiful girl with delicate features and dark hair. Mark found that he was unable to forget her.

The following December on a visit to New York he met Langdon again, and at his invitation called on his parents and sister, who were in the city for the holidays. "It was 40 years ago; from that day to this the sister has never been out of my mind nor my heart," he wrote.

—Readers Digest

*M*rs. Washington combines, in an uncommon degree, great dignity of manner with the most pleasing affability, but possesses no striking marks of beauty. I learn from the Virginia officers that Mrs. Washington has ever been honored as a lady of distinguished goodness, possessing all the virtues which adorn her sex, amiable in her temper and deportment, full of benignity, benevolence, and charity, seeking for objects of affliction and poverty, that she may extend to the sufferers the hand of kindness and relief.

—A Colonial Army Officer

*N*o one did more toward solving this problem [medical care for women in the pioneer West] than Dr. Ellis R. Shipp, "Utah's Grand Old Lady," unquestionably the outstanding woman of her time... The West owes her a debt of gratitude... [Her great contribution] was made by conducting systematic, thorough, and complete instruction classes in nursing and obstetrics. She was kind, considerate, and patient with her pupils, but she never gave a certificate of graduation to any student who did not have the mental and personal qualifications necessary to make a good, practical nurse and midwife. It is impossible to compute the number of graduates from her classes during the fifty-nine years she maintained her school.

—Dr. Ralph T. Richards

*A*nd God said unto Abraham, As for Sarai thy wife, thou shalt not call her name Sarai, but Sarah shall her name be. And I will bless her, and give thee a son also of her: yea, I will bless her, and she shall be a mother of nations; kings of people shall be of her.

—Genesis 17:15,16

368

*A*rkansas fiddler who made it to the Met, Sarah Caldwell [was] the first woman to conduct the Met... "Once in a while," says Sarah Caldwell, "when everything is right, there is a moment of magic. People can live on moments of magic."

—Life

[*T*he wife of a patient] stood numb and immobile for several minutes after being told her husband had passed away. She stood perfectly quiet after I told her. Tears welled into her eyes, but her face remained inscrutably calm and impassive... Then through her tears came a wonderfully sweet and genuine smile. She spoke simply and slowly, pausing thoughtfully between every sentence:

"Paul was a wonderful man. It has been a great privilege to have been able to live with such a person... He would want me to bear up and to go on as though he were still here. And I am going to keep him and his influence here by trying to be as he would have been... He has given me so much. And now I guess I am going to have to give the children and other people the same spirit he gave me, and that he gave them." She did exactly that.

—Dr. John A. Schindler

*A*nd Jacob set a pillar upon her grave: that is the pillar of Rachel's grave unto this day.

—Genesis 35:20

*M*other Teresa, who has become a legendary humanitarian figure of our time, was born of impoverished Albanian parents in Yugoslavia. Albania, where there has been no public worship of any kind for decades, is the most hard-core Communist nation in Eastern Europe... From such an unlikely background came this beautiful person who ministers grace, loving-kindness, and mercy to the destitute and dying in Calcutta, the dirtiest, filthiest city in Asia. She is loved by the mighty and the lowly alike. Visit her Home of Mercy next to the wretched Kali Temple in the heart of the slums of this slum city...and you will encounter a slice of heaven on earth. Here, because of Mother Teresa's concern and care, the beggars, the indigent, and the homeless die with dignity—and the word whispered in their ears is that God loves them.

—Ted W. Engstrom

369

*W*hen Ramsay MacDonald, onetime Prime Minister of Great Britain, was sitting by the bedside of his wife as she was dying, she said to him, "Ramsay, put romance into the lives of our children. Teach them to see the beauty, the charm and the fascination, the indescribable wonder of the world."

—Norman Vincent Peale & Smiley Blanton

❧

*R*ahab had two known vocations, that of innkeeper and weaver. She hid Joshua's two spies... Later she let them down by a scarlet cord through a window. Rahab is also called a harlot. But whatever Rahab's vices, she later redeemed herself... She is honored as one of the heroines of faith.

—Edith Deen

❧

*A*nnie Smith Peck...drifted around the world seeking heights "where no man has previously stood" and lecturing on classical languages. In 1908, at 57, she became the first to scale Peru's Mt. Huascaran, then believed to be the highest mountain in the western hemisphere... Her last climb was up the steep ascent to the Acropolis when she was 85.

—Life

❧

[*Of* Florence Nightingale:]
Lo! in that hour of misery
A lady with a lamp I see
Pass through the glimmering gloom
And flit from room to room.

And slow, as in a dream of bliss,
The speechless sufferer turns to kiss
Her shadow as it falls
Upon the darkening walls.

—Henry Wadsworth Longfellow

370

$\mathscr{I}$t is safe to say that practically every American who ever went to school will recognize Miss Dove. The terrible Miss Dove, she was called by generations of children of the small town of Liberty Hill. She was the teacher who was held in awe and dread for her rigid discipline and her standards of perfection. It was not until disaster threatened Miss Dove that the whole town realized how deeply she had affected everyone in it.

—*John Barkham*

$\mathscr{N}$arcissa Whitman was one of the first two white women to cross the American continent. Beautiful, blonde-haired, courageous, this girl in her twenties married a young doctor and set out with him in 1836 from her home in New York State for the almost unknown western county which is now Oregon... Beyond St. Louis nearly two thousand miles of wilderness lay between them and their goal. But the Whitmans did reach Oregon and there established a mission which became one of the first outposts of civilization in the Northwest... Narcissa Whitman kept a journal and wrote many letters to her family and friends far away in the East... Narcissa's journals, the letters she wrote...are still available.

—*Book Jacket, Harcourt, Brace & Company*

$\mathscr{A}$nne Lindbergh is small of stature, and has a charming dignity when surrounded by people... Her dress is simple, like her direct manner... About her mouth a smile always seems to lurk.

—*Amelia Earhart*

$\mathscr{F}$anny Van de Grift fell in love and married a young unknown writer [Robert Louis Stevenson] who was ill of tuberculosis. She knew instinctively that he was a true genius and that if she could but keep him alive she would give to the world an immortal name...

She fought a losing fight in many lands until advised to get him on salt water and keep him there... A sensitive woman, she once had to live on a tiny trading schooner with 15 men, exposed to a pitiless lack of privacy; sleeping in the leaking aftercabin crowded with wet human beings... She slept on the floor beside her husband's berth so as to be ready in an instant to minister to him... In spite of all these hardships she took heart, for she could see that the invalid was slowly regaining a measure of health... In the decade and half of their married life...[he wrote over 30 books].

—*Austin Strong*

371

*M*ary Hogarth, younger sister of Catherine Hogarth Dickens, lived in Dickens' home [and died suddenly at age 16]. Of her Dickens said, "I solemnly believe that so perfect a creature never breathed..." After she died, Dickens removed a ring from her finger and wore it the rest of his life.

—Charles Haines

❦

I am glad the friendship with Aunt Mary [Moody Emerson] is ripening... By society with her, one's mind is electrified and purged. She is no statute book of practical commandments, nor orderly digest of any system of Philosophy, divine or human, but a Bible, miscellaneous in its parts, but one in its spirit, wherein are sentences of condemnation, promises and covenants of love that make foolish the wisdom of the world with the power of God.

—Ralph Waldo Emerson

❦

*P*resident Theodore Roosevelt described her [Jane Addams] as nothing less than "the most useful citizen in America." Others spoke of her as "Saint Jane"... Addams at 29 took over the shabby Hull mansion in Chicago's tenement district, renamed it "Hull House," and in 1889 opened its doors to the oppressed and underprivileged... Addams, its resident director for nearly 50 years, became the model for those who felt they could serve the needy best by living, as well as working, among them... [She] fought for the legal protection of immigrants, for the regulation of child labor, for women's suffrage. A deeply committed pacifist, she was the central figure in the international women's peace movement during World War I. In 1931 she was co-winner of the Nobel Peace Prize. Characteristically, Jane Addams directed that her prize money be utilized to help create a better life for all of human kind.

—Life

*S*he [wife Margaret] was a better soldier than I was.

—Zachary Taylor

Through faith also Sara herself received strength to conceive seed, and was delivered of a child when she was past age, because she judged him faithful who had promised.

—*Hebrews 11:11*

Madame Chiang was her husband's teacher—and his follower. She gave him of her mind, and she partook of his courage... She saw for the first time, in the hinterland of China, the pitiable living conditions of the millions of coolies, and the more she saw of the filth and the ignorance and the degradation, the more she became determined to clean it all up... She inspired her husband with plans for a crusade of morality and cleanliness among the Chinese masses... The Chinese had perpetuated during all the modern centuries their ancient superstitions. She was determined that they should perpetuate only their ancient virtues—courtesy, responsibility, honesty, good will. She enlisted the aid of all the missionaries in China...to help her emancipate the Chinese masses.

—*Henry & Dana Lee Thomas*

Here at the summit of our world community is the lady whom we respect because she is our Queen; whom we love because she is herself.

—*Winston Churchill*

She [Abigail Adams] would have made a better president than her husband.

—*Harry S. Truman*

In every scheme of happiness she [wife Martha] is placed in the foreground of the picture, as the principal figure. Take that away, and there is no picture for me.

—*Thomas Jefferson*

At 90, Ruth Rothfarb is the oldest runner in the Boston Marathon. She started running when she was 72; eight years later she ran her first marathon. "Oh, I have the usual aches and pains," she admits, "but I've learned to overcome them." Rothfarb's fastest marathon was 5:28:33, when she was 82.

—*365 Days*

*N*obody fought harder to reconcile Indians and whites than Paiute "Princess" Sarah Winnemucca... From lecture platforms, in negotiations with government officials, with President Rutherford B. Hayes himself, she pleaded for her people's basic rights. The promises made to her were never kept, and Winnemucca is remembered for her poignant pursuit of a losing cause.

—Life

*O*ne of the most popular nurses [of Frontier Nursing] was a red-haired young woman from Ireland, named Nancy O'Driscoll... Her bubbling sense of humor and her repertoire of lilting Irish songs won the hearts of the children. Sometimes she rode to the center with six of these little ones on her horse, three before and three behind...

At times she suffered from a pain in her side... One morning she had a rather severe attack but rode off without mentioning it. That day she visited three maternity patients, made a number of other calls, and held a clinic as well. It was dark when she got home. She went to bed without supper, saying she was not hungry... On her last ride her appendix had ruptured. There was nothing [the doctor]...could do for her. Nearly three hundred mountaineers followed the stretcher taking her to Lexington for burial. Nancy was the first of several nurses who gave their lives for the Frontier Nursing Service.

—Robin McKown

I knew her [Joan of Arc] in my youth as long as she remained with her parents. She was very hospitable to the poor, and would even sleep on the hearth in order that the poor might lie on her bed. She was not fond of playing, at which we, her companions, complained. She liked to work; and would spin, labour with her father, look after the house, and sometimes mind the sheep. She was never seen idling in the roads; she was more often in church at prayer.

—Isabellette [Wife of a laborer]

[*D*edication of his last novel to his wife Fanny:] Take thou the writing; thine it is, for who burnished the sword, blew on the drowsy coal, held still the target higher; chary of praise and prodigal of counsel...who but thou?

—Robert Louis Stevenson

One evening as Stephen [Foster] sat alone he thought longingly of Jane. He remembered her as she had been in the days when Old Black Joe carried bouquets down the hall to "Miss Jinny." Thinking of her beautiful laughing eyes and her soft brown hair, he began to scribble words and music...*Jeanie with the Light Brown Hair,* a graceful little song of yearning and regret.

—*Claire Lee Purdy*

Lena Marie Johansson of Sweden [was] born with no arms... "My parents treated me like a normal person, never as a handicapped person," Marie testifies... Today...[she] eats and works with her feet. She drives a car with special equipment. She has won swimming competitions. And she has a beautiful voice. After she sang recently at Robert Schuller's Crystal Cathedral, she was given a standing ovation. Watching her sing, one forgets that she has no arms and marvels instead at her radiant positive personality.

—*Norman Vincent Peale*

It would not have been possible for any man in public life to get through what I have gone through without the devoted assistance of what we in England call our better half [wife Clementine Hosier].

—*Winston Churchill*

When Harriet Beecher Stowe was introduced to President Lincoln, he exclaimed, "What! are you the little woman that caused this great war?"

—*Grace Humphrey*

The most important day I remember in all my life is the one on which my teacher, Anne Mansfield Sullivan, came to me. I am filled with wonder when I consider the immeasurable contrasts between the two lives which it connects. It was the third of March, 1887, three months before I was seven years old...

I felt approaching footsteps. I stretched out my hand as I supposed to my mother. Someone took it, and I was caught up and held close in the arms of her who had come to reveal all things to me, and, more than all things else, to love me.

—*Helen Keller*

On a plain Celtic cross, behind the mausoleum of Douglass of Glenfennert, on the almost severe, bare stone is written: In loving memory of Elizabeth Blackwell, M.D., born at Bristol, 3rd February, 1821, died at Hastings, 31st May, 1910. The first woman of modern times to graduate in medicine (1849) and the first to be placed on the British Medical register (1859).

—Rachel Baker

Even in her prose her words were poetry... The world...discovered her [Emily Dickinson's] verse only after she died. In her lifetime seven of her poems saw print; there were hundreds more in her room, and they have earned her acclaim, from students of literature, as the greatest woman poet in the history of the English language.

—Life

Miss [Marian] Anderson stood as a symbol for the emergence of the Negro... Those who remember her at her height can never forget that big resonant voice, with those low notes, almost visceral in nature, and with that easy, unforced ascent to the top register. A natural voice, a hauntingly colorful one, it is one of the vocal phenomena of its time.

—Harold Schanberg

Gladys Aylward saw herself as a simple woman... A British citizen, Alyward left her home in 1920 and sailed for China. There she bought orphans who were being systematically discarded, children who had been displaced by the political upheavals of the time and left to starve or wander on their own... Gladys gave these children a home.

When the Japanese invaded China she was forced to flee the mainland with 100 children. She ended up on the island of Formosa with her charges. There she continued to devote her life to raising children who knew no other mother.

—W.B. Freeman Concepts

I could not hold up for you a better pattern for your imitation than presented to you by your dear mother. You never saw her course marked with precipitation, but on the contrary... Brought before the tribunal of her judgment...all her actions are founded in prudence.

—John Tyler

*M*iriam, Deborah, Huldah, and Esther achieved front rank as national leaders. Miriam stood beside her brothers Aaron and Moses in the highest office of the state. Deborah, one of the so-called judges, exercised authority over limited tribal areas and led her people to victory in battle against the Canaanites. Huldah, the prophetess, teacher, and preacher, identified for King Josiah the Book of Law, the brilliant work of a group of prophets and priests who recorded Yahweh's spiritual ideals. Esther averted a general massacre of her people... It is quite remarkable that all four of these women lived in several of the most critical periods of their nation's history.

—Edith Deen

*S*onia Schlesin [his secretary] is one of the noblest beings I have known.

—Mohandas Gandhi

[*M*any "blue babies" owe their lives to Helen Taussig.] It was Dr. Taussig who found the cause of this disorder—inborn heart defects—and suggested a treatment: the operation that...has turned blue babies a healthy pink.

—Life

❦

*W*hen the Russian empire was still a totalitarian menace, Stalin's daughter Svetlana, in her thirty-fifth year, began to sense the reality of a spiritual world. She said, "I looked for the words to express this new sensation and found it in the Psalms of David. Since then I have found nothing that better expressed the Higher, Eternal Life... Nowhere have I found words more powerful than those in the Psalms. Their fervid poetry cleanses one, gives one strength, brings hope in moments of darkness."

—Norman Vincent Peale

*T*he Seventh International Red Cross Conference was held in St. Petersburg in 1902. Clara Barton, as a most honored guest, was welcomed by Nicholas II, Czar of Russia, and his Empress. It was one of many tributes which royalty paid to the President of the American Red Cross, now one of the most celebrated women in the world.

—Robin McKown

During the Queen Mother's visit to a British youth center, one of the boys at a pool table placed his cue into Her Majesty's hand. "Would you like a shot?" he inquired, smiling.

The Queen Mother fingered the cue reluctantly. If she refused, this nice young man might be hurt. "Which do you suggest I aim for?" she asked.

"The red one," he replied, indicating a ball close to one of the pockets.

So the Queen Mother lined up for the shot. Peering through the silk veiling of her hat, she whispered to the boy, "It would be awful if I missed."

Wham! The ball was soundly potted, and the Queen Mother straightened to face amazed cheers. "She didn't hit it," gasped one teenager. "She slammed it. No way could my grandma do that!"

—Susan Maxwell

She [Eleanor Roosevelt] walked in the slums and ghettos of the world, not on a tour of inspection, nor as a condescending patron, but as one who could not feel complacent while others were hungry, and who could not find contentment while others were in distress... She would rather light a candle than curse the darkness, and her glow has warmed the world.

—Adlai E. Stevenson

❦

Gertrude Palmer, 105-year-old Senior Adult Student of the Year, tries to learn something new every day.

—Living

Most people think the Holocaust camps were like snake pits—that people stepped on each other for survival. It wasn't like that at all. There was kindness, support, understanding. I often talk about a childhood friend of mine, Ilse. She once found a raspberry in the camp and carried it in her pocket all day to present to me that night on a leaf.

Imagine a world in which your entire possession is one raspberry, and you give it to a friend. Those are the moments I want to remember. People behaved nobly under unspeakable circumstances.

—Gerda Weissmann Klein

378

In 1876 he [Alfred Nobel] met Bertha Kinsky (later Baroness von Suttner), a Bohemian noblewoman. She became one of the world's leading pacifists. In letters to Nobel over several years she developed his ideas for world peace. Nobel's bequest for a peace prize was largely in tribute to her.

—Compton's Encyclopedia

Though she had passed her eighty-fifth birthday, she [Dr. Ellis R. Shipp] conducted a class in obstetrics from a sickbed, where she had to lie for three months after a heart attack.

—Claire Noall

In 1962, when biologist Rachel Carson was dying of cancer, she celebrated her love of nature by writing of the day when the long-term effects of DDT and other poisonous chemicals might "still the song of birds." Her vision so changed our consciousness, that the title, *Silent Spring*, still haunts even those who have not read the book.

—Life

❦

Mahalia [Jackson] sang the Gospel, and only the Gospel, at Carnegie Hall, on television, at the 1959 Democratic Convention for Eisenhower, Kennedy and Johnson, and for audiences all over the world.

She was resolute not only about what she sang, but where she sang. At the peak of her career, with more than 22 million record sales [she]...was not too proud to sing in the humblest of churches. But an offer of $25,000 a performance could not lure her to a Las Vegas nightclub— which she reckoned to be the place of the devil.

—San Diego Union

George VI was sustained by the strength of his wife [Elizabeth Bowes-Lyon who] was a living "testimony to the power of loyal and unquestioning affection."

—Robert Lacey

She [Oveta Culp Hobby] is the type of woman you'd like to have for a daughter or sister, a wife or a mother, or a trustee of your estate.

—Lyndon B. Johnson

*W*atching for five long months over the dead, unburied bodies of her two sons and Saul's five grandsons, all of whom had been hanged and accursed after King Saul's death, Rizpah, his concubine, showed infinite patience. She, who had worn regal robes, now sat silently, alone and weary on a rock, with death all around her until King David learned of her sacrifice and then had her loved ones buried in a family grave. Although she suffered long and tragically, her patience never faltered.

—Edith Deen

*S*uch discipline in non-violence as I have had, was given at home by my wife.

—Mohandas Gandhi

*N*o one who saw the actress named Maude Adams at the turn of the century ever forgot her portrayal of Napoleon's son...or her flute-voiced appeal in James Barrie's *Peter Pan*... Even into the 1930s, when she occasionally acted in radio plays and taught drama at Stevens College, Maude Adams was regarded with very special awe.

—Life

*H*annah, who lived at Ramah and went once a year to see her son Samuel, traveled fifteen miles each way.

—Harry Emerson Fosdick

*T*wenty years ago, Liz Christy looked at the abandoned lots in her New York neighborhood and decided to plant a garden. She and fellow gardeners hauled out the garbage and carted in soil and seeds. The city accused them of trespassing, but Christy's Green Guerillas persevered. Today that lush garden...is one of 1,000 community gardens in the city.

—365 Days

I have been singularly fortunate in marrying a woman who has never given me any perplexity about anything she said. I have never had to explain away words of hers. She has been so prudent that I have never been diverted from my work for one minute to take up any mistakes of hers. When things get worse and there is the most public clamor and the most anger to me and to us, then she is the coolest. Sometimes it looks a little blue before me, but I get courage from her perfect bravery.

—James A. Garfield

$\mathcal{I}$do not think my eyes are blinded by affection when I say that she [Edith Roosevelt] has combined to a degree I have never seen in any other woman the power of being the best of wives and mothers, the wisest manager of the household and at the same time the ideal great lady and mistress of the White House.

—Theodore Roosevelt

$\mathcal{E}$ver since the Crimean War she [Florence Nightingale] had been an invalid, much of the time confined to her bed or chaise lounge. On rare occasions she left her home on London's South Street for some important mission, always in great secrecy... In a curious way her illness was useful. She had a splendid excuse for not seeing people who would waste her time, including members of her own family. Her very seclusion increased her fame. Generals and statesmen had to beg an audience with her. Royalty from foreign countries saw her at the time she named, or not at all. Important cabinet ministers trembled at her wrath or basked in her infrequent praise. No other woman, with the exception of Queen Victoria, was regarded with such awe and reverence.

—Robin McKown

❦

$\mathcal{H}$ere stood the true woman [Lucy Stone] pure, noble, great-hearted, with the light of her good life shining in every feature of her face.

—Julia Ward Howe

$\mathcal{I}$love Madame Gandhi... [She is] a saint, who has a wonderful loyalty to a man, a woman of unrivaled readiness to endure danger and suffering for him.

—Madame Nayyhar

❦

$\mathcal{S}$he [Barbara Streisand] has the profile of an undernourished Aztec, a personality of pure Carborundum, a singing voice of amazing range and nuance. Her manner...inspires people in the seats to identify, to celebrate her success, and serves to confirm their trust that plain folks, given artistic gifts, can fit in at the top, too.

—Life

*H*elen Steiner...was only sixteen when her father died in the flu epidemic that followed World War I. Graduating that year from high school, she went to work to help her mother and younger sister. Helen soon became director of public relations for the Ohio Public Service company and became one of the few women speakers of the time...

Helen caught the eye of a handsome young banker named Franklin Rice and married him before the Great Depression. Caught up in the euphoria of the times, he put everything he could borrow into the stock market when it crashed and took everything he owned. One morning Helen woke up to find Franklin gone, leaving her only a suicide note... Out of that experience Helen Steiner Rice began writing verses that have helped make the Christian faith a practical reality in the lives of thousands of her readers.

—Norman Vincent Peale

[*G*eorgia] Griffith has been blind since birth... She became the first blind student to attend classes at Capital State University... After she graduated cum laude in 1954, Griffith, who could play 12 instruments, including piano, flute and trumpet, returned home to teach music...

At age 39, Griffith contracted infection, and her world went silent. A depression followed. "Friends helped me through it. Once I had something worthwhile to do, things brightened." In 1971 she became a Braille music proofreader for the Library of Congress. She also taught herself Russian, German and a handful of other languages in order to help a friend write a braille music dictionary... She came across a VersaBraille machine, a computer that translates text into braille on a tactile display board. It changed her life... She plunged into the brave new world of computers...off in what she calls her real world—the land of the Internet.

—Marjorie Rosen & Leah Eskin

*M*y dear, [wife Harriet] you must be a literary woman. It is so written in the book of fate. Make all your calculations accordingly. Get a good stroke of health and brush up your mind... Write yourself fully and always "Harriet Beecher Stowe." Then, my word for it, your husband will lift up his head in the gate, and your children will rise up and call you blessed.

—Calvin Stowe

382

*W*hen gold was discovered in Alaska and hordes of greedy men rushed to the Yukon...Evangeline Booth knew the Salvation Army would be needed there. So she headed north... Five men were killed the day Evangeline Booth arrived. There were shortages of everything—blankets, food, equipment, clothing—men were quick-tempered and surly and in no mood for sermons. But Evangeline Booth knew what to do. That evening she and her little band stood on the banks of the Yukon River and sang "Nearer, My God, To Thee," and lonely men began to gather by the hundreds—by the thousands—until nearly twenty-five thousand were lustily singing the hymn! There was singing every day after that...and much less disorder, many fewer shootings.

—Lillian Eichler Watson

[*A*t presentation of Nobel Prize:] Mrs. Pearl S. Buck, you have...advanced the understanding and appreciation in the Western world of a great and important part of mankind, the people of China; you have taught us by your works to see individuals in this great mass of people; you have shown us the rise and fall of families, and the land as the foundation upon which these families are built. In this you have taught us to see those qualities of thought and feelings which bind us all together as human beings on this earth.

—Herr Lindblad

*S*he [wife, Abigail Smith Adams] was a constant feast. Tender, feeling, sensible, friendly. A friend. Not an impudent, not an indelicate, not a disagreeable word or action. Prudent, modest, delicate, soft, sensible, obliging, active.

—John Adams

*J*anette Oke, best-selling novelist with more than 40 books to her credit, is considered the modern "pioneer author" for Christian fiction. Her books have sold millions of copies since her first novel was published in 1979...

She refused to compromise her principles. Although she would write realistically, her stories would be "wholesome and good and encouraging." Many thought that approach was doomed to failure at the outset, but a shelf of novels later...Janette Oke has proven "God can teach spiritual truths through fictional characters."

—W.B. Freeman Concepts

*T*ania Aebi was only 18 when she started her 27,000-mile voyage alone in a 26-foot sloop in May 1985. When she returned 2 1/2 years later, she was the youngest person—and the first American woman—to have sailed solo around the world.

—365 Days

*A*t the christening of Prince Charles in 1948, it was Queen Mary who stole the show with her gift. She noted in her diary: "I gave the baby a silver gilt cup and cover which George III had given to a godson in 1780, so I gave a present from my great-grandfather to my great-grandson 168 years later."

—Anthony Holden

*T*he diary [of Anne Frank] became world famous... The book has been published in fifty-five languages, more that 20 million copies have been sold, and plays and films based on the book have been produced. Throughout the world, streets and schools have been named after Anne Frank... [She] became a symbol of the six million Jewish men, women, and children who were murdered by the Nazi in the Second World War.

—Ruud van der Rol & Rian Verhoeven

*I*n 1898, Frau Schumann-Heink came to America...[to sing in the Metropolitan Opera House]. When her ship arrived in New York, Mr. Grau greeted her—and paled. Confound this woman! She was always with child at the wrong time... "Nonsense," she replied. "What do you know about babies? I have had them many a time. I shall sing regardless. You will see how I shall sing!"

...When she walked upon the stage in Chicago, the entire cast stood breathless because of that little life that was only a month away from making its own debut. Could she sing and kneel as Orturd in *Lohengrin*? They didn't realize the strength and the big stout heart of an Austrian mother. She carried the whole world within her as she sang. The audience shrieked and stamped hysterically. Twenty times the curtain rose and fell... People rushed in with flowers and telegrams. Grau was shouting and dancing like a maniac. "Heink, you are a wonder! You are a wonder!" he kept on saying, "Baby or no baby, you are a wonder, Heink!"

—Henry & Dana Lee Thomas

384

*N*ine generations of her [Ethel Barrymore's] family had been in the theater, and "we became actors," she once said, "not because we wanted to, but because it was the thing we could do best." She made her debut at 15, and for decades she and her brothers, Lionel and John, were acknowledged members of U.S. theater's Royal Family. Ethel seemed ageless: at 43 she was a captivating Juliet. And she was indomitable: with her husky contralto and commanding personality, she easily made the transition from stage to film and won an Oscar at the age of 65.

—Life

*Th*e only woman in the Bible who was placed at the height of political power by the common consent of the people was Deborah. Though she lived in the time of the "Judges," some thirteen centuries before Christ, there are few women in history who have ever attained the public dignity and supreme authority of Deborah. She was like Joan of Arc, who twenty-seven centuries later rode in front of the French and led them to victory...

"Go," [she told the fainthearted general Barak]... "and take with thee ten thousand men"... [He answered] "If thou will go with me, then I will go: but if thou wilt not go with me, then I will not go." That is one of the most unusual passages in the Bible spoken by a man to a woman.

—Edith Deen

[*In* Brazil] The Albergue Santo Antonio was opened in February 1960 [by Sister Dulce Lopez Pontes]. It was a three-story building and held 150 beds. From their planks in the old chicken coop [which had been their shelter], the incredulous patients were led or carried to the Albergue, and each assigned to a real bed with a straw mattress. Three months later all the construction bills were paid; only Sister Dulce could say how. In its first twelve months 8,765 children, 21,562 men, and 6,601 women received care there. Four nursing nuns helped Sister Dulce look after them.

—Robin McKown

*M*rs. [Pearl S.] Buck is that rarest of rarities: she is wise. And yet she is not sad, for wisdom frequently gives birth to sadness. Mrs. Buck, instead, has hope... She is, no question about it, the best informed individual in the world today on what ails the world and what can be done about it.

—Jason Lindsey

385

The work which Miss [Alice C.] Fletcher did in allotting the land to the Omahas was so successfully handled that she was appealed to by the Government to serve in the same capacity for the Winnebago and Nez Perce Indians. The law whose passage was secured by her zeal was the forerunner of the Severalty Act of 1885 which marked a change in policy of the Government and ushered in a better era for all the Indian tribes.

—*Mary R. Parkman*

Once I had occasion to see her [Mother Teresa] off... When the train began to move, and I walked away, I felt as though I were leaving behind me all the beauty and all the joy in the universe. Something of God's universal love has rubbed off on Mother Teresa, giving her homely features a noticeable luminosity, a shining quality. She has lived so closely with her Lord that the same enchantment clings about her that sent the crowds chasing after him in Jerusalem and Galilee, and made his mere presence seem a harbinger of healing... This love, this Christian love...shines down on the misery we make, and into our dark hearts that made it; irradiating all, uniting all, making all one stupendous harmony.

—*Malcolm Muggeridge*

❦

Sarah Josepha Hale believed that Thanksgiving should be a national patriotic holiday. She was the editor of a popular woman's magazine called *Godey's Lady's Book*. She began her campaign in 1846. Year after year she wrote editorials and sent letters to the President, to the state governors, and to other influential persons... Finally Sarah Hale was able to win the support of Abraham Lincoln... [He] and every president who followed him proclaimed the holiday each year... In December 1941, a joint resolution of Congress specified the fourth Thursday in November...as Thanksgiving Day.

—*Compton's Encyclopedia*

I commend unto you Phebe our sister... That ye receive her...and that ye assist her in whatsoever business she hath need of you; for she hath been a succourer of many... Greet Priscilla and Aquila my helpers in Christ Jesus; Who have for my life laid down their own necks... Greet Mary, who bestowed much labour on us.

—*Romans 16:1-6*

386

The news of his [Generalissimo Chiang Kai-shek's] capture had electrified the world. Panic had swept over Nanking, China's capital city. The only one who remained calm was Madame Chiang Kai-shek. She spoke to the people over the radio and told them to hold their peace. When the government offered to send an army...she warned against bloodshed...and flew straight to Sian in order to negotiate with her husband's captors for his release...

Charmed by her daring, the captors allowed her to come into the presence of her husband. He looked up from the bed where he was confined. "Why have you come here?" he asked in alarm.

"I have come to see you," she answered with the nonchalance of a schoolgirl. The eyes of the Generalissimo filled with tears. Only that morning he had opened his Bible at the sentence, "Jehovah will now do a new thing: He will make a woman protect a man." The kidnapers had lost heart for the adventure. And on Christmas Day—thanks to Mayling's diplomacy—the Generalissimo was released, unharmed.

—*Henry & Dana Lee Thomas*

❧

We have seen an American woman [Harriet Beecher Stowe] write a novel which...was read with equal interest to three audiences, namely, in the parlor, in the kitchen, and in the nursery of every house.

—*Ralph Waldo Emerson*

❧

Waking in the gray of the next morning, [Julia Ward Howe]...lay waiting for the dawn [and] the words came to her. "Mine eyes have seen the glory of the coming of the Lord."

She lay perfectly still. Line by line, stanza by stanza, the words came sweeping on with the rhythm of marching feet, pauseless, resistless. She saw the long lines swinging into place before her eyes, heard the voice of the nation speaking through her lips. She waited till the voice was silent, till the last line was ended; then sprang from bed, and groping for pen and paper, scrawled in the gray twilight the "Battle Hymn of the Republic."

—*Daughters of Julia Ward Howe*

[*M*arian Anderson's] astonishing contralto voice transported her to the highest realms of musical acclaim, a position from which she dramatized the fulfillment of black's dreams. Whether singing Verdi...in her debut as the first black to perform with the Met—or [singing] the old, sad spirituals of her people, Anderson's rich range and tender power transmuted the familiar into art freshly her own... When the D.A.R. barred her from performing at Constitution Hall in 1939...her government gave her the Lincoln Memorial instead. [She] later revealed her greatness in the simplest, quietest way: "If you are all right on the inside, you don't have to worry about things like that."

—*Life*

I have come to present to you [Massachusetts Legislature] the strong claims of suffering humanity. I come as the advocate of the helpless, forgotten, insane men and women held in cages, closets, cellars, stalls, pens; chained, naked, beaten with rods and lashed into obedience.

—*Dorothea Dix*

❧

[*The* governor called Gladys Alyward and said,] "There is a riot in the prison... We can't go in, they will kill us. And one of the worst men in the prison is berserk. He has a huge meat cleaver in his hand and has already killed two men and terrified the others. We want you to go in and take the meat cleaver out of his hands..."

She stood at the prison door and they unlocked it and quickly shut it... She could see men wildly running about, shouting and cursing... She...saw the mad man, the meat cleaver dripping with blood, chasing a man. Suddenly he was in front of her. They stood facing one another: the little woman and the giant. She looked into his wild and feverish eyes and calmly said, "Give me that weapon." There was a moment of hesitation; then, with utter docility, he handed it to her. "Now," she said, "get in line, all of you men—get back in line." Quietly they lined up. Addressing them, she said, "What are your complaints? I will tell them to the governor and I assure you in his name that where possible they will be corrected."

—*Norman Vincent Peale*

Settlers in their letters, speeches and memoirs told and retold the story of what the Whitmans did for Oregon. Narcissa was the heroine of all these narratives... Under the most primitive conditions [pioneers] found Narcissa Whitman an unforgettable experience. Magically in the wilderness they were welcomed at the gracious home she had created; there they shared once more civilized ways of living... Not for her beauty nor her lovely voice was her memory most cherished; not even for the affection she shed on every child who passed through the station... They would never forget how her faith brought radiance to the things of every day, exalted her love for Marcus, and at the last glorified her death [in a massacre by Indians].

—Jeanette Eaton

❦

Trudy Ederle's conquest of the storm-blown English Channel in 1926, in a time two hours better than any man had done, was high achievement. Songs were written about her. A newspaper gave her a red roadster. Marriage proposals poured in, and President Calvin Coolidge called her "America's best girl." She was indomitable. When her trainer had urged her to give up in midchannel she replied, "What for?" In later years, after she suffered a serious back injury...and lost her hearing, she interrupted her quiet life only to teach deaf children to swim. "They feel I'm one of them," she explained, "and they trust me."

—Life

❦

The Civil War battle of Fort Donelson was officially over... On the battlefield the wounded lay with the dead. It was bitterly cold. Stretcher bearers literally had to chop them from their icy bed. Encased in frozen mud and blood-stiffened uniforms, the first casualties were carried over rutted roads to the Cumberland River, where the hospital ship, *City of Memphis,* and Mary Ann Bickerdyke were waiting for them.

She was the motherliest woman imaginable, big and stout and hearty, with work-worn hands, a broad and friendly face, and a cheery voice. In her gray calico dress and Shaker bonnet over her thick brown hair, she looked like the kind of mother some of the boys had left at home on the farm. And the kind nearly all of them would have liked to have.

—Robin McKown

$\mathscr{R}$ebecca Adamson, an Eastern Cherokee Indian, started the First Nations Development Fund to help Native Americans become economically self-sufficient. First Nations worked with the Lakota Indians to help them create a small enterprise loan program, then to build their own health clinic. They've also taught Navajo rugmakers how to price their work.

—365 Days

❧

$\mathscr{J}$oseph Pulitzer was impressed with Nelly Bly's ideas. She wanted to get stories from the inside; to work as a shopgirl, a factory girl, a servant, and then to write these stories for the *World*... She had the same itch to get the facts... He hired her—on condition she get herself committed to Blackwell's Island, the notorious asylum for the mentally deranged of New York, in order to report honestly on conditions there.

She succeeded in fooling doctors and even judges who committed her. When she came out ten days later she wrote a story that was a bombshell, exposing the harsh treatment and the horrible conditions on the island... She became America's first accredited newspaper woman...[with] the nation's biggest newspaper. Pulitzer raised her to international fame when he arranged for her to make a trip around the world to beat the record of Jules Vern's fictional hero of *Around the World in Eighty Days*. Nellie made it in seventy-two days, six hours and ten minutes and set a new world record!

—Iris Noble

❧

$\mathscr{O}$ne [of life's blessings] was our nurse, Lizzie Endicott, in whom even the exacting memory of childhood can discover no flaw—nothing but kindness, gaiety, and good sense... [To her] I owe my lifelong immunity from the false identification which some people make of refinement with virtue... Lizzie was, as nearly as a human can be, simply good.

—C.S. Lewis

Clara Barton suffered nervous breakdowns, and at times, according to her diaries, an almost paralyzing sense of uselessness... Recuperating... she first heard about the International Red Cross, recently formed to alleviate the horrors of war and already subscribed to by several European countries. As soon as she could, Barton undertook what became a lonely and interminable one-woman campaign to persuade Congress and the White House to let the U.S. participate... Barton finally succeeded in 1882, chiefly by emphasizing the value of the Red Cross in peacetime. And for the next 22 years she ran the American Red Cross, rushing her forces to the rescue wherever disaster struck.

—Life

ح

[After Dr. Ellis R. Shipp's graduation from medical school in 1878:] The birth of five additional children in her own life did not interfere with her work. Her family of ten living children did not keep her from teaching obstetrics nor from practicing medicine...

She lost but one mother, though she waited on five thousand women in confinement. This person was in convulsions when Ellis was called to see her. Ellis never refused to return to a home where her former services remained unpaid... She traveled from Canada to Mexico teaching obstetrics, and from Colorado to Nevada... In each town she visited she remained three months.

In the summer of 1935, in response to an invitation from her college, Ellis went to Philadelphia, where she headed the fifty-seventh procession to cross the campus of her Alma Mater since her own triumphal day. She was then the oldest living graduate of the Women's Medical College of Philadelphia... At the age of ninety-one...she was elected to Utah's Hall of Famous Women.

—Claire Noall

And the word of the Lord came unto him [Elijah] saying, Arise, get thee to Zarephath...and dwell there; behold, I have commanded a widow woman there to sustain thee.

—I Kings 17:8,9

391

*M*argaret Fuller's flame burned early, brightly, briefly. She knew five languages at 15, was a leader of the Boston circle that included Thoreau and Emerson, served as critic for the *New York Tribune* and also managed—in that incredible burst of accomplishment before her death at 40 in a shipwreck—to write a feminist manifesto, *Woman in the Nineteenth Century.*

—Life

❦

*A*ll the art, the thought, and the nobleness in New England related to her [Margaret Fuller] and she to it.

—Ralph W. Emerson

❦

[*A*fter her three years' exile in the United States] to the people of Veracruz the coming of Doña Margarita [de Juarez] was an event in itself. They had not forgotten her walk through the wilderness with her [eight] children, nor her care for them and her courage under siege in the two years she had spent in their city. [They]...crowded the streets to welcome her warmly as the victory was being celebrated in Mexico City.

With flowers, banners, bells and fireworks, all of Veracruz came down to the dock. It is said that the people also brought Empress Carlota's gilded coach, which had been left in Veracruz, for Margarita to ride in.

Then they saw her coming down the gangplank, dressed in black, surrounded by her daughters and leaning on the arm of Bene, her only remaining son. Margarita was still beautiful and gracious, but all the gaiety they remembered was gone. The rumor swept through the subdued crowd that she had brought with her the coffins of her two dead sons— Pepe, who had walked the streets of Veracruz with Don Benito, and the little one...[who never knew his father].

The trumpets were silent; the fireworks stayed in their wrappers; the gilded coach stood forgotten on the side street. Veracruz paid Doña Margarita a tribute better than cheers and music—a tribute of love.

—Emma Gelders Sterne

$\mathcal{I}$ believe Wang Amah [our servant] was what people call not a good woman and I am afraid she will never understand very much of the gospel. But I have never seen her unkind to one of the children, nor have I ever heard her speak an evil word, and if there is no place in heaven for her, she shall have half of mine—if I have one.

—Pearl S. Buck

❦

$\mathcal{T}$hen Esther bade them return Mordecai this answer, Go, gather together all the Jews...and fast ye for me, and neither eat nor drink three days, night or day: I also and my maidens will fast likewise; and so will I go in unto the king, which is not according to the law: and if I perish, I perish.

—Esther 4:13-16

❦

$\mathcal{J}$oan [of Arc]...finds no equal in a thousand years. The records of her trial present us with facts alive today through all the mists of time. Out of her own mouth can she be judged in each generation. She embodied the natural goodness and valour of the human race in unexampled perfection. Unconquerable courage, infinite compassion, the virtue of the simple, the wisdom of the just, shown forth in her. She glorifies as she freed the soil from which she sprang. All soldiers should read her story and ponder on the words and deeds of the true warrior, who in one single year, though untaught in technical arts, reveals in every situation the key to victory.

—Winston Churchill

❦

$\mathcal{E}$dith Cavell had been condemned to death before a German firing squad.] It is said that the men of the firing squad, unwilling to kill a woman, all fired high in the air, and that an officer took over and shot her in the heart with his revolver... Women in England, learning of Edith Cavell's death, tore up their black petticoats and draped them from their windows in mourning. All over the world, people wept for her.

—Robin McKown

393

There came unto him a woman having an alabaster box of very precious ointment, and poured it on his head as he sat at meat. But when his disciples saw it, they had indignation, saying, To what purpose is this waste? For this ointment might have been sold for much, and given to the poor... [Jesus] said unto them... Wheresoever this gospel shall be preached in the whole world, there shall also this, that this woman hath done, be told for a memorial of her.

—Matthew 26:7-10, 13

❧

Epilogue

Epilogue

I wish to further recognize the women to whom this book is dedicated.

My mother, Rhea Allred, at twenty married my father, Morris Q. Kunz, and bore him eight children. In addition to rearing her family during the challenging times of the Great Depression and its aftermath, she was a teacher, poet, and historian with several published volumes of work.

My paternal grandmother, Maren Sophia Nielsen, left Denmark with her parents at the tender age of four. Soon after their arrival in America, her mother died. At nineteen she married my Swiss immigrant grandfather, David Kunz, and bore him eleven children. Her industry and cleanliness were a great asset to him as a pioneer cheesemaker.

My maternal grandmother, Charlotte Susannah Pead, was childhood sweetheart to Grandfather Byron Harvey Allred, Jr., and married him shortly before she turned eighteen. She was noted for her beauty and was a talented pioneer singer and actress. She also bore eleven children.

The deaths of these two grandmothers occurred within two days' time. Although we have no record of their ever having met, it was as if their lives were linked years before my parents would become adults and marry. The grandmothers have left their mark—both by their presence and absence.

For the following poems honoring these three woman, I wish to thank my sister, Donna K. Mackert.

—Compiler

Rhea A. Kunz

Everything That Was You

Mama, I remember our first new home.
When we moved in, the only siding
was black tar paper held by lath
until Daddy could earn money for stuccoing.
The only heat was the Great Majestic
coal-burning range in the corner in the kitchen.
Orange-crate cupboards were covered
with flour-sack curtains.

You lit kerosene lamps.
Over drafty cracks that gaped
in one-by-twelve subflooring
you spread throw rugs
made from folded squares of wool
sewn onto gunny sacks
as you treadled your old Wheeler Wilson.

You kept pneumonia at bay with mustard plasters
and a steaming eucalyptus pot.
In the old wool coat that was your robe,
three times during every cold night
you left your brick-warmed bed
to check us children,
to retuck under hand-pieced quilts
an escaping arm or shoulder.

Before dawn you sat,
your feet on the lowered oven door,
and in a five-cent Scholastic notebook
wrote poems in neat Palmer penmanship.

Twice a week you shampooed our hair
in an enamel basin on the washstand.
Then beside the Great Majestic,
in a galvanized number-three tub,
you bathed us one-by-one
in communal precious warm water.
You banished germs with clean rinse water
poured over us from a tin cup.

You rode the trolley to town,
combed secondhand stores for books.
Longfellow and Whittier,
Shakespeare and Shelley became friends
who lived on shelves of a small glassed cabinet.

You never had a matched set of china
or cooked a gourmet meal,
but you fed us with your brown bread
and home-churned butter,
nourished us with music and words.

To the end of your life
your home was open to the less-fortunate.
You had no bank account,
left no money to dispense,
but when you died
I was heir to everything that was you.

—*Donna K. Mackert*

M. Sophia Kunz

December Night

In her white house,
between her white sheets,
thirty-nine-year-old Sophia
lay pale and sweating
with a ruptured appendix.

The doctor from Montpelier
sped over frozen white landscape
in his bobsled.
He must boil instruments
on Sophia's kitchen range,
must operate to save her.

Four-year-old Morris stirred
under woolen quilts
in Aunt Lou's attic,
where he had slept with Nick,
her fourteen-year-old son.

There were voices downstairs.
Someone was saying
that his mother was dead.

Kettles and dishes rattled
as Aunt Lou prepared breakfast.
Upstairs Morris was weeping.
Nick put muscular arms around him,
told him not to worry.

After the haunting funeral,
Morris was sickened by the scent
of chloroform which lingered
for days in Sophia's house.

—*Donna K. Mackert*

Charlotte P. Allred

One Last Look

Two days after Sophia's death,
thirty-eight-year-old Charlotte,
her dark hair clinging to her face,
her pillow damp with perspiration,
struggled in hard childbirth
in her brick home at Blackfoot.

In frail health, with a weak heart,
she had feared this labor.
To comfort her, Harvey had promised
to bring the loved and trusted doctor
who had cared for them in Garden City
on the shores of Bear Lake,
where they grew up
as childhood sweethearts.

The doctor stumbled out of his bobsled
and staggered into the house.
His breath reeked of alcohol,
He spoke brusque words,
his bedside manner was brutal.
Harvey was nearly wild with fear
as the doctor jerked two baby girls
from Charlotte's body
and she gasped her last breath.

"My wife is dead! You have killed her!"
he cried in anguish.
Grief-stricken and battling rage,
Harvey laid out
Charlotte's beautiful body
with the help of a woman friend.
They closed dark, sightless eyes,
positioned the mouth
that could smile and sing no more,
placed hands that could not
tend the babies
nor again strum her guitar.

Tender care from Relief Society sisters
did not save the twins.
They were placed in the coffin,
one on each of Charlotte's arms.

Harvey bent to pick up
Lottie's living baby,
two-year-old Rhea, his Little Rosebud.
He held her so she could see
the two lifeless little sisters
with whom she could not play
and have one last look
at her mother.

—*Donna K. Mackert*

Charlotte K. LeBaron has had a life of varied experience. She is an avid journal-keeper, and in addition to *Words and Wisdom of Women*, has two historical family journals nearing publication.

She attended the University of Utah on scholarship, and though she did not obtain a degree, was granted a standard teaching credential by the State of California on the basis of her work experience and did further study there. She has taught in public and private schools for 27 years, during which time she served as director of a bilingual school for six years. One of her cherished experiences was teaching in a one-room school with a dirt floor in Nicaragua and washing her clothes in a nearby river.

She married Verlan M. LeBaron in 1951, was widowed in 1981, and is mother of nine children and grandmother of fifty-six. She counts sewing and quilting as hobbies, her most recent project being wedding quilts for three grandchildren. She enjoys traveling and recalls with pleasure two trips to Europe. An articulate public speaker, she is active in church and civic affairs—*women* being her special subject.

The Artist

Sketching has been inherent since early childhood for Linda Marlene Farrar. "I had to draw everything I saw," she recalls. She drew so much in kindergarten and the first grade that her teacher called her mother, saying they would have to do something about Linda. Her mother responded by taking the paper out of the house. Undaunted, Linda drew on envelopes, sacks, or any scrap of paper she could find.

As she studied art her great love became portrait painting. During the administration of President Ronald Reagan she painted his portrait, which a senator presented to him for his birthday. She received a letter of commendation and thanks from the White House.

She is also adept at florals, still life, folk art, landscapes, and illustrations for children. Her oil paintings, watercolors, and sketches have been displayed in nine showrooms throughout the nation. A skilled photographer, she specializes in portraits and video photo art.

David S. McCullough ~ Digital Art Director

For information or additional copies write

Woodbine Books
P.O. Box 923
Deming, N.M. 88030
www.cameolady.com